PANDEMONIUM

Jack Horgan-Jones is a political reporter at the *Irish Times*. He previously covered business, news and current affairs for the *Business Post* and TheJournal.ie.

Hugh O'Connell is a political correspondent with the *Sunday Independent* and *Irish Independent*. He has previously worked for the *Business Post*, TheJournal.ie, the BBC and Newstalk.

PRAISE FOR *PANDEMONIUM*

'The pandemic was not just a public-health crisis – it was also a great test of Ireland's systems for making decisions and wielding power. This gripping, fast-paced, sometimes breath-taking narrative acts as a blazing searchlight, illuminating all the corners of our institutions that are usually able to operate in the dark. It helps us to understand not just an extraordinary moment in our recent history but Ireland itself.'

Fintan O'Toole

'This is a page-turner, and provides an exceptional insight into the behind-the-scenes politics of an exceptional period in Irish life and the personalities and thinking behind crucial decisions. I thought I was well informed because of my own position covering these events, but it turns out there was a lot more to know … and this book delivers an essential service in that regard.'

Matt Cooper

'In *Pandemonium*, an unflinching and unrelenting account of Ireland's response to the pandemic, Jack Horgan-Jones and Hugh O'Connell provide a searing and scrupulous examination of the personal and political calls made during Ireland's emergency. No stone is left unturned in a gripping tome that exposes the extraordinary impacts of Covid-19 on citizens and interrogates the institutional implications of a public health crisis whose lasting impacts will remain unknown for some time to come. *Pandemonium* is a sobering non-fiction book that reads like a Hollywood blockbuster.'

Dearbhail McDonald

'If a movie is ever made of how Ireland responded to the Covid-19 pandemic, *Pandemonium* may well provide the script. Horgan-Jones and

O'Connell give us a hugely authoritative and compelling blow-by-blow account of how the various groups of experts, most notably NPHET, interacted with the government in this most difficult of times. You will feel as if you were in the room when key conversations happened and decisions were made that hugely affected all our lives.'

Professor Luke O'Neill

PANDEMONIUM

Power, Politics and Ireland's Pandemic

Jack Horgan-Jones
Hugh O'Connell

Gill Books

Gill Books
Hume Avenue
Park West
Dublin 12
www.gillbooks.ie

Gill Books is an imprint of M.H. Gill and Co.

978 07171 93981

Designed by Bartek Janczak
Edited by Jane Rogers
Printed by CPI Group (UK) Ltd, Croydon, CR0 4YY
Illustrations by Derry Dillon
This book is typeset in 11 on 16pt, Minion Pro.

A CIP catalogue record for this book is available from the
British Library.

5 4 3 2 1

For Kate, Olivia and Eve – JHJ
For Theresa and Mary-Jane – HOC

CONTENTS

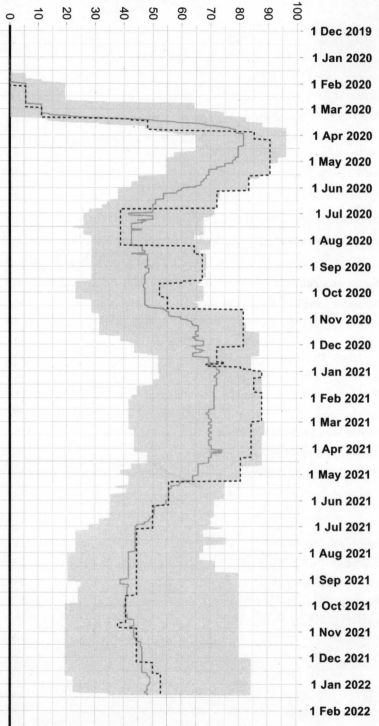

Stringency Index

Range of EU-27+UK

—— EU-27+UK Median

- - - Ireland

AUTHORS' NOTE

From early 2020 to early 2022, Ireland endured three harsh lockdowns that severely curtailed every citizen's daily activities. Outside of these lockdowns, some form of public health restrictions was retained as the Covid-19 pandemic dominated the political and economic life of the State.

An analysis of data from the Oxford University stringency index, which measures how tight restrictions were at a given time, shows that Ireland had the most restrictive regime of comparator countries – the EU27 and UK – for 121 out of the 685 days between 1 March 2020 and 14 January 2022: just over one-sixth of that nearly two-year period. The analysis was undertaken for the authors by Kevin Cunningham, a statistician and lecturer in TU Dublin.

The State had heavier restrictions than the median country in the EU for 69 per cent of the time, and fewer restrictions than the median country for 18 per cent of the time.

It's clear that Ireland's lockdowns were extraordinarily tight, measured on this index, but it did not have the harshest restrictions on aggregate. When compared to Europe, Ireland was joint fourth with Portugal, after Italy, Greece and Germany. Those other four countries have the highest share of their population aged over 65, whereas Ireland has among the lowest share of that demographic. At the same time, Ireland has significantly fewer intensive care beds than many of these countries, not least Germany, yet restrictions have been broadly the same. On some measures, Ireland was closer to the top – 2nd on workplace closures – but on others it was lower: on school closures and restrictions on gatherings or public events, Ireland was 10th or 11th in Europe; on international travel controls, Ireland was markedly more relaxed, coming in 21st of the countries measured.

When compared to the EU and UK, Ireland had significantly fewer deaths attributed to Covid per one million of population.

The index tells us some things about Ireland's experience of the pandemic, but no one index can adequately capture the full impact of restrictions across society. Every way of measuring experiences as all-encompassing as lockdowns or tight restrictions has some weaknesses. The combined impact of the public health measures on delayed care, or the mental health of the population, cannot be neatly captured in one graph. Each decision taken by the government during the pandemic has had incalculable ramifications throughout a period when the entire resources of the State were mobilised to one end, the only comparison for which in recent history is a state of war.

This is the inside story of that war with Covid-19.

PROLOGUE

'It is important to understand that the future is not like the past.' A short message with a two-page attachment dropped into Leo Varadkar's private email inbox just before 5.15 p.m. on Wednesday, 4 March 2020. Kevin Cunningham, a Dublin-born, Oxford-educated statistician, political pundit and pollster, was so worried about the coronavirus that he felt compelled to write to the Taoiseach.

For a few days, Cunningham had been part of a loose band of commentators, medics and experts loudly warning about coronavirus on Twitter. The whole process made Cunningham uncomfortable; he had been gaining credibility as a pollster, but now he risked coming across as just another overexcited guy, outside his professional lane, shouting about something on the internet.

It made him more uncomfortable to be one of those people who also randomly emailed the Taoiseach with their concerns. But the two men had history. Cunningham had performed polling analysis for Varadkar when he ran for Fine Gael leader in 2017, and the pair had corresponded when Cunningham was working on the People's Vote, a British grass-roots campaign seeking a second referendum on the UK's decision to leave the EU. The statistician had political capital, and he decided to burn it.

I really don't think we can wait.

The UK may play around until it gets to 100 cases because they've 160k beds. We've obviously got 14k, which are full. So we must act earlier. We know where this is going to go. We must use this time.

Panic will be much, much worse than when there's no room in hospitals for people who cannot breathe.

The attached document began by outlining 'statistics versus experience':

It is important to understand that the future is not like the past. When World War 1 began they thought it would finish at Christmas. When people look at past elections they presume it will be like similar elections. The sample sizes of identical events are too low to recognise things that will occur that don't reflect our life experience. The medical profession experiences the winter flu on a regular basis and are treating this epidemic as if it were similar, but more difficult.

The numbers do suggest that the issue is much worse than this and the numbers should be treated in their own right as important in the same way the winter flu follows the data. I'm not going to suggest that I know more than others in this sphere … That said, the mathematics are fairly straightforward.

Cunningham included a small table showing that the virus was growing at a rate of anything from 3 per cent in the previous nine days in Singapore to 52 per cent in the previous seven days in France. It was at 37 per cent in the previous nine days in Italy, and weak public health measures in Germany, Spain and France were failing to prevent rapid growth. The wave would 'overflow' Italian hospitals within weeks – but with decisive action, it could be stopped. He then outlined in stark terms what needed to be done in Ireland:

The scale of the disaster is avoidable by taking the precautionary measures early. As per the WHO recommendations: 'It's worth trying to slow the pace of the outbreak with measures to keep the number of patients from overwhelming local hospitals'. I would recommend all of the following immediately, on a daily basis the longer we wait the worse it will be:

- Ban all mass gatherings immediately
- Close all schools and universities – helping people to stay at home (there is a theory that young kids are spreading it without) immediately
- Advise the public to work from home where possible
- Close the airports and ports to ordinary passengers
- Inform supermarkets (maximum spend of 50 euro per person per visit)

I know the damage this will do to the economy but I also know the damage that delaying will do. Imagine Wuhan without a strong government. It will be lawless.

If we don't do this I believe people will start taking things into their own hands.

Varadkar did not respond to the email. Nearly twenty months later, he had moved jobs. Sitting in the last office on the left of the Tánaiste's ground floor corridor in Government Buildings, he looked through the paper sent to him by Cunningham. 'I remember Kevin Cunningham being in touch with me about it,' he said. 'There were a few people very early on who were warning that this could be a big thing.'

Before working in politics, Cunningham had spent time at the United Nations, building statistical models of human migration for its population division. He gained experience of working with messy data on people and populations – similar to that used when modelling disease outbreaks – on how large groups of people change and behave over time, and how rates of change work in the real world.

When he was doing his undergraduate degree at Oxford, swine flu was seen as a significant threat to global health, and he became interested in epidemiological statistics. His great-grandmother and her baby died of the Spanish flu in 1918, and so he took an interest in the area whenever it came up in his studies.

He also understood exponential growth, a phrase commonly used to describe something growing quickly. In statistics and disease modelling it has a narrower definition. It means that a single infected person might infect another two on day zero. If those two infected people infect another two people, who in turn infect another two people, the scale of the infection will double rapidly – and continue to double.

Coronavirus was highly infectious and would make a small percentage of people sick enough to require hospitalisation. Exponential growth in this context would mean disaster. In late February and early March 2020, Cunningham crunched numbers, examining the relationships between testing and cases, reading deeply, and becoming more worried.

While still in his twenties, he had risen to a senior position in the British Labour Party, and after leaving the UK, he was briefly involved in helping to set up the Social Democrats in Ireland in 2015. He worked closely with the then Independent TD Stephen Donnelly until the two fell out when Donnelly asked Cunningham to decant into one document his entire approach to political polling and strategy. Cunningham felt he was being bypassed. Being asked to, in effect, turn his job into a document would make him redundant. He lost all faith in the Wicklow TD and quit the nascent party before it was launched.

He applied unsuccessfully for the role of general secretary of the Irish Labour Party. During the process, he struck up a relationship with Ed Brophy, Tánaiste Joan Burton's chief of staff. After Labour was nearly annihilated in the 2016 general election, both men were in need of work. They founded the Ireland Thinks polling company, which carved a niche for itself with punchy, topical polls. Cunningham had featured heavily in RTÉ's coverage of the general election, parsing results as they came in, providing a statistical and thematic backbone to the uncertain election outcome.

Brophy, meanwhile, went back into government, as an adviser to finance minister Paschal Donohoe. That meant that Varadkar was not the only person inside government with whom Cunningham was able to burn his political capital, as his concerns mounted.

He watched the government prevaricate over what travel advice to give to punters bound for the Cheltenham horse racing festival, and the debate over whether St Patrick's Day festivities should proceed. All that clearly told him one thing: 'No fucking way they were on top of this.'

Cunningham had a little more purchase with Brophy than with Varadkar, and was more willing to strafe him with texts and emails. So on 26 February, the day after he first discussed his concerns about the virus as part of a panel discussion on RTÉ Radio 1's *Late Debate*, he texted Donohoe's adviser, 'Nobody will blame the government for taking too many precautions on coronavirus.'

'Totally,' Brophy responded.

In the days that followed, Cunningham besieged Brophy with more texts and phone calls. The longer the government delayed, he argued, the more people would die. Brophy was increasingly irked by the volley of WhatsApps. 'Translating the "something should be done" narrative into reality raises 100s of questions,' he wrote back.

But the message was landing. Early in March, the pair spoke at length on the phone while Brophy paced the sidelines at his son's football game. Afterwards, Brophy was nearly in tears. Hundreds of thousands of people were going to die, he thought; people would not be able to see their parents and grandparents in their final hours. In the days after that conversation, Brophy texted the Taoiseach with his view that it was time the government acted. 'We really need to fucking move on this,' was how Brophy would later characterise his text to Varadkar.

Brophy urged Cunningham to take his concerns offline and directly to the Taoiseach, and offered to circulate them in government. 'Send me a few reasoned/evidence-based paragraphs & I will bring it to the attention of those making decisions,' he told Cunningham. When there was no response to his first email, Cunningham wrote to the Taoiseach again on Tuesday 10 March:

Please undertake these measures today. Tell people how serious this is. People will find a way to work and for the economy to continue to function. Real disaster is if hospitals were overwhelmed. France will be the same as Italy in a week. Spain the week after. Please don't wait.

Brophy approached Varadkar with his concerns. 'Do you really think so?' the Taoiseach replied. 'This isn't the advice that we're getting from our public health people at the moment. They're not saying cancel the parade. They're not saying stop the flights from Italy.'

It's not unusual for a taoiseach to receive conflicting advice on a big issue. Varadkar was being told, on the one hand, that this was SARS or MERS or swine flu all over again; and on the other, that it was a very different type of pandemic.

Varadkar was inclined to take his counsel from the chief medical officer (CMO). 'It seemed kind of sensible to me.' The advice of CMO Dr Tony Holohan and his National Public Health Emergency Team (NPHET), set up in late January 2020 by Holohan himself, was not to cancel the St Patrick's Day festival and not to impose major public health restrictions.

Not yet anyway.

—

That view – 'not yet' – was based on the orthodoxies of public health, a division of medical practice that is almost like a mix of medicine and social science and involves its fair share of subjective judgement. When the medical advice is for a whole population, part of it is about holding steady, striking at the right time, ensuring the public's buy-in and compliance.

In the early days of Covid-19, even as it became increasingly inevitable that the country would shut down, this view spread across government. 'Part of "not yet" was the view at the time that people would only be able to tolerate very strict restrictions for, you know, twelve weeks,' Varadkar later recalled. 'Yes, we could shut down the schools or yes, we could do a "stay at home" order. But you could only do this for a certain number of weeks, people would only tolerate it for so long.'

The corollary of that strategy is that it allows the virus time to spread. In Ireland, the pandemic response was split into three phases: Delay, Contain and Mitigate. It involved tracking the growth of the disease before imposing harsh restrictions if it looked as if it was getting out of control. But Ireland's nascent testing system was picking up only a small fraction of the cases in the country. Early testing criteria focused on travel from an area of concern or close contact with a confirmed case – and on being symptomatic.

On 25 February, a man was brought by ambulance to Cork University Hospital (CUH) with a headache – he had previously been diagnosed with a brain tumour. He had no travel history, hadn't had contact with a Covid case, and didn't fit the criteria for testing for Covid. He was, in any case, tested for Covid on 2 March and notified as positive to regional public health on 5 March. Later testing of a swab that had been taken when he was admitted showed he was already infected. In the interim, he had been shuttled around the hospital, infecting people on at least three separate occasions, a subsequent public health report found. Eventually, he was transferred to another hospital, where he later died.

That report identified three 'transmission events': one when he was in the emergency department, where he was on a trolley for two days; another in a medical short stay unit he was transferred to; and another in the ICU itself. The report also found that he had been recently discharged from another hospital in the city, and concluded that he had most likely acquired Covid-19 there. The other hospital was contacted, but medics there concluded, after reviewing case files of patients who were contacts of the case, that none of them was likely to have carried Covid-19. But these patients were never swabbed or tested for Covid-19.

The public health report into the CUH case would eventually find 780 close contacts of the patient, 405 of them in the hospital, where 64 cases were later diagnosed during an outbreak – 9 had been close contacts of the patient. The outbreak control team in CUH brought the disease under control, but it caused significant staffing issues in the ICU, requiring an exemption for asymptomatic staff who were close contacts to continue working. It was an early and jarring warning of what Covid-19 could do. Public health doctors concluded that the man had probably had the virus for around a week before he checked into CUH, meaning he likely acquired it in mid-February.

Dr Cillian De Gascun, the State's top virologist and a member of NPHET, later said that the CUH case (and one more death from around this time later shown to be a Covid-19 infection with no travel history) showed something else. 'It would seem that the infection was seeded far more widely than certainly I appreciated, or we appreciated at the time,' he said. 'Looking back, we have to assume that the pockets of infection we identified in near real time were in fact being replicated all over the country.'

Using a case fatality ratio – the proportion of people with a disease who die from it – it can roughly be determined how many cases are present in the community based on those two deaths alone. Rather than the six cases that had been detected by 4 March, De Gascun believes the two community-acquired Covid-19 deaths by early March meant that people were being infected on a greater scale than was being detected. 'We can presume they acquired their infections in February, so unless you are very unfortunate and two of the first three cases just happen to be susceptible to infection and die, that suggests there were at least a few hundred cases circulating in the community in February 2020,' he said.

It will never be possible to tell just how widely Covid-19 was spreading in Ireland before the first public health restrictions came into force. The 2019/2020 flu samples in the National Virus Reference Laboratory (NVRL), which could have retrospectively indicated the prevalence of undetected Covid-19 in people with flu-like symptoms, were discarded in the second half of 2020 as part of a routine space-saving protocol. There was just no room in the freezers.

In the UK, an academic study later found around half its first-wave deaths could have been avoided by locking down one week earlier. Ireland did move faster than the UK and many other countries, introducing a lockdown that just about contained the first wave of the virus and prevented the health system collapsing. But it is also the case that it did so after the virus had been afforded a chance to spread, unobstructed. As the pandemic took hold in spring 2020, the words of Irishman Dr Mike Ryan of the World Health Organization (WHO) became a maxim in Ireland: 'Speed trumps perfection.' The first wave of Covid-19 still hit a country that was mentally, politically and medically unprepared.

—

The consultant oncologist and former Independent senator John Crown was another person warning the Taoiseach to move early. He contacted Varadkar in early March and told him that he must cancel the St Patrick's Day festival. The danger, he said, was not the parade itself but people congregating in pubs afterwards. 'Leo from day one really did take this seriously,' Crown later said. 'But I think there were some people around him who were not taking it as seriously. I worried that he was getting other advice that was not taking the public health aspect of this seriously.'

On 10 March, Crown appeared on *The Tonight Show* on Virgin Media Television. He would later reflect on how anxious he was to sound the alarm on everything from restrictions to face masks – and how he thought it made him unpopular. But that night, Crown sat in the middle of a crowded five-person TV panel with Dublin City University (DCU) academic Professor Anthony Staines and De Gascun to his right, and Fine Gael TD Jennifer Carroll MacNeill and Stephen Donnelly, who was then Fianna Fáil's health spokesperson, to his left.

'The real danger is that we're going to be doing battlefield-level triage here if the extrapolations from Italy are correct, and the stories that we're hearing from Italy are horrific,' Crown said with a sense of urgency.

Matt Cooper, the co-host, asked what this would mean in practice.

It would mean turning people away from hospitals, Crown responded.

So what could be done?

'Adopt the extreme measures now,' Crown insisted.

'Close everything?' asked the other co-host, Ivan Yates.

'Yes.'

'Stop travel?'

'Yes.'

Cooper and Yates were visibly taken aback, as were some of the panellists. But within 24 hours it would become a reality for everyone in the studio.

It was only the beginning. Across 2020 and 2021, Ireland would be locked down three times, with less onerous public health restrictions constantly in place, even when lockdowns were eased. It was unprecedented – the future would not be like the past.

CHAPTER 1:

THE PHONEY WAR

24 January 2020
Cases: 0
Deaths: 0
Seven-day average of new cases: 0

aul Reid was on the second hole at Carrick-on-Shannon golf
course in Leitrim and his phone was hopping. There were cases
of coronavirus infection associated with travel in Paris and
Bordeaux. 'This was here and it was in Europe. It had reached
us and it was for real,' he would later recall.

The chief executive of the Health Service Executive (HSE) soon had
to give up on golf. 'Lads, this just isn't working, I have to pack it in.'
He was getting nowhere, and, in any case, his golf buddies had already
moved forty yards ahead of him.

It would be a long time before Reid would get back out on the course.
A small group within the HSE – the High Consequences Infectious
Diseases Group – had been meeting since early January, but now the
decision was being taken to elevate the response.

Reid pulled together a National Crisis Management Team (NCMT).
Much like its counterpart in the Department of Health – NPHET – there
had been NCMTs before, periodically formed in response to disease outbreaks in hospitals, severe weather events, or other unpredicted threats.
This would be different.

—

The first ripples of Covid-19 reached Ireland in early February. Passengers on a flight arriving from Moscow late on the evening of 1 February were greeted with the unexpected sight of public health doctors in hazmat suits, who had scrambled after being alerted that a passenger could be carrying the virus. Passengers were told to 'avoid contact with other people as much as possible tonight'. The person suspected of carrying the virus was taken to the Mater Hospital, tested negative, and released.

In early 2020, the official position in Ireland was that the State was ready for whatever might be coming. On 28 January, the Cabinet was told of the Department of Health's view that 'Ireland is adequately prepared to address any potential cases of the novel coronavirus (2019-nCoV)'.

A full two weeks later, a briefing note by the Health Threats Coordination Group, a high-powered gathering of officials from across government departments, the Defence Forces, the HSE and elsewhere, said there were 'advanced plans in place as part of its comprehensive preparedness to deal with public health emergencies such as novel coronavirus'. They were, the note said, the plans that had previously been used for pandemic influenza, SARS and MERS. 'Ireland is, therefore, well-positioned to detect and respond to any case of the novel coronavirus (2019-nCoV) that might arise here,' it concluded.

Through January and February, diplomatic cables from China detailed the advance of disease, but it was not a headline on the dispatches. It was there if you looked for it, but it 'wasn't up in lights or anything like that', a source in the Department of Foreign Affairs later said. As days turned into weeks, no single urgent communiqué received in Iveagh House, the Department of Foreign Affairs headquarters on St Stephen's Green in Dublin, sounded alarm bells about Covid-19. But a drumbeat was beginning to signal trouble.

On the eve of the general election, 7 February, it was confirmed that an Irish couple were passengers on the *Diamond Princess*, a cruise ship that would become a real-life petri dish for what the virus could do in an enclosed setting. Fourteen deaths would eventually be linked with 712 infections on the ship. In fact, six Irish passengers were on board the cruise ship, two of whom caught the virus. Nine more Irish citizens were later caught up in an outbreak on the *Westerdam* cruise ship in Cambodia. Irish people were being flown out of Wuhan, which had been placed under a severe lockdown on 23 January, but in small numbers. The Chinese city was the epicentre of the coronavirus outbreak and had by this stage reported more than 10,000 cases and nearly 550 deaths. Gradually, the virus was moving from being stock content in diplomatic cables to something more substantial. Something was out of step with the normal hubbub of activity and intelligence gathered from across the globe.

Early NPHET meetings were small gatherings of experts who were usually called upon in the face of public health threats. The meetings were held in person in room 631 on the sixth floor of the Department of Health, a sprawling complex of buildings at Miesian Plaza in the heart of Dublin 2. The first meeting was chaired by Tony Holohan, who had served as chief medical officer for over a decade. There were ten people there, largely drawn from the HSE and the Department of Health.

In addition to what one participant later recalled as an 'optimism bias' in the wider health system at the time, members of the team were unsure how reliable information emerging from China was. In early February the Health Protection Surveillance Centre (HPSC) began engaging with the Chinese embassy, which shared documents on the characteristics of the new virus, including one that said that, to date 'there is no reliable evidence from the field investigations that the disease is contagious during the incubation period'. This assessment would later prove to be devastatingly wrong. Equally, documents suggest the Chinese didn't always get prompt responses from the Irish side. On 11 February, the first secretary of the embassy emailed the HSE to say that a 'Chinese patient' had been trying to get in touch with their local Department of Public Health in Ireland. The embassy said, 'We are also concerned that the phone calls made [...] were not answered after 13:00 on Saturdays and Sundays.'

The first meeting of NPHET on 27 January discussed how supplies of personal protective equipment (PPE) were 'sufficient', with contracts in place to access more 'as required'. While the European Centre for Disease Control's assessment of risk to the EU was 'moderate', the threat of onward transmission of the virus was rated as 'low'.

On the evening of 26 January, the first messages began to flow out from HSE headquarters to the hospital network. 'The CEO is calling an emergency meeting in the morning about the Chinese coronavirus,' a senior HSE official emailed an executive in the Dublin Midlands Hospital Group. 'Can I check if there's any major red flags or gaps in your hospitals around PPE or preparation levels that we need to be aware of?' the official asked, before almost casually pointing out that this was landing amid the chronic chaos of winter in the Irish health system: 'Apart from the obvious that your [emergency departments] are likely out the doors and isolation facilities are full up already. Thanks.'

In the Department of Health, Holohan's team were working on pandemic preparedness plans based on old models for other diseases, in a vacuum, with limited information about the new threat. They were looking back at work done for influenza, as well as SARS and MERS. Holohan would later admit to being 'troubled' by the lack of real disease modelling as he began to assemble a larger team in early March. But in February it was, one senior department official later recalled, still a 'phoney war'.

The parts of the State apparatus that were nominally supposed to plan for and react to medical threats were gradually warming up. Holohan, his deputy, Ronan Glynn, and their small team worked away in Miesian Plaza, as did the HSE in its Dr Steevens' Hospital headquarters in Dublin 8. But the brain, the heart and the soul of the system was elsewhere – because, in late January and early February, everyone else was off having an election.

—

Faced with a motion of no confidence in Minister for Health Simon Harris, Leo Varadkar called a general election in mid-January just as

4

the Dáil had been due to return from its Christmas recess. In so doing, he called time on the confidence and supply agreement with Fianna Fáil, a deal that had spanned the previous four years. It involved Micheál Martin's party abstaining on Dáil votes in return for the delivery of certain key priorities, which were laid out in a short document that the two parties had agreed in summer 2016.

For the two parties that emerged from the ashes of the Civil War nearly a century earlier, the 2020 general election was a period of intense pressure. Their leaders had to make good on promises not only to the electorate, but also to their own parties.

For Varadkar, the thrust of his leadership campaign in 2017 had been that Fine Gael seats were safer with him in charge – and that he could deliver more of them. His allies believed his reputation as a straight-talking politician who was not afraid to be blunt and to court controversy, who would transcend party lines and win new voters. Alongside this was his compelling backstory as the son of an Indian doctor and an Irish nurse, who grappled with his sexuality before publicly revealing in 2015 that he is gay.

But the local and European elections in 2019 had been the first, and unconvincing, test of his pitch. Varadkar then hesitated over calling a general election when, on the crest of a wave after helping to secure a Brexit deal in late 2019, he stood to benefit. Yet in early 2020, the post-Brexit shine had worn off and Varadkar's hand was being forced by the political vulnerability of his health minister.

His government was also deeply unpopular, a position compounded by a disastrous attempt to hold a commemoration event for Ireland's pre-partition police forces. After the emergence of the plan caused wide-spread anger and claims that Fine Gael were in effect commemorating the brutal regime of the Black and Tans, the idea was abandoned in early January 2020.

The damage was done in the minds of an electorate who were already deeply frustrated with Fine Gael's handling of seemingly intractable housing and health crises. It hammered home a deeper Fine Gael vulnerability: the sense that it did not understand the electorate, and that it was remote, detached from them after nearly a decade in power – a well-trodden path for many political parties after two terms.

Meanwhile, Micheál Martin, the only true veteran of government in the senior echelons of Fianna Fáil, faced being the first leader of his party not to occupy the Taoiseach's office. The local and European elections had been largely positive for Fianna Fáil. The party retained its position as the largest in local government, taking back council seats ceded to Sinn Féin five years earlier and making gains in Dublin, where its fortunes had nosedived since 2011, including winning a European Parliament seat.

But large swathes of the Fianna Fáil parliamentary party and the wider membership had been unhappy with the confidence and supply arrangement. They fumed at Martin's unilateral decision to extend it in December 2018 – without consulting the party – because of his concerns about creating political instability as Brexit loomed. But as the election dawned, it still seemed Martin stood a chance of leading the next government and closing the book on one of the most remarkable recovery stories in Irish political history.

On the campaign trail, ministers were briefed to expect questions on Covid-19, but it didn't feature. Instead, the election was dominated by housing issues. Health featured, as always, but it was the stock barrage of issues around waiting lists, clinical outcomes and the fallout from recent scandals like that surrounding CervicalCheck, the State's screening programme for cervical cancer. Countless debates, interviews and doorsteps with leaders, frontbench members and ministers came and went, but coronavirus received scant attention.

While out canvassing in Dublin towards the end of the campaign, Micheál Martin told a group of young Fianna Fáil members, 'Watch out for this, there's not much comment on it now, but this could be something.' He had read a newspaper report about the new virus emerging from China and had what he later described as 'a hunch'. Martin had been health minister when SARS emerged in 2003. It had left an impression on him.

To most others the new virus was something that was 'over there' – in China. 'Everybody in the West did not pay enough attention to what was going on in the East,' Professor Mark Ferguson, the government's chief scientific adviser at the time and a future member of NPHET, later said. 'I would say that's collective Western arrogance. We didn't look carefully enough at what was happening in China and elsewhere.'

Both Fine Gael and Fianna Fáil failed to capture the public appetite for change. There was a surge of support for Sinn Féin, and the two Civil War parties' bitter and personal attacks on each other continued, while they also expanded into the familiar territory of targeting Sinn Féin's murky links with the IRA.

Their stuttering campaigns led to dramatic setbacks on 8 February when Sinn Féin surprised itself by gaining 15 seats and winning the popular vote. 'Mary Lou for Taoiseach' became a popular refrain among its buoyant supporters. The party proceeded to hold a series of post-election rallies across the country that would soon have to be curtailed.

After the election there was no clear route to power for any party, while the caretaker government was shattered. The ranks of Cabinet were depleted – Shane Ross, Katherine Zappone and Regina Doherty had lost their seats – but they retained their Cabinet seats until a new government could be formed. Finian McGrath was a lame duck minister who had not sought re-election. Housing minister Eoghan Murphy, once the architect of Varadkar's successful campaign to lead Fine Gael, was an opposition hate figure and although he had clung on to his Dáil seat, he would resign it a year later. Varadkar's demeanour after the election, Cabinet colleagues thought, ranged from despondency to acceptance that Fine Gael would be going into opposition. Most of his parliamentary party demanded Fine Gael get out of government. It was just about the worst time for an identity crisis, given what was coming over the horizon.

Worldwide, the virus was stealing a march on governments and healthcare systems that failed to grasp its insidious nature. The election compounded this in Ireland, creating a political vacuum.

CHAPTER 2:

'AN EXPLOSIVE EFFECT'

13 February 2020
Cases: 0
Deaths: 0
Seven-day average of new cases: 0

Simon Harris, his adviser Joanne Lonergan and Dr Colette Bonner, one of Tony Holohan's deputy chief medical officers, boarded the government jet at Casement Aerodrome just outside Dublin. They were bound for Brussels and a meeting of EU health ministers, known by the acronym EPSCO. Three days earlier, on 10 February, Harris had been re-elected as a TD for Wicklow on the fifteenth count without reaching the quota. At the age of 33, the Minister for Health was embarking on his third Dáil term, having been just 24 when he was first elected in 2011, but the election outcome meant this could be the last time he was on board the Learjet 45. Some of the party took selfies to mark the occasion.

At the EPSCO meeting, Croatia's health minister Vili Beros confidently told journalists that there was a 'high degree of preparedness' within the EU for the emerging Covid-19 threat. Briefing materials circulated to journalists afterwards focused on information sharing and co-ordinated action to avoid shortages of medicine. There were presentations from the WHO and the European Centre for Disease Prevention and Control (ECDC), which brought home the growing seriousness of the emerging situation surrounding the virus. Harris's public comments mirrored the bravado of his colleagues on the continent. He told the *Irish Times* that he was satisfied Ireland had a 'significant level of preparedness' for the virus.

But on the plane home, the mood was darker. At the summit, EU member states had wrangled over the wording of a joint declaration. For all the affirmations about common cause, health was not a core EU competency, with member states retaining autonomy; in a pinch, some countries could go it alone. 'We were having all these meetings, but Europe didn't act as a cohesive bloc; that had devastating consequences,' Harris later said. 'We were suspending normal rules in our own country and everywhere else, we didn't seem to suspend the normal rules in Europe. We left ourselves really exposed as a geopolitical bloc.'

On 20 February, Harris signed an order designating Covid-19 a 'notifiable disease', meaning that doctors would have to inform the HSE when a case was diagnosed. There was a growing acceptance that Covid-19 would come to Ireland, but the view remained that it would be controlled, and perhaps only a few cases would be reported.

'Even public health officials thought this was something we could kind of weather,' Harris would later recall. 'There was a period from January to mid-March where there was a sense of "this is a pandemic, we've had lots of difficult times before, Minister – SARS, whatever else – we got through it, we'll get through it, [even though] we'll probably see cases".'

But before a case was even diagnosed in Ireland, the power of the virus to stop life in its tracks would be vividly illustrated.

—

Late on the night of Sunday 23 February, Austrian authorities stopped a train from Italy crossing the border through the Brenner Pass on suspicion that two passengers might be infected with Covid-19. Later that evening, the authorities stopped all services crossing the border. Deaths from the virus were now being reported in Italy, and 50,000 people were quarantined across the Veneto and Lombardy regions.

The Department of Foreign Affairs would soon issue advice against travel to northern Italy as the virus began to strike at the commercial and industrial heartland of the country. The north of Italy is the centre of much of the country's power and wealth, home to its fashion and automotive industries. In Milan, the biggest city of the region, the Borsa Italiana saw billions wiped off its publicly quoted companies as panic took hold. It was also home to a lot of Italian rugby fans.

That Sunday evening in Dublin, Tony Holohan called an emergency NPHET meeting. Just eight members attended via teleconference, but there was a clear shift in tone and emphasis. Events in Italy made the threat of the virus tangible, and Holohan told the meeting of his concerns. The ECDC had just published a threat assessment on Italy which reported that there was 'third generation' transmission of the virus across multiple towns, cities and regions. The report highlighted that, 'once imported, the virus causing Covid-19 can transmit rapidly. This may emanate from cases with mild symptoms that do not provoke healthcare-seeking behaviour.'

Holohan told the meeting that Ireland now had to consider how to deal with high levels of infection. The current model for dealing with cases suggested that all patients would be hospitalised, but they needed to think about home testing and self-isolation. The subtext was obvious: if there are a lot of cases, only the sick ones could be hospitalised. What was happening in Italy could happen in Ireland, even though not a single case had yet been detected. For the first time, the group discussed cancelling mass gatherings. 'In general terms experiences had an effect on actions taken,' Holohan would later recall. 'Northern Italy had an almost kind of explosive effect.'

In his own mind, Holohan had already formed the view that the forthcoming Six Nations rugby match between Ireland and Italy in Dublin could not go ahead on 7 March as planned, but a larger meeting of NPHET two days later would be needed to formally adopt the recommendation. Simon Harris was anxious to get in on the act and promptly turned up at the meeting in the Department of Health that Tuesday, 25 February. Holohan did not like this because he doesn't like politicians at his meetings. It was an article of faith for him that the formulation of advice needed to be separate from the consideration of that advice. Holohan had always been of the view that ministers in meeting rooms have one of two effects on officials: either they don't want to disclose things; or they try to show off in front of their political master. In either case, it becomes more challenging to ascertain clear advice. Officials speak more freely when there is no minister present. So on that day, Holohan made it clear, either Harris would leave quickly, or he would.

Members of Harris's team recalled feeling intensely uncomfortable. Nonetheless, Harris was allowed to address the meeting on the understanding that he would depart before NPHET got down to business. TV cameras were brought in for the show. Some amused NPHET members furtively took photos with their phones of Harris enthusiastically addressing the room with a cranky-looking Holohan beside him.

After Harris left the room, the discussion about cancelling the match was straightforward. There was little debate or dissent, given that Holohan had flagged concerns to a smaller group the previous Sunday. Paul Connors, the HSE head of communications and a huge rugby fan, was somewhat horrified. As he pointed out of the window in the direction of the Aviva Stadium, he said that the Irish Rugby Football Union (IRFU) would have to be briefed. His nephew Will Connors, a tearaway flanker who plied his trade for Leinster, was in line to win his first international cap against Italy.

Outside the room, Harris was booked to appear on RTÉ's *Six One News* that evening, and he and his team grew anxious as the meeting dragged on. 'I got messages to say that the outcome was awaited from the minister's team, [on] pieces of paper as I am chairing NPHET,' the CMO later recalled. But Holohan was not running the NPHET meeting so that Harris would have a result in time for the evening news. 'In the course of the kind of work I do, I'd often get messages from the minister of the day – and I've had many of them – and they're looking for something and I am not in position to give it and I don't get too worked up about that.'

Nonetheless, the meeting adjourned just before 6 p.m. There was a scramble to tell the IRFU of its decision, but the Department of Health's communications chief Deirdre Watters could not raise her counterpart in the IRFU, Stephen McNamara, or its chief executive Philip Browne, who was on a plane. Sarah Bardon, Harris's press adviser, tried unsuccessfully to contact Varadkar's staff, and Harris texted the Taoiseach. But it was too late. Harris's announcement during a live interview on the main evening news caught everyone cold. The IRFU released a terse statement seeking a meeting with Harris. Sports journalists were pointedly briefed on how the IRFU was caught unawares by the announcement.

Later that evening, Harris rang Shane Ross, the Minister for Transport, Tourism and Sport, to apologise and acknowledge that the affair should have been better handled. Ross recalled speaking with Browne about the cancellation. The IRFU boss does not do effing and blinding, but Browne made clear in a measured way his displeasure at what had happened. 'He's not the type of guy to fly off the handle,' Ross later recalled, 'but he was very cross.' At the same time Ross, so often a thorn in his Fine Gael Cabinet colleagues' sides over the previous four years, was in total agreement with the decision. Early on he had become very concerned about the threat Covid-19 posed. 'Lives, lives, it's simple human lives,' he would later say. Ross duly went on *Morning Ireland* the following day to defend the cancellation.

But that was not the end of the matter. Later that week, Holohan, Harris and his team were summoned to the Department of the Taoiseach where Leo Varadkar rounded on his health minister. He was furious that Browne hadn't been notified, and told them that there could never again be a situation where a decision was made involving a key sectoral body that wasn't told in advance. 'Leo tore a new one for Simon and Tony for cancelling it,' one person in the room later recalled.

Varadkar queried whether the match could have gone ahead with Italian fans told not to come and their tickets resold. Could it have gone ahead behind closed doors? Holohan would later be described by one participant as bemused by these suggestions, while Harris's team wondered whether Stephen McNamara, the IRFU communications chief and a friend of Varadkar's, had been in the Taoiseach's ear.

The following Sunday a story in the *Sunday Business Post* outlined how the Taoiseach had 'reprimanded' his health minister over his handling of the matter. Harris's team blamed Varadkar's team for leaking the details of the entire meeting.

Even though the match was cancelled, there was never a substantial discussion about stopping Italian fans coming to Ireland. The travel advisory for Irish citizens against going to Italy did nothing to stop Italians from landing in Dublin. 'I don't know how many [came], but I'd say a lot did,' Varadkar later said.

Around this time, on NPHET's recommendation, HSE staff were sent to Dublin Airport to review the steps they were taking to police the advisory. Very little, it turned out. At one point, a senior HSE executive literally walked around the airport with a member of DAA staff pointing at spots on the walls where posters with advice for arrivals from Italy could be put up. In retrospect, it seemed futile – but this was the playbook from previous pandemics.

On the week the rugby match would have taken place, 3,585 people still flew in from Italy, and 7,640 had preceded them the week before.

—

On Saturday evening, 29 February, the Department of Health confirmed Ireland's first case of Covid-19, diagnosed in a teenage boy who had come home from a school trip. Within hours of parents being told, the name of the school became public knowledge. Scoil Chaitríona, a gaelscoil in one of the leafier parts of the Dublin Central constituency, was attended by children of, among others, Sinn Féin president Mary Lou McDonald. The boy concerned had just returned from a skiing holiday in northern Italy, and therefore was eligible for testing.

Testing had been under way at the National Virus Reference Laboratory for weeks, and its director, Cillian De Gascun, was quietly unnerved by the fact that nothing had yet been found. Just one case was detected from 460 tests carried out between 7 February and 2 March.

There was almost a sense of relief in the lab when the first positive test was returned because it meant the kit was working.

But the situation in Scoil Chaitríona was complicated. There had been discussions about testing the contacts of confirmed cases, but with four hundred students in the school, that was discounted. Instead, contacts identified by public health doctors were asked to restrict their social interactions, and the school was closed for 14 days. The student was never seriously unwell – the hospital told senior HSE managers he was ready to be released, but he was kept in isolation because they didn't know how contagious the disease was.

At a hastily arranged meeting held in Croke Park a few days later, several senior HSE staff fielded questions from a packed room of parents. Paul Connors chaired what turned out to be a highly volatile event. Concerned parents demanded to know the identity of the student so they could assess their own and their children's levels of risk and exposure. Many of those present wanted to be tested even though they didn't fit the criteria for testing. Some complained about having to cancel or delay weddings because of concerns about the virus, which was then seen as a major and unusual imposition. But the large indoor gathering did not itself appear to set off alarm bells, even among those from the HSE at the top of the room, showing just how little was known at that stage.

As a parent, but more relevantly as a political and community leader, Mary Lou McDonald was not going to remain silent. She read the riot act to the HSE executives, telling them that she wanted absolute assurance that her family and the families of those in the room were safe; and she had heard nothing in their presentations that provided that assurance.

Connors called on Professor Martin Cormican, the HSE's head of infection control, to respond to McDonald from the stage. Based in the small village of Clarinbridge in south Galway, Cormican, softly and precisely spoken, has a black belt in karate and would frequently practise by himself in his back yard late at night. Or he would go out running, finding that physical activity of whichever kind helps take his mind off the pressures of the day job. In 2019, at the age of 57, he completed the Dublin City Marathon in a time of 3 hours 36 minutes. Colleagues observe that he has an almost monk-like discipline and is congenitally unable to tell a lie.

On that tense night in Croke Park, Cormican calmly but firmly told the Sinn Féin president that he would love to give her absolute assurance that everything would be all right. But that isn't the way medical advice works, he said. She and her family would probably be okay, but in a pandemic, total guarantees could not be provided. He was unfazed by what he later described as a 'confrontational sort of manner' from McDonald. It was just her style, he concluded. Cormican's view on this was clear. He used to tell his students, 'Never promise patients the sun will come up in the morning.' Certainty is not the business of medics – 'Our business is managing uncertainty.'

The Croke Park meeting was, a participant later recalled, a harbinger of things to come. People were upset, disoriented, seeking reassurances that they and their families would be protected from infection, that someone, or something, would stop the disease. One HSE participant later recalled thinking, 'I hope there's not too many more cases, because if we've many more meetings like that, we'll be fucked.'

—

The HSE was not just trying to address growing public concern about the virus. In early March, Paul Reid had begun to warn the Taoiseach more explicitly about the need to protect the health service. 'My concern was growing, that something was needed to protect the health service,' he later said.

Over the course of the months that followed, Reid's approach would, at times, divide and frustrate others involved in the pandemic response. Some on NPHET, a body rammed with PhDs, medical doctors and university-educated civil servants, would mischievously call the HSE chief executive – who left school at 16 without a Leaving Certificate – 'Professor Reid'. Others who observed him closely as he settled into the role he had been appointed to in April 2019 on a pay and pension package of over €420,000 a year, felt he struggled initially with his lack of a clinical background.

Reid's reporting structure was also far from straightforward. In addition to the HSE board, he had effective reporting responsibilities to the political system – Taoiseach, Tánaiste and Minister for Health – and relationships to manage with the Department of Health, its secretary general, and the chief medical officer. The fate of his predecessor, Tony O'Brien, who had been forced to resign over the CervicalCheck scandal, showed how exposed the position could become. 'I think he was pulled in a dozen different directions,' observed one HSE source who interacted with Reid across the period.

Later in the pandemic, there was a feeling in some quarters of the HSE and NPHET that Reid would exceed his brief as chief executive of the health service, his responsibility being solely to protect healthcare provision in the State. He would often appear in the media, much more so than his predecessors. He was fond of referring to how the HSE existed within a society and an economy, and how the welfare of the health service would be impacted by all these elements. While undoubtedly true, this provoked the ire of some, who felt Reid should stick to the knitting. 'He's the head of the HSE, he's not the head of a multi-agency organisation cross-checking the economy,' an HSE contemporary later remarked.

Reid's style frustrated some. He would speak in generalities, both in public and in private, saying that the health system was 'coping' and referencing conversations with clinicians as evidence for his position. Members of NPHET were particularly irked – they felt they were held to a higher standard than the HSE chief executive; they had to be more precise, and if they were wrong, the criticism was unbridled. Meanwhile, they felt, Reid got away with a communication style that was one part sloppiness and one part an elaborate manoeuvre to avoid being pinned down, or aligned too closely with any one policy response, lest it prove politically unpopular. In the months ahead, NPHET members would form the impression that Reid was a domineering presence in the HSE, looming over his senior team, and that at key points, he didn't identify threats from Covid-19 coming down the tracks. 'Paul "Everything-is-going-to-be-all-right" Reid' became another moniker.

However, for all that some people chose to criticise him – and rarely to his face – there was a steeliness to Reid. HSE veterans believe he galvanised the organisation within months of taking over, simplifying top-heavy reporting structures and ruthlessly cutting out unnecessary feedback loops that perpetuated the HSE's speciality: inertia. He also knew how, and when, to fight his corner, and had an assertive leadership style. He is a 'pugnacious street fighter [who] operates on the principle that the only way of avoiding being weak is to attack', observed a senior HSE source.

True to this characterisation, in the early days of March 2020, Reid was warning the political system that something needed to be done. 'This is getting really serious, we need to do something, there needs to be some restraint put on it, we need strong messages,' he told Varadkar in one phone call. The HSE chief executive was reflecting the growing anxiety at board level around the planned St Patrick's Day festival but also the risk associated with the Cheltenham festival, which thousands of Irish racing fans flock to every year. Board members had asked Reid that their concerns about mass gatherings be passed on. Reid was concerned that NPHET was 'maybe not as strong' on the mass gatherings, with St Patrick's Day a particular cause for concern.

Around 500,000 people were predicted to flood into Dublin for the parade. The Department of Arts was 'panicky', one source later recalled, and had argued that if a cancellation wasn't decided by a certain date, it could not be cancelled. St Patrick's Day was the showpiece event for the State for the entire year and to cancel it would be tantamount to declaring Irish tourism closed.

On Friday, 6 March, Tony Holohan stood next to Leo Varadkar in the courtyard of Government Buildings as the Taoiseach told reporters that Ireland was still in a containment phase, that decisions would be proportionate, and that at this stage, major events, including St Patrick's Day, were not being cancelled.

Watching the footage at Dublin Airport was Simon Harris and his team, who had just returned from another meeting of health ministers in Brussels – this time flying Ryanair. The meeting had heard more of the same urgent messages about the EU needing to act together. The ECDC warned ministers there had been a hundred-fold increase in cases since their last meeting, and that this trend would continue. Cases were being reported without links to affected areas or cases that had already been diagnosed, which signalled that the virus was likely far more prevalent in the community than testing was picking up. The WHO warned EU ministers that the measures being taken now would determine the course of the outbreak.

Harris and his team were, at that stage, firmly of the view that 'Paddy's Day' could not go ahead. Sweden had cancelled its parade and the Irish permanent representative in Brussels had cancelled its St Patrick's Day gathering. Harris's special adviser Joanne Lonergan relayed the minister's concerns to Varadkar's chief of staff, Brian Murphy, and another of the Taoiseach's advisers, Clare Mungovan, including his belief that a call should be made that Friday afternoon to cancel St Patrick's Day.

But the message that came back from Murphy was to hold tight through the weekend. He believed the decision would be best made the following Monday at the inaugural meeting of the Cabinet subcommittee on Covid-19, which had been set up a few days earlier. Although agreeable to waiting a few days, Harris wanted to join a press conference being organised for Varadkar and Holohan later that day once he returned from EPSCO. But coming off the plane he saw Varadkar and his chief medical officer signalling that it was all systems go for St Patrick's Day. He wasn't happy that the event had happened without him, and that night Harris told the Taoiseach as much in a phone call.

Within 48 hours, however, Holohan had brought forward a NPHET meeting to discuss the St Patrick's Day festival originally slated for the following Wednesday to that Sunday night, 8 March. The only people physically present at the ad hoc meeting in the Department of Health were him and Dr Colm Henry, the HSE's chief clinical officer, with every other member joining via teleconference. The official minutes record a 'robust' discussion on cancelling the festival. However, participants remember it as a straightforward call to cancel that came from Holohan. The broad shape of the decision had been emerging for some time. NPHET had discussed whether just the Dublin parade could be cancelled, with local festivities going ahead, but the fear was that the congregation due to take place in Dublin would just spread outwards, with attendance at regional parades swelling and the risk of mass transmission increasing.

That evening the political briefings to the next day's newspapers conveyed that there were at that stage no plans to postpone the St Patrick's Day parade. However, the exact opposite was in fact the case. Holohan would carry the recommendation under his arm into a meeting that few present would ever forget.

CHAPTER 3:

THE BLACK LINE

9 March 2020
Cases: 24
Deaths: 0
Seven-day average of new cases: 5

Tony Holohan projected a slide on to the wall of conference room 242 in Government Buildings. It showed the number of people who would be hospitalised with Covid-19 in a worst-case scenario. The line shot upwards on the slide before curving – this was representative of tens of thousands of people ending up in hospital. Below this curve was a straight black line tracking right across the page.

'What's the black line?' asked Simon Coveney, the Tánaiste and Minister for Foreign Affairs.

'That's the hospital capacity,' Holohan responded. 'That's ten thousand beds.'

The gap between the two was massive. 'It was scary, actually, because I knew what that meant,' Leo Varadkar would later recall. It was the moment the scale of the threat became real for the Taoiseach, and for many others.

The cold reality of these numbers, graphs and charts, laid out before ministers, was that in a few short weeks people would be turning up at hospitals with no space for them. They would die in the car park or, just as bad, they would die at home because the ambulance service would be so overwhelmed it would not be able to reach them in time to transport them to a hospital that probably couldn't admit them anyway.

This would be northern Italy – or worse.

—

The occasion that day in conference room 242, more commonly known as the Sycamore Room (because of the large oval sycamore table in the centre) was the first meeting of the Cabinet subcommittee on Covid-19. It was, in part, a communications set piece designed to show the public that the new virus was being taken seriously. Television cameras and photographers had been invited into what was yet another packed indoor gathering. 'There were at least fifty people in that room, around the walls and at the table,' Regina Doherty, the Minister for Social Protection who had lost her Dáil seat a month earlier, later said. 'We just crowded in. It was just bizarre. It was as if we knew the seriousness of the decision we were making but not the impact that the actual virus would have on us.'

For some in the room a sense had been dawning that Covid-19 was more serious than any infectious disease the State had previously grappled with. Simon Harris and his team had been embedded in the issue for weeks. Paschal Donohoe had been hearing horror stories from his Italian counterpart, Roberto Gaultieri, at meetings of EU finance ministers. 'He said what's happening on the ground in China is grave, exceptionally serious and if it's not on your radar screen, it needs to be,' Donohoe later recalled. The affable Minister for Finance and Public Expenditure had also been part of a smaller group of ministers, the Taoiseach himself and senior civil servants, including the likes of Martin Fraser, the Taoiseach's secretary general, and Robert Watt, the secretary general of the Department of Public Expenditure, who had seen some of the grimmest projections around mortality that were based on early, rough modelling.

The memo prepared for ministers for that meeting on 9 March noted that 'mathematical modellers are using data from the Covid-19 outbreaks already seen in more severely affected countries to predict what the impact in Ireland is likely to be.' After the cameras left, Holohan's PowerPoint presentation focused on the evidence from China and Italy. The disease was highly infectious and people were dying. Rough modelling indicated that as many as 20,000 people in Ireland could die. The presentation was reliant on basic calculations done by Breda Smyth, the HSE's director of public health in the west of Ireland. Some of the modelling had already been leaked to Susan Mitchell, the health editor of the *Business Post*, the previous day. But ministers were shown the full extent of the damage the disease could wreak. It was not sophisticated, and the message was not complicated, but it shocked most of those in the room.

People briefed on early modelling recall how it showed that up to 80 per cent of the population could be infected, and 40 to 50 per cent would have a clinical disease. Some two million people could be sick. While 80 per cent of those would have relatively mild symptoms, 15–20 per cent would require hospitalisation – somewhere in the region of 400,000 people. Another 100,000 would be in high-dependency or intensive care units. Tens of thousands could die. It was a nightmare scenario of unprecedented proportions. 'Obviously a situation where there are two thousand deaths is entirely different from a situation where there are twenty thousand deaths, and we need to avoid twenty thousand deaths,' Varadkar told the meeting.

The modelling showed clearly that closing the country would make a difference – a significant difference – in suffering and death. Suddenly this was no longer a difficult call for self-described civil libertarian Varadkar. The decisions he finds difficult in politics are the ones with many moving parts, and no obvious clear option – sometimes just an array of bad choices. Combining that with the intangible calculus of electoral politics – the trade-offs, the judgement calls, the inexactitude and the high stakes – is difficult. Even though the decision to lock down would be momentous – and in the room, Varadkar admits, it was 'scary' – it wouldn't actually be that difficult.

Varadkar is known for being analytical to a fault; almost calculating. What's undeniable is that he runs the numbers. Hundreds of people can die from seasonal flu in a bad year, but this was not a seasonal flu. Avoiding 20,000 deaths would likely require the imposition of public health restrictions. 'We would never shut down the country, put people out of their jobs, and close the borders for the flu season. But twenty thousand to eighty thousand [deaths] was a whole other ball game,' Varadkar later said.

The memo given to ministers that day was blunt. Options were being narrowed as one outcome became unavoidable.

There is currently a moderate to high risk that Covid-19 will become established in Ireland in the coming weeks in a manner similar to that seen in Italy and it is expected that Ireland will see a rapid increase in numbers of confirmed cases. If it does become established here it is likely that this will happen quickly and that most cases will occur over the following twelve weeks.

The document noted that evidence from other countries was that 'Covid-19 will affect the most vulnerable in Irish society, and specifically older people and people with pre-existing medical conditions.' It went on to note that experience of the disease in China and globally showed that while it 'spreads rapidly in some regions' it had 'developed more slowly in others'. This, the memo said, indicated that with an 'appropriate, con-certed and co-ordinated national response, there is scope for Ireland to influence the spread and progression of infection'. But, it added, Covid-19 infection 'places extraordinary pressure on the health system, whatever the level of the health service's development and resources'.

To that end, the subcommittee agreed on a €2.4bn package of reforms for sick pay, €200m for businesses, and €435m for the HSE. The decision to cancel St Patrick's Day, which the government had publicly agonised over for weeks, was a mere footnote to the discussion. The money and the cancellation of one mass gathering paled in comparison to the numbers that Holohan had presented.

Like bankruptcy, the seriousness of the situation was becoming clear first very slowly, and then all at once. The State could only slow the spread of the disease. 'There's a lot about this virus that we don't know,' Varadkar told the media after the meeting, ashen-faced alongside a drawn-looking Harris and the equally grave business minister, Heather Humphreys. 'But it is possible we're facing events unprecedented in modern times.'

—

For three years, Paschal Donohoe's mandate as Minister for Finance and Public Expenditure meant he oversaw every euro that was raised and spent in the State. While he was caricatured as 'prudent Paschal' for his parsimonious attitude to spending, for much of this time he had been held in high esteem by his Cabinet colleagues. That esteem had begun to fracture, though, the previous October, when he refused spending requests during budgetary negotiations, even as the odds on a general election shortened. Frustration with Donohoe grew in ministerial ranks during that campaign, for which he was director of elections. One TD remembers having a row over campaign resources and strategy on the day the election was called, and knowing then – correctly – their seat would be lost. Even if his standing had been dented, however, Donohoe's words still carried great weight for those in Fine Gael.

In an interview with Seán O'Rourke on RTÉ Radio 1 on 10 March, the day after the Cabinet subcommittee meeting, he outlined the new stance: 'Whatever resources we need to mobilise to help deal with this, the government will do.' This was the new fiscal stance – although the Dublin Central TD was at that stage only talking about the €2.4bn that had been allocated for Covid spending, and only conceding that it 'may' be spent.

For many in Fine Gael, it wasn't so much what Donohoe said about the gravity of the situation, but the political departure he signalled that really caused ears to prick up. For weeks in the aftermath of the election Fine Gael had been resisting entering talks to form a new government. From the Taoiseach down, the leadership of the party was expecting – publicly and privately – to enter opposition. Now, Donohoe told O'Rourke, the political context 'had very significantly and fundamentally changed' and could be changed for 'quite a while'.

Privately, Donohoe had begun communicating this to Michael McGrath, Fianna Fáil's finance spokesman, with whom he had developed a close working partnership under the confidence and supply deal. The pair had hammered out four budgets in total. 'I want to do this,' he would say to McGrath. Donohoe saw the emerging Covid crisis as a war-like threat to the State and that it was inconceivable that his party could remain off the pitch.

'We were facing a threat of the highest magnitude. We were going to be building morgues for people. I knew the work was under way to build those emergency facilities,' he would later say. 'It wasn't so much a potential threat – I already knew our welfare systems couldn't deal with it – it was an existential threat. That just led me to form the view that whatever we had to do, we were going to do it. I absolutely did believe it was an existential crisis for the State.'

The clear signal that the situation could force Fine Gael and Fianna Fáil into coalition grabbed people's attention, but a meeting of ministerial advisers called by Brian Murphy, Varadkar's chief of staff, rammed the point home. Murphy, who first joined Varadkar's staff when he was transport minister, was a veteran. Gregarious and shrewd, he was seen by colleagues as politically sharp, and possessing an emotional savviness – a human side, where his boss was notoriously weak. He was hugely protective of the Taoiseach, softening his hard edges by being likeable and pleasant to all comers. Varadkar, staffers recall, could walk past you in a corridor without acknowledgement half the time and look right through you the other half. Murphy would make the effort: 'He humanises Leo's political operation,' one colleague said. For all the friendliness, though, Murphy carried a big stick. His power across Fine Gael in government was almost without parallel. When he spoke, people listened. Many of the advisers were battle-weary after years in government and bloodied by the election result; and they faced losing their jobs if their bosses had lost their seats, or if they failed to retain Cabinet roles even if Fine Gael did stay in government. At the meeting Murphy delivered a series of blunt and shocking messages: there were going to be a lot of cases, a lot of sickness; and a lot of people were going to die. Notwithstanding how tired or unmotivated people were, the message was, one participant recalled, 'That you guys are paid by the Irish taxpayer, and the shit is about to hit the fan, so everyone to your posts'. Murphy told the group that Covid was likely to be with them for between three and six months. Steps like those then being taken in Italy were going to happen, and businesses were going to close, he said, giving a bleak assessment of the outlook for the economy. The best case suggested by modelling, he told the room, was that 25 per cent of the population would be infected. However, Murphy said that steps like closing schools and restricting travel would be held in reserve; they would devastate the country, and could only be done at the right time, otherwise public compliance would slip. His message was that the State only had so many arrows in its quiver, and couldn't shoot them all at once. Some would have to be held back, he said. But a little over 24 hours later, many of these arrows would be fired.

That day, 10 March, NPHET gathered in the Department of Health for its regular Tuesday meeting. It was clear there was a step change coming – the need for improved modelling, changing the policy of hospitalising every case as numbers increased, and increasing testing were all flagged. Most important, the meeting discussed measures that would, in a very short time, become key pillars of lockdown – that mass events could be cancelled or restricted, and that schools and universities would be shut. It was also a meeting at which the first death from Covid-19 in the State was confirmed (although it would not be publicly confirmed until the following day). It was a sad and symbolic moment. However, there was still no sense of how imminent things were: the meeting discussed NPHET's inputs into the State's National Action Plan, still being drafted, and agreed to sign off on them on Thursday 12 March.

Then, everything changed.

CHAPTER 4:

'PAY ATTENTION'

10 March 2020
Cases: 34
Deaths: 0
Seven-day average of new cases: 5

Leo Varadkar arrived in Washington DC having cancelled both the New York leg of his St Patrick's Day trip to the USA and his attendance at an earlier business leaders' lunch in DC. There had been doubts about whether he would travel at all. The trip was going ahead because of concerns relayed by the Irish ambassador in Washington, Dan Mulhall, that if it did not happen in some form, the annual tradition could be scrapped altogether. That would be a disaster, losing Ireland vital annual bilateral access to the White House and the president of the day. There was another crucial reason in that neither the Taoiseach nor his team wanted to give any impression that a lockdown was imminent – and spark public panic – by doing something unusual like cancelling the annual trip to the USA. 'If you're not ready to do it [lockdown], you should not start doing things that look unusual,' one senior official later recalled.

Having deputised for him at the business leaders' lunch, that evening Mulhall met with Varadkar at Blair House, the US president's official guest house across the road from the White House. The pair, along with Varadkar's travelling delegation – Brian Murphy, Secretary to the Government Martin Fraser and assistant government press secretary Sarah Meade – were due to attend the Ireland Funds dinner. The $1,000-a-plate black tie fundraising event in the National Building Museum is a staple of the DC Beltway circuit, and the high point of the year for Irish America, attended by the great and the good of its business and political worlds.

Mulhall, a veteran diplomat who had previously served as Irish ambassador to London and Berlin, had already decided to cancel an Irish embassy event he was due to hold the following day in a large basement area of a DC restaurant. He had invited 800 people and expected 600 to turn up, but he felt that many people in a confined space would not be a good idea. By contrast, the organisers of the Ireland Funds dinner were determined their event should go ahead. The vast high-ceilinged open plan room in the National Building Museum was perhaps a safer venue, but fears over the virus had already dissuaded some guests from coming. Attendance was notably down for a mediocre dinner – an artisan charcuterie display of various meats and cheeses; a main course of pavé of beef tenderloin or smoky herb panko-crusted salmon; and a dessert buffet. Attendees were promised special entertainment. What they got was a bizarre musical interlude from a guitar-wielding former US Congressman Joe Crowley, whose career on Capitol Hill was ended by Alexandria Ocasio-Cortez in 2018.

By that stage the dinner had already been overshadowed by Donald Trump's sudden announcement that the US would, from that Friday, suspend all travel from Europe, excluding the UK, for 30 days in response to the escalating coronavirus outbreak. At the top table, Varadkar sat with, among others, US House Speaker Nancy Pelosi. A short time before the ban was made public, a member of Pelosi's staff had tapped her on the shoulder. 'Speaker, you have to come out and take a call, the White House is looking for you,' the aide told the veteran California congresswoman. She left the room and returned 15 minutes later, informing some of those around the table that Trump was going to ban travel from the Schengen area. 'What is the Schengen area?' she was overheard asking.

As news of the travel ban broke across Twitter, a sense of panic took hold among some attendees who had travelled from Ireland and now wondered if they would be able to get home. The room started to empty. Brian Murphy's dinner had already been interrupted by Martin Fraser: 'Look, I need to talk to you.' But it wasn't about the travel ban.

Fraser had been at another table, sitting alongside Diane Dodds, the Northern Ireland economy minister, simultaneously trying to hint to her that Covid was likely to cause major issues while not letting on about imminent restrictions in the South. As he was having his dinner his phone rang. It was Liz Canavan, one of his key lieutenants in the Department of the Taoiseach. There was news from Dublin. After he went over to speak to Murphy, a short time later Fraser came for Varadkar, whispering in the Taoiseach's ear. 'We have to go,' he said urgently. 'I have to talk to you about something.' Fraser wanted to extricate Varadkar from the room in a manner that would not cause a fuss, but the Taoiseach's abrupt exit prompted a flurry of tweets from Irish journalists in the cheap seats on the edge of the main hall. They assumed he had been whisked away to be briefed on the implications of the Trump travel ban (Ireland, it would later transpire, was not on the initial list of banned countries). But in an empty private room at the National Building Museum, the Taoiseach, along with Murphy and Fraser, was being given an update from home … and it was not good.

—

That evening in Dublin, Tony Holohan called an emergency meeting of NPHET. Cillian De Gascun had relayed news of a sharp increase in the number of new cases. The 27 new cases NPHET would publicly report the following day represented a trebling of the previous day's numbers. It was enough to prompt Holohan to take action. 'We need a meeting,' he said. 'We can't sit on this. We need a meeting of the NPHET tonight, we need to get everybody in.'

Simon Harris was putting his dinner in the oven at home in Greystones when Holohan rang. 'I'm really concerned,' the CMO said.

'I wouldn't be holding this meeting if I wasn't.' As he changed back into his suit, Harris rang Brian Murphy and briefed him on what was happening back home. At 8.40 p.m., Harris texted Varadkar with what he described as 'very worrying developments' with Covid-19. An emergency meeting of NPHET had been called, there was significant community transmission and very ill patients, Harris told his boss, and it was likely that very serious decisions would have to be taken that night. Varadkar asked what those decisions might be, but Harris texted him back to say he wasn't sure at that point.

As they grappled with the news in DC, Harris contacted Simon Coveney, the Tánaiste and most senior member of the government in Ireland that night. Coveney offered to come into the Department of Health.

With Harris's driver gone home for the night and knowing he needed to be back in quickly, he got into his own car and drove himself the 30 kilometres from Greystones to the department in around 30 minutes. By contrast, Coveney was in Dublin city centre, staying in what he later described as a 'small apartment' on Holles Street that was just an eight-minute walk from the department. 'Simon said to me, "You're the Tánaiste, head of government when the Taoiseach is away. You have to come into the Department of Health, there's going to be some very impactful decisions this evening,"' Coveney later recalled. Rather than make the short walk from his apartment to Miesian Plaza, Coveney recalled getting a lift over to the Department of Health.

On the seventh floor of the department, the NPHET meeting ran for some three hours. The data was pored over. Sources later remembered how some of the cases were linked to an outbreak in a Dublin Airport hotel, where trainee flight attendants from Italy were staying as part of an exercise run by their airline. Was this an isolated cluster, they wondered, or was the sudden increase evidence of community transmission?

NPHET had already done groundwork on what the next phase of response to the virus would look like. At that stage, Ireland was in the containment phase, attempting to detect early cases and tracing their contacts in a bid to limit the spread. But now the delay phase was being contemplated, in which measures like restrictions on mass gatherings would be recommended to limit the spread of the virus. Elsewhere in Europe, lockdowns were beginning to roll out, first in Italy, which had been badly hit. It was 1 a.m. before the NPHET meeting broke up.

Holohan made his way downstairs to the sixth floor where Harris, Coveney, their advisers and department officials had been waiting for several hours, drinking copious cups of tea and snacking.

Accompanied by two Department of Health assistant secretaries, Tracey Conroy and Fergal Goodman, Holohan sat to Harris's right and opened his zipped brown leather folder. The chief medical officer later recalled feeling a sense of 'genuine trepidation' at this moment. He had been in the role for over a decade, advising numerous health ministers, but he had never proposed shutting down the economy. 'I don't mind admitting I was nervous, but I knew this was necessary,' he said.

He handed the minister a piece of paper with a printed list of NPHET recommendations for the government to consider and implement. For the next twenty minutes he ran through an emphatic presentation with a series of severe proposals for government to consider. Schools, colleges and childcare facilities should close, along with cultural institutions. Indoor mass gatherings of more than 100 people and outdoor gatherings of more than 500 people should be cancelled.

Holohan told Harris that this needed to happen early the next day and that communication of the measures would be vital in order to avoid widespread chaos. A decision was taken not to ring Minister for Education Joe McHugh to tell him or his department that schools would have to shut for fear it would leak. When he was told early the next morning, McHugh assumed he would be part of a press conference taking place later that morning, but he soon discovered this was not the case. His staff hit the roof.

The softly spoken Donegal TD had to phone the Taoiseach and insist on his involvement. 'Simon [Coveney] is in charge,' Varadkar told him. When McHugh rang Coveney he was not asking to be part of the press conference; he was declaring that he would be there. Coveney later acknowledged McHugh's legitimate grievance but insisted there was ample reason for not briefing him in advance or inviting him to the press conference. 'The idea that a journalist could have got a scoop to say the country's about to go into lockdown at three a.m. or four a.m. or for *Morning Ireland*, without any context around that, would have really triggered potential panic,' Coveney would later recall. 'The country needed the Taoiseach to tell them why.'

What's more, there were concerns in government that the Department of Education could be leaky. A false alarm over the closure of schools had already been reported in local media in recent days, and the department was suspected as being the source of the garbled messaging.

Back in Washington, Varadkar was grappling with the news Liz Canavan relayed to him of the need to shutter large parts of society. Coveney, whom Varadkar spoke to that night, later recalled that the Taoiseach was 'deeply frustrated that he wasn't in Ireland'. Varadkar maintains he was not annoyed, however. 'We thought this was going to happen, we knew the direction of travel in terms of the restrictions, at the time,' he later recalled.

However, the bigger problem right there and then in the National Building Museum at 10 p.m. DC time and 2 a.m. in Dublin, was trying to get the Taoiseach back to Blair House without arousing suspicion among the travelling Irish press corps. Fortunately, Varadkar had a Secret Service detail assigned to him who were skilled in the art of clandestine extractions. As their boss was quietly removed from the building, Fraser and Murphy went back down to the main function. 'We all need to go for a few pints here now,' Fraser told everyone who was with him. The intention was for the Taoiseach's team to drink in plain sight of the fourth estate – it was vital that nothing gave the game away. Press aide Sarah Meade calmly told the hovering Irish journalists that the Taoiseach would speak to them early the next morning. A leak, a tweet or a stray word from Varadkar if he was buttonholed by the Irish media could cause chaos at home. It was, in the view of senior officials that night, a moment of great peril. It could have caused 'an absolute catastrophe', one said. Controlling the message of imminent major restrictions was crucial to the pandemic response, and so they tried to give the impression of normality. But they drank bottles, not pints. There was important work to be done in the morning.

That night, the Taoiseach lay in bed in his Blair House guestroom tapping out a short speech on his iPhone before sending it to Meade in the small hours of Thursday morning. The Taoiseach would address the nation at the bottom of the steps leading up to the president's guest house. Flagpoles had to be sourced from the Irish embassy and brought over as dawn broke across the US capital.

Just before 7.30 a.m. Washington DC time, Fraser, Murphy and the rest of the Taoiseach's delegation emerged from Blair House and walked down the steps. The grave looks on their faces said it all. 'Pay attention,' Fraser told a waiting journalist, pointing to the podium where Leo Varadkar arrived moments later.

'I need to speak to you about coronavirus and Covid-19,' the Taoiseach began.

—

As the nation back home grappled with the mid-morning announcement from Varadkar that unprecedented restrictions would come into force from 6 p.m. that evening, the Taoiseach's day took a surreal turn.

He headed for the White House, where he was to have meetings with US Vice President Mike Pence and then President Donald Trump. He was preoccupied, musing to those around him about how he would re-register as a doctor to help in the Covid effort. But those he encountered recalled how unnaturally calm he seemed. He doesn't often get excited or emotional.

At the White House, Donald Trump greeted Varadkar. 'It feels strange not to be able to shake your hand, but I am told we shouldn't, so we won't,' the President told his guest before ushering him into the Oval Office. The waiting media were brought in. The room was packed with journalists on top of each other, scrambling for a good position. For the next 25 minutes President Trump repeatedly insisted to the assembled media that the virus would 'go very quickly'.

Varadkar would later recall that he told Trump in their private meeting how important it was to take the virus seriously. 'There was a perception at the time that he wasn't because he had been previously dismissive of it,' Varadkar later said. 'His kind of view was that the reason why the virus was in America was because the Europeans hadn't cut off travel from China, that's how it got to Italy and got to Europe.' From Varadkar's perspective it seemed that Trump was blaming Europe and China for the virus landing on US shores.

The Taoiseach disagreed with this view, but admitted he was reluctant to get into a row with Trump. He had a 35-minute private meeting with the most powerful man on the planet and many topics to touch on. In the same meeting, Trump was his usual confident, assertive self. 'We just have to get out of this,' one participant remembers him saying of the emerging Covid-19 threat. He was facing re-election in November and could ill afford a public health and economic crisis.

Varadkar already had the verdict of his electorate and was facing an uncertain political future at the same time as the State was facing the biggest public health emergency in its history. But to those who observed him that day, 12 March 2020, in Washington DC, the Taoiseach seemed, again, strangely calm. It wasn't a feeling shared by all the Taoiseach's staff, some of whom sat sleepless on the entire flight back to Dublin, contemplating the awful reality that awaited them at home.

CHAPTER 5:

COMPLEX RELATIONSHIPS

14 March 2020
Cases: 90
Deaths: 1
Seven-day average of new cases: 16

I n the days leading up to his election as Taoiseach in June 2017, Leo Varadkar was advised by close allies to sack Simon Harris from Cabinet. Harris had backed Simon Coveney for the leadership of Fine Gael after briefly toying with the idea of running himself. Following a fractious campaign rife with briefing and counter-briefing, some of Varadkar's allies felt Harris could not be trusted. The new Taoiseach ignored the advice and reappointed him as Minister for Health – a move that would eventually make Harris one of the longest-serving health ministers in the State's history.

Harris had been just 29 when then Taoiseach Enda Kenny appointed him to the notoriously troubled Department of Health in May 2016. Kenny rated Harris highly, but his hand had been forced somewhat. Varadkar, the then incumbent of the office, had refused to go along with what he viewed as the annual farce of a health budget being set and blown before the year was out, necessitating a supplementary funding stream. He wanted more money. Kenny felt there would be less strife if he moved Varadkar to Social Protection and moved an ally, like Harris, into Health.

The job of health minister had significant political drawbacks, with the occupant usually becoming the media and opposition scapegoat for everything from the annual trolley crisis, waiting lists, strikes and historical scandals. These were more frequent in Health, making the work unrelenting. There were no weekends off and even going away for a few days could be hazardous, as Varadkar found out at Christmas 2014 when he went to Florida on holiday as the winter trolley crisis unfolded back home.

No politician, or their team, leaves the Department of Health without the marks on their back to show for it. One official who worked there remembers waking up every morning and looking at the front page of the *Irish Times*. Two of four stories might be clearly related to health; the other two might have roots in the department that just weren't public yet. Another recalled dreading 4 p.m. on Friday afternoons when, typically, some middle-ranking official would walk into their office to inform them of a looming crisis – a misdiagnosis, perhaps, or a horrendous maternity care case – likely to break in the media over the weekend. When he came into office, Stephen Donnelly would go running in the middle of the night to deal with the stress.

On his first day as health minister in May 2016, Harris turned up on his own with no adviser and no idea what awaited him in Hawkins House, the crumbling edifice that housed the department at the time. He walked up to his office where his new private secretary put a pile of draft answers to parliamentary questions in front of him to clear. It was a sobering moment. In the years that followed, he encountered no end of difficulties, from the long-delayed delivery of a new National Maternity Hospital to a monstrous overspend on the National Children's Hospital.

In 2018 the major controversy over the national screening pro-gramme, CervicalCheck, convulsed the political system and resulted in the resignation of HSE Director General Tony O'Brien. The scandal left a long and bitter legacy. Some at a senior level in the HSE felt Harris used the controversy to try to undermine Varadkar, querying how much he had known about an audit that was carried out when the Taoiseach was health minister. 'He'd have thrown anyone under a bus to save himself,' one person claimed. While Harris would strongly dispute this, it was the case that there was constant talk in political circles that the ambitious young Fine Gael minister was on manoeuvres against his boss. Varadkar had got used to these stories and rumours of plotting against him over the course of his three years in the Taoiseach's office. Often people would tell him that Harris was behind it. Sometimes the minister was briefing against his leader, sometimes he wasn't. The same was true of Varadkar when Enda Kenny was Taoiseach.

The relationship between Harris and Varadkar has always been complex. They were rivals and yet on so many issues pre-pandemic they had to be allies, including the successful abortion referendum in 2018. One person who has worked closely with both of them believes they share many of the same character traits. They both know and understand the unique pressure of being health minister. They are also both fiercely ambitious, highly intelligent, analytical, deeply political and media savvy. They are both demanding to work for and tend to work long hours, always switched on. 'They think they're chalk and cheese, and they hate the suggestion that they're like each other,' one insider said.

Despite the tensions over cancelling the rugby and St Patrick's Day, the friction between Varadkar and Harris dissipated in March 2020 as the first public health restrictions took hold and Covid cases rose, and the pair agreed a broad framework for managing the disease. 'There's a basic principle for managing Covid that actually, Simon Harris and I agreed very early on and there were to be two pillars,' Varadkar would later recall. 'One was the NPHET advice and one was what we saw happening in other countries and we'd always try and make sure that we didn't hit either side.'

In other words, the aim of the political side would be that Ireland's pandemic policy would be closely aligned with NPHET advice and with what other countries were doing.

—

How Harris handled CervicalCheck tainted him in the Department of Health. The charged debate was reductive and polarising – it was a complex story that was often played out in inaccurate or misleading soundbites or headlines. It centred on scores of women who had cervical cancer and were not told that previous smear test results showing them to be in the clear were inaccurate. The results of an audit that uncovered these inaccuracies were kept from these women for years. Tony Holohan, who was at the centre of the controversy, and his team had a stubborn view of what was going on, and stuck doggedly to their guns. 'The public narrative around CervicalCheck is wildly at variance with facts,' Holohan said later.

Harris had a more difficult task. He had to handle the nuanced healthcare implications of the scandal, while feeling personal responsibility to the women affected. Then there was the political angle: the plight of the affected women was political kryptonite and he could end up becoming collateral damage. It was an intense, fraught, upsetting and charged time for all involved, but Harris's strategies left a bad taste in the mouth for some.

Harris had told the media in late April 2018 that while he had full confidence in the screening programme, he could not say the same for Gráinne Flannelly, who ran the programme, or other members of its senior management. The health minister's comments precipitated Flannelly's resignation within 48 hours. Tony O'Brien was enraged: he told Harris that he had treated Flannelly 'abominably'. 'When someone goes way off the reservation like he [Harris] did he needed to be told. I couldn't allow him to continue behaving like that, in a way that could lead to the next set of senior clinical leaders being thrown under the bus,' O'Brien later recalled.

He believed that, as director general of the HSE, it was his duty to have that conversation with Harris. 'I wasn't being nasty. He was behaving in a way that he needed his cards marked, and I did that,' he said. 'It's what anyone in my position would have to do. What he did was unprecedented in terms of ministerial behaviour. There was another senior clinical leader who had to go out on the radio the next morning on CervicalCheck, and I needed to know that they wouldn't get thrown under the bus.'

Ironically that clinical leader was Colm Henry, the HSE's chief clinical officer whom O'Brien had appointed just weeks earlier. He would later become a household name during the pandemic.

Harris said he did not recall any conversation like that with O'Brien and defended his handling of the CervicalCheck issue: 'I chose to put the concerns of the women impacted first. Perhaps that upset some in the system, but I had to put the concerns of the women first and I don't regret that and never will.'

In May 2018, at the height of the controversy, Harris said publicly that accountability would be required not just of politicians but 'other people who work in the public service, in the civil service, in jobs that are well remunerated'. Holohan believed there was no basis for the minister to say this and told him of his displeasure with the public comments. 'I said it in clear and unequivocal terms,' Holohan said later. 'Let me put it this way, if I had a displeasure with him, and what he might have said in relation to me in public, I would let him know. You can be sure of that.' Friends of Holohan's believe he felt Harris had hung him out to dry. There was a 'strain in the relationship', Holohan revealed. Harris later admitted, 'There was tension but we both got on with the job.'

By late March 2020, as Ireland settled into lockdown, the nightly vigil over push notifications detailing climbing case numbers and deaths, and as pressure on the hospital system grew, NPHET – and more specifically Holohan himself – moved to the centre of the public discourse; and Harris moved in lockstep with him.

With no effective treatment, no vaccine and no approach outside draconian restrictions being seriously countenanced, Harris would back Holohan all the way. 'Anything coming out of my mouth at [that] point in the pandemic was directly from Tony Holohan,' Harris recalled later. Cabinet colleagues saw this too.

Regina Doherty later remembered how Harris 'completely 100 per cent believed and sold whatever was told to him by his medical advisers'. This played to Harris's strengths as a communicator. Just as he had during the abortion campaign two years earlier, he came across as genuine, empathetic, convinced and convincing. 'It wasn't like I had all the answers but I knew people were scared so I just kept talking to them and telling them what I knew,' Harris said later. His chief medical officer, meanwhile, was bolstering his team.

—

One weekend morning in early March, Tony Holohan was out walking in Bushy Park close to where he lives. This would become a familiar pattern for him; rising early and walking around the park, thinking about the pandemic and ringing people up to talk about it.

That particular morning he was troubled by the lack of modelling that could help predict the trajectory of the virus in various scenarios. It was not safe for NPHET to stay in that space. The modelling presented to the Cabinet subcommittee on 9 March had been preliminary, comparatively crude, and based on extrapolations and reverse-engineering of British and Swedish models. It was illustrative rather than scientific.

Holohan wanted something more bespoke and more sophisticated for Ireland to better track the disease trajectory. He rang Philip Nolan, the president of NUI Maynooth. The pair had known each for years, having finished their final year of medical school in 1991 together. They weren't social friends, and both had drifted away from frontline medicine – Holohan to the Department of Health, and Nolan to the university sector. Nolan's public profile was serious, austere and measured, but it belied a personable side and a sense of humour. The pair hadn't spoken in the decade before 2018, when Holohan had asked Nolan, whose research expertise was in physiology – specifically the control of breathing and the cardiovascular system during sleep – to chair a review of cardiovascular services in the State. And it was Nolan who came to mind almost two years later.

'We have access to some of the work being done in the UK, but we can't keep looking in their copybook. We need to do our own homework,' Holohan told Nolan, who was still in bed that weekend afternoon. Nolan agreed to reach out to colleagues in Maynooth University, and more widely across the sector, who could help, and to speak with Breda Smyth, the HSE's director of public health in the west of Ireland.

Over the 18 months that followed, Nolan would be a key ally for Holohan during pitched battles over Covid-19 policy, and the face of the effort to forge some statistical basis for the choices that were to be taken – to extract signal from the noise of the pandemic.

The models built by him and his team, the Irish Epidemiological Modelling Advisory Group (IEMAG), set up on 11 March, would become the focus of scorn and frustration, at turns dismissed or embraced by the political system and the wider public, as the choices became harder and the atmosphere more charged. 'People are looking at me as if I were the national epidemiologist, and I am not,' Nolan later mused. 'But I never claimed to be.'

Building modelling capacity also had a more subtle but long-lasting impact. Being able to measure something gave NPHET a huge capacity to shape the public debate around the pandemic, setting the backdrop for every policy action that would follow.

As well as the actual modelling, Holohan needed raw materials, like data, to feed into the newly minted IEMAG. Often this took the form of near-diktats to the HSE. At a 16 March meeting of NPHET, he 'stressed strongly' the vital role of surveillance data – information that indicated how and where the disease was spreading, and the impact it was having on people and healthcare systems. This, he felt, was needed for real-time reporting within 24 hours to support detection of Covid-19, and contact tracing to try to control the spread of the virus. 'This needs to be addressed by the HSE as an immediate priority with work to increase capacity to upscale if this is necessary,' the meeting was told. Less than a week later, this point was rammed home by Harris in a letter to Ciarán Devane, the HSE chair, which was largely based on Holohan's input. There was an 'urgent and critical necessity for real-time and robust epidemiological, surveillance and clinical data and information in respect of Covid-19', the letter stated. The government – but via NPHET – had to have this data, Harris wrote.

These demands irked the HSE, where officials developed techniques to take the wind from Holohan's sails; for example when Paul Connors, the head of communications, withdrew from NPHET and was replaced by his deputy, David Leach. This meant that anything asked of the HSE's communications team could not be signed off in the room. Leach would have to run it past Connors. It was a minor, but deft, way of redressing the power imbalance.

Holohan was frequently looking for 'reassurance' about the HSE's capabilities. 'Who can give me reassurance that the HSE has in place sufficient capacity to do X, Y or Z?' recalled one person involved in the HSE response, months later, impersonating Holohan's voice. 'Reassurance my eye. We were making it up as we were going along, putting it together like MacGyver, with a couple of matches and an elastic band making a nuclear warhead.'

Holohan's call to Nolan, the demand for data, the rapid accumulation of power and functions, was part of building something bigger. It was already clear in early March that Covid-19 was going to consume more time, energy and resources than any other previous threat. And that it was going to be done under immense public scrutiny as the pandemic inserted itself into the daily life of every citizen in the country.

At the first NPHET meeting there were just 11 attendees, but it would grow and grow. At one point during the pandemic, its membership, largely determined by the chief medical officer, totalled more than 40. The meetings could become the centre of the news agenda. At their most paranoid, politicians and civil servants privately feared that the concentration of agenda-setting power in NPHET was a subversion of democratic power. To the outside world, the disrupting effect on the policy-making space was clear.

The Economist Intelligence Unit (EIU), in its 2020 Democracy Index, wrote that, while many countries had seen their ranking for civil liberty and political culture tumble due to lockdowns, in Ireland 'a more specific factor has been disputes between the government and [NPHET]'.

The government's adoption of NPHET recommendations, despite disagreeing with them, 'indicates its weakness and the extent of public discontent with politicians, together with greater trust in scientific expertise', the analysis stated. 'The Government's willingness to depict its decisions as having been made by scientists, rather than merely being informed by them, risks obscuring the accountability of technocrats to the democratic process and has spurred controversy.'

Behind the curtain, the reality could be a bit less racy. The first hour (or more) of a NPHET meeting might typically be taken up with a survey of the epidemiological situation – an 'epi report' that would examine the key indicators of the disease and its spread. Then there were questions and answers, taking up to 90 minutes or more, often followed by a discussion of advice, modelling work, projections, and reviewing minutes and correspondence. Holohan was far from the only voice at the meetings themselves, but almost everyone who attended NPHET meetings agreed they were one thing above all others: a Tony Holohan production.

When a big decision was to be made, contributions would be solicited from upwards of 40 people, seeking a kind of collective acclamation on the path ahead. Holohan allies saw it as consensus-forming leadership; others saw it as a form of attrition warfare. Even supporters suspected a degree of gamesmanship from Holohan. If NPHET were seen to be divided, if members were to individually speak out afterwards against a decision, it could damage the whole enterprise.

Holohan would frequently contact members, especially before big meetings, to take soundings. 'He would do his walk around Bushy Park and make his phone calls,' De Gascun later said. 'Similarly, I think if he felt there were people uncertain or unsure, or if he perceived that people had alternative perspectives, he would try and contact them and talk to them either before or after the meeting to hear them out.'

De Gascun admired this approach, but others weren't so sure. Many viewed it as a calculated move – the CMO trying to pre-emptively iron out any views that might jar with his own sense of what the NPHET decisions should be. 'He clearly comes in having worked his way through the process with pre-ordained thoughts, and it's very difficult to get past those,' said Kevin Kelleher, a NPHET member and at that time the HSE's assistant national director of public health. 'I felt the debate was controlled to ensure certain outcomes were achieved.' Kelleher felt frustrated, for example, when arguing that testing policy should look more like how the HSE tests for other infectious diseases – testing a sample of people, rather than every single case, to help figure out how prevalent a disease is. 'I felt ignored. I felt this happened overtly, to myself and others,' he later said.

A source who worked closely with Holohan believes he does not entertain questions, challenge or argument. 'He doesn't split the difference. It's very black and white,' they said. Some NPHET members, speaking privately, are more blunt: 'autocratic', said one, and then another: 'His style is very dictatorial and autocratic. Very.' If someone was making a point he didn't agree with, he could 'effectively throw his eyes to heaven on Zoom'; or, as one NPHET member recalled, 'he would give these little laughs', which showed that he didn't think much of a particular idea. A political source who worked with him at first hand said he is 'intolerant of alternative views'.

Mary Favier, who joined NPHET during the first wave, has a slightly different view, arguing that 'in some ways Tony Holohan likes people he can't bulldoze' and that he has 'an odd admiration for them'. Of course, the obvious corollary of that is that he can and does bulldoze others. 'If he didn't want to listen, he is well able to make [a topic appear] small, or show impatience,' Favier said.

NPHET members also wondered why there were some notable absentees from the group, most conspicuously Martin Cormican, the HSE's clinical lead for infection prevention and control. Cormican himself said the absence of someone with his skillset from NPHET is 'beyond my understanding'. He had worked with Holohan before, but not always harmoniously: 'We've had significant differences of opinion', although the relationship was 'civil and courteous' the vast majority of the time, Cormican insisted. People have suggested to Cormican that his initial absence from NPHET was due to Holohan's and Cormican's history, but he doesn't have any evidence to support that. He was quietly added to NPHET in 2021 following a request to Holohan from the HSE's chief clinical officer, Colm Henry, in late January. Much later, Holohan reflected that it may have been a mistake not to add Cormican to NPHET sooner, insisting he had 'the height of admiration' for him. But their differences of opinion would emerge again. On at least one occasion, Cormican asked that the minutes of a meeting be changed and circulated more quickly. 'The decisions of the meeting are often communicated to the government before the meeting has had an opportunity to review the draft minutes,' he said. 'There have been occasions where the content of the letter [to government] wasn't what I understood at the meeting.'

Holohan was calloused, according to people who know him well, by multiple health scandals in which he had fought rear-guard actions against legal cases, public controversies, and endless turf wars across the health ecosystem. 'In his world, you have to be right about everything because if somebody else invents what's right, you're fucked,' said one person who has worked with him at close quarters.

Tony O'Brien, a personal friend of Holohan's, said that for a time, particularly at the start of the pandemic, the CMO was the leader the country looked to. 'Everyone stopped what they were doing and watched him live on RTÉ. He needed to carry people's confidence. He needed to be sure of himself.' Holohan was utterly convinced of his own analysis at a time when a frightened population was looking for someone authoritative.

He was 'Churchillian', Colm Henry later said. 'He has a set of skills; he has an understanding of the pandemic which is unparalleled. He has an understanding of what needed to be done. He's never afraid, he would never compromise.'

For Philip Nolan, a close Holohan ally, the CMO is a 'very strong leader, a very strong personality – but that's what we needed [...] There are people who would disagree from time to time with his approach, and perhaps there are some people on NPHET who felt pushed around by him. My view is that those people needed to be pushed.' Nolan said that in almost all circumstances, consensus was achieved. Consensus, one official later remarked, might not always mean unanimity – but it meant that members would not vote against a measure.

—

The scale of the crisis meant that public health policy was present everywhere. Outside NPHET, the health service and the political system, Holohan was, on occasion, asked to attend meetings of the highly secretive National Security Committee, an interdepartmental group that is responsible for ensuring that the government is kept informed on security, intelligence and defence matters. The group, chaired by the Taoiseach's secretary general, Martin Fraser, included the Garda Commissioner Drew Harris, the Chief of Staff of the Defence Forces Mark Mellet, as well as other departmental secretaries general. Their meetings are the kind where participants are asked to leave their phones outside the room.

In spring 2020 the meetings were a place to kick around ideas and raise issues about the State's initial response to the pandemic. Drew Harris came away from one of the earliest briefings, before the first restrictions were announced, and relayed a 'doomsday scenario' to colleagues in Garda headquarters.

Harris, a former deputy chief constable of the PSNI, whose father, a senior RUC officer, had been killed by an IRA car bomb, had for years encountered terrorist plots, but the earliest briefings on Covid-19 left him cold and concerned that it could lead not just to a high number of deaths, but also potentially civil unrest. He offered Holohan any assistance he could in a series of phone calls.

The pair had a good relationship. But the CMO could not get everything he wanted. In one meeting, Holohan stressed the need to find a way to ensure that movement of people across the country was curtailed. 'There was a sense in some parts of the country that "Dublin people are going to come down here and infect us all" and certainly restricting movements [was] advised and the [hope was] that Gardaí could reinforce [that …] that's all that we would have been looking for,' Holohan later said.

But Drew Harris interpreted the comments as Holohan effectively looking for the guards to put, what he described to colleagues as, 'a ring of steel' around Dublin and prevent people from leaving the capital. It was something the commissioner was reluctant to do on the basis that it could lead to Ireland becoming a police state. Gardaí preferred to police by consent. Charlie Flanagan, who was then the justice minister, would later recall that there 'were reservations as to the impact' of policing the public health restrictions 'on the capacity of the Gardaí'. This would be a constant theme throughout the pandemic.

As March progressed into April, Holohan had suddenly become a household name, a figure whom the public relied upon and trusted. It was far beyond what Deirdre Watters and her communications team in the Department of Health had envisaged in early January, when they presented a plan to the board to build the voice of the CMO in a way similar to the US Office of the Surgeon General, whose messages appear on cigarette packets in the United States. The plan would take three to five years to implement, Watters told the department's board in a communications strategy presentation on 7 January. But three months later the CMO was telling the public to stay at home – and people were staying at home. Holohan had transcended the normal boundaries for the profile of a civil servant, no matter how senior. During the financial crisis, Central Bank governors or high-ranking mandarins in the Department of Finance had achieved a degree of fame (or notoriety) outside the bubble, but nothing like this.

On the side of Devitt's pub on Dublin's Camden Street, artist Niall O'Loughlin painted a mural of Holohan springing into action from an old-style Telefón box, tearing open his shirt to reveal a superman-style 'TH' logo. Watters showed Holohan pictures of the mural. 'This is amazing,' she told him.

'Don't worry,' Holohan responded. 'That will change.'

CHAPTER 6:

NO MASKS

17 March 2020
Cases: 292
Deaths: 2
Seven-day average of new cases: 37

The request was rushed, messy: 'If providing individual packs 100 packs pls. If not – 10 boxes of gloves/100 aprons/20 masks sorry 20 Google's [*sic*] and 20 boxes of masks (we have no masks left)'. It was the afternoon of St Patrick's Day, 17 March 2020, several hours before Leo Varadkar would make a speech to the nation laden with imagery of doctors and nurses hard at work on the frontline of the pandemic – in hospitals.

The email that came into David Walsh's inbox was from Glenaulin Nursing Home in Chapelizod, Dublin. It is around a ten-minute drive from Dr Steevens' Hospital, the HSE headquarters where Walsh, its national director of community operations, had an office. He would direct much of the health service's response to Covid in nursing homes during the first wave. Glenaulin was among the first nursing homes to detect a case of Covid-19 in the country, reporting one on 12 March.

Five days later, it had five cases, and staff were out of PPE. An HSE office in Waterford dispatched the order because closer community healthcare organisations could not, due to the pressure they were under to support testing centres. 'ETA one hour,' Walsh was told. By 6 p.m., the delivery had been made and signed for. 'That is a great response,' Walsh emailed his colleague. But this was only the beginning – it would not be that straightforward again.

By January 2021, the HSE was sending well over 20 million pieces of PPE to nursing homes per month – the large majority for the private sector. From April 2020 to January 2021, €132m was spent on PPE for nursing homes, over €95m of which was for the private sector. The government approved a total of €92.5m in emergency funding for the nursing home sector in 2020, and another €42m in 2021.

But one number mattered above the rest: by early May 2020, there would be at least 877 confirmed deaths as a result of Covid-19 in nursing home outbreaks, at least a further 64 probable deaths, and at least 101 possible deaths from the virus.

By St Patrick's Day 2020, Ireland was midway through a month where catastrophe in nursing homes would unfold slowly, but surely, until suddenly, it was too late.

—

Shortly after the first restrictions were announced on 12 March, images began to emerge from northern Italy showing that its health system was overwhelmed. 'Italy has a well-developed health service,' Professor Mark Ferguson, the government's chief scientific adviser, would later note. 'This is not a third world country. When you saw those people being completely overwhelmed, and you saw the human angst and grief, you thought, My God, this has happened very quickly, and it's happened on our doorstep – and it's spread from China so rapidly.'

The images conditioned Ireland's early response to Covid. The focus narrowed to a hospital system that was pressured at the best of times, and had a chronic shortage of intensive care beds. Taoiseach Leo Varadkar was told that the healthcare system could come to resemble a battlefield hospital. It reminded him of his medical school lectures. 'In wartime triage, you've one person who's really badly injured and you have four other people,' he later explained. 'So do I spend all my time saving that one person and the other four might die, or do I try and save the other four?'

This threat was made vividly real by the images of military trucks being brought in to relieve the overwhelmed morgues in the northern Italian city of Bergamo. Ireland's initial pandemic response was forged in this heat, Simon Harris said later. 'It was a constant refrain. How do you not become Italy?' The HSE's Colm Henry said the mindset – and fear – at the time was 'Bergamo is coming.'

To avoid this, the State and its agencies set about constructing field hospitals and temporary morgues, and sourcing extra staff. The hospital system was going to do everything it normally did, but for just one disease, and it was going to have to be temporarily reorganised to do it. That meant finding space.

For years the Irish healthcare system has been bedevilled by a system in which patients who are ready to leave the acute hospital system get stuck there, for a myriad of reasons. They are unkindly known as bed blockers, but the official jargon is 'delayed transfers of care'. As Covid-19 bore down on Ireland, they were seen as a major threat to the hospital system's ability to withstand a Bergamo-style wave of infection.

On 10 March, NPHET's acute hospitals group noted that three days earlier, '379 of the just over 600 delayed discharges require[d] nursing home beds'. On the same day, the Health Information and Quality Authority (HIQA) – which is responsible, among other functions, for regulating nursing homes – told another NPHET subgroup that, as of 1 January, there were 7,000 vacant beds in the nursing home sector and that was unlikely to have changed very substantially since then. 'This provides potential for accommodation for appropriate discharges from the acute hospital setting,' HIQA said.

Infection prevention guidelines for the sector were developed, and NPHET established a Vulnerable People subgroup which included older people in its brief. But there was a parallel systematic effort under way to find beds in nursing homes. On 13 March, HIQA cold-called all nursing homes. All bar five replied, confirming vacant beds. Early HSE plans for distributing PPE contain no reference to nursing homes, according to briefings given to the board. Expediting discharges from acute hospitals into nursing homes would soon become official policy.

The government's Covid-19 plan, published on 16 March – the same day the first cluster of Covid-19 cases was registered in a nursing home – referenced how nursing homes would accommodate delayed discharge patients and early discharges. Even as late as the end of March, department officials involved in looking at the nursing homes sector outlined the strategy baldly:

> [Nursing homes have] been identified by the health system as a source of capacity for egress from acute hospitals. In preparedness arrangements, a significant reduction in Delayed Transfers of Care was identified as a key measure in generating capacity within the acute system. To realise this, the NHSS (Fair Deal) [the Nursing Homes Support Scheme, known as 'Fair Deal'] and associated nursing homes were utilised to free up space in hospitals.

Under the Fair Deal, a resident contributes towards the cost of care and the HSE pays the balance.

The strategy worked. By 24 March, delayed transfers of care were at their lowest point since national reporting began. This was in large part driven by a flood of patients out of hospitals and into nursing homes. Between the Fair Deal and a separate scheme under which patients in need of convalescence were discharged to nursing homes, there were 1,363 transfers approved in March, almost 65 per cent higher than in an average month in 2019, and 40 per cent higher than in February 2019.

Simon Harris conceded later that, in the first instance, Ireland had 'a pandemic [plan] based on the Italian model, but the idea [that] nobody cared about nursing homes, that's just not true. From the very first Cabinet subcommittee meeting, nursing homes were on the agenda. A huge amount of work had been done by department officials before that.'

It's true that materials given to ministers on 9 March outlined the need to develop supports for vulnerable groups, including those in residential facilities. But the same material outlined how the 'first step' was to 'optimise capacity in the acute environment', including 'moving all delayed discharge patients'.

While the focus on the hospitals was unrelenting, Covid-19 was stealing over the threshold in nursing homes all over the country.

—

On 20 March, Dr Brian Creedon, a palliative medicine consultant at University Hospital Waterford, emailed Michael Fitzgerald, the HSE's chief officer in the Cork Kerry Community Healthcare division. There was an 'unexpected issue'.

Private nursing homes in Waterford were refusing to take patients from the hospital, including some who were their own residents, on the basis they were 'presumed Covid-19 negative, i.e. asymptomatic'. Forwarding Creedon's email to the Department of Health, Fitzgerald wrote, 'Contrary to Dr Creedon's view that the refusal is a Waterford only issue, it is in fact similar to issues in Cork that we have been dealing with over the past few weeks. It's another sign of the sector's anxiety as there is no clinical indication to refuse admission back into what in effect is the person's home.'

The reality of Covid-19 was now beginning to cause panic in some nursing homes, which were refusing to accept hospital transfers solely on the assumption – and not the confirmation via a test – that these discharges were not carrying the virus because they displayed no symptoms. But this was at odds with the health service's desire to clear out hospitals for the coming wave – and there had to be a way to keep that strategy on track.

Nursing homes around the country had been raising the issue for some time, as nervousness about the volume of hospital discharges grew. Earlier in March, when the first case of community transmission in the country was identified in Cork University Hospital, the hospital was forced to write to local nursing homes assuring them that discharges were safe. 'There are no grounds for greater concern about discharges from the CUH at this time as every possible risk assessment and medical assessment necessary will have been carried out before a patient is confirmed suitable for discharge,' the hospital wrote.

In his email to the Department of Health on 20 March, Fitzgerald bluntly suggested that the nursing homes would have to play ball in exchange for support payments. 'We will need as I said previously to tie in the nursing homes to non-refusals of readmissions and indeed admissions in terms of any financial package and indeed any more directive measures that we may take if we are to keep the hospital system going,' he wrote.

The idea gained traction and, according to the sector's chief lobbyist, Tadhg Daly, the chief executive of Nursing Homes Ireland (NHI), it appeared in the draft terms of the financial deal for the sector that was ultimately approved by the government in April. Daly pointed to a clause which reads, 'We the applicant Nursing Home confirm that we will be open and available for admission and readmission of patients to long-term residential services and short-term transitional care services, in line with any guidance issued.'

The clause was removed from the final deal, Daly said, but, speaking in late 2021, he was still angered by it, arguing that in effect it would have meant that funding was contingent on doing whatever the State wanted, 'taking away the ability of the registered provider or the person in charge to make a judgement on an individual admission'. He and NHI members firmly believe that patients leaving the hospital brought Covid-19 with them into nursing homes. It's not hard to see how this might have happened. For months, testing of hospital discharges was partial.

Initial strategies focused only on people, including close contacts of confirmed cases, with symptoms that met what was then the clinical definition of Covid-19. As more was learned about the virus, it became clear that symptoms were different in older people, and would not always have met the criteria for testing. 'Older folk don't necessarily show the same range of symptoms, for any infection,' explained Professor Dermot Power, a consultant geriatrician in the Mater Hospital. At the start of Covid, some symptoms, such as the loss of taste, that would later be recognised in all groups, weren't considered indicators of infection. In older people, there were more symptoms. 'Basically anything can be Covid in an older person; [a] new onset in falls, incontinence, classic chest and cough or fever.'

The testing issue compounded this, Power said. Some nursing homes wanted multiple tests, but hospitals were short of equipment. 'You have a bit of a recipe for trouble,' he said. 'Obscure symptoms, unknown symptoms, and there was almost a rationing of tests.' There would not be blanket testing of people being discharged from hospital into nursing homes until June 2020.

In May 2020, NPHET argued in a paper that if nursing homes adhered to guidance that new arrivals had to isolate if they had been exposed to the virus, then 'the risk of transfer to and subsequent spread of Covid-19 to Long Term Residential Facilities would have been low'. But there is evidence that this did not always happen. Simon Carswell later reported in the *Irish Times* that Covid-positive patients in one facility in Cork shared rooms with patients who had not been diagnosed with Covid-19. Patients with dementia could also wander from their isolation rooms, while in the real world, many needed care that required close physical contact. Seamus McCormack, the owner of Glenaulin, the home that had emailed the HSE seeking help on St Patrick's Day, remembers how challenging this was. 'You're trying to ask the symptomatic ones to wear a mask, but they don't understand why, what the virus is. All they want to do is continue in their activities, shaking hands, hugging you. That was the huge trouble,' he said, months later. For residents without dementia, it stripped them of their independence. McCormack remembers how, in pre-Covid times, some would have got the bus into town for the day, returning later to Chapelizod. That was no longer possible, with residents confined to their rooms or to certain parts of what was their home. Gone, too, were the visits from family members, or musicians to entertain them, and group activities. Familiar faces disappeared behind masks and visors. Life in the homes became dour, and terrifying.

—

Infections in nursing homes peaked in late April, raising a question over how strong the link was between discharges from hospitals – which mostly occurred during March – and infections in nursing homes. A research paper by HIQA and the HPSC later in 2020 found that the main determinant of a nursing home outbreak was the prevalence of the disease in the wider community. There is a broad truth in that – the more Covid-19 there is, the harder it is to keep it from vulnerable groups.

Similarly, Simon Harris later argued, 'When an infectious disease takes hold in your country, it is almost impossible to keep it out of congregated settings, which nursing homes are. We see it with the flu every year.'

But the authors of the paper also acknowledged that they lacked the data to identify causes, including whether issues like staff transfers, training and hospital discharges played a role. It's also not clear that a complete picture of infection was being painted in real time by the State's embryonic testing system. Many outbreaks were identified in the early days of April and reflected in reports drawn up by and for the HSE and NPHET.

It was not until a system-wide testing blitz of the entire nursing home sector took place on 18 April that a fuller picture emerged: the spike in nursing home cases recorded seems likely a function of how testing was carried out, rather than a true reflection of when the disease spread into the homes. A paper from NPHET in late May noted, 'The peak in numbers of newly confirmed cases seen in LTRC [long-term residential care] residents in late April coincides with the implementation of the expanded testing programme of LTRC residents and staff.'

Deaths, ultimately, may tell the fullest story of what happened in Ireland's nursing homes. Data from weeks after the first surge suggests Covid-19 was beginning to take hold in nursing homes from around the time the first public health restrictions were introduced – or even before. A census of mortality undertaken in early May 2020 identified a small number of 'probable' Covid deaths in the last week of February and the first two weeks of March; eight such cases were identified across this three-week period.

Data compiled by the HPSC in autumn 2021 suggests there were at least 51 confirmed or suspected deaths linked to nursing home outbreaks that were identified in the week beginning 16 March – the week Glenaulin sought PPE and four days after the first nursing home outbreak was reported to HIQA. Not all these deaths took place that week, but, due to the way the statistics are gathered, they were linked to the outbreak reported to health authorities that week. What they do show is that Covid was in these nursing homes in a way that would ultimately claim hundreds of lives. The number of infections and deaths grew rapidly thereafter. There were 138 confirmed, probable or possible deaths linked to outbreaks identified the following week; 383 the week after; and 359 the week after that.

Documents obtained by the authors suggest this was underestimated at the time decisions were being made. HIQA told a meeting of an internal Department of Health working group on 26 March that it was aware of just 28 confirmed cases across 8 nursing homes, a further 13 homes with suspected cases, and just 4 deaths. The more recent HPSC data suggests clusters identified that week ultimately claimed up to 138 lives.

There's no way of knowing just how many infections were introduced by discharging patients, and it's almost certain that Covid would have infected swathes of nursing homes even if the discharges never happened. But while the risk to older people was part of early government planning, contemporary documents show the focus of action was on hospitals.

There's also evidence from contemporary materials that testing was not always done, or that it failed to catch infections. A submission from HIQA to the Oireachtas Covid-19 committee in June 2020 outlined how there had been 'requests to admit new residents from the acute sector without evidence that Covid-19 tests had been carried out'.

Meanwhile, an unpublished report by public health doctors on ten nursing home outbreaks completed in early May 2020 noted that the source of the infection in one home was believed to be a resident returning from an in-patient stay for a non-Covid-19-related illness. The resident developed symptoms a few days after returning and tested positive, despite having tested negative on their discharge from hospital.

Among the findings of that report was that a factor driving infection or spread was the 'discharge of hospital in-patients who were contacts or undiagnosed cases of Covid-19 into [residential care facilities], particularly more in the earlier stages of Covid-19.'

Martin Cormican, the HSE's clinical lead of the antimicrobial resistance and infection control team, said later, 'I don't think anybody doubts, now, that there were instances where people who were transferred from one healthcare facility to another were infected, and the virus went with them. That's happened in transfers between hospitals and nursing homes, it happened between hospitals and hospitals, it's happened pretty much throughout the world, and it happens with other infections as well.'

Jim Daly, the Minister of State for Older People, would later say that discharges into nursing homes was an error. 'I saw that in real time, where people were discharged from acute settings in a panic to clear them, into nursing homes, and brought the virus with them,' he said. 'It was a case of build capacity at all costs.' The true costs would emerge rapidly in the days and weeks of spring 2020.

CHAPTER 7:

NO SWABS

20 March 2020
Cases: 683
Deaths: 3
Seven-day average of new cases: 85

'We have no swabs. Our GP has no swabs.'
The manager of Tara Winthrop, a 140-bed nursing home in north County Dublin, was speaking to a room full of civil servants. The officials had been brought together to plan out how the State was going to support nursing homes. The agenda for their Friday afternoon meeting was purely practical: to plan reports, funding schemes and workflows for the group, which was due to produce an urgent report for NPHET.

But as part of the meeting, Nursing Homes Ireland, the sector's lobbyist, had arranged for a call with Tara Winthrop. The officials got an unexpectedly chilling first-hand account of how Covid could rip into a nursing home. Eight days earlier, on 12 March, 2 staff members at Tara Winthrop had reported symptoms. The following day, 3 residents were swabbed. By St Patrick's Day, 4 of the 5 were positive. Three days later, on 20 March, 26 were symptomatic and 15 had tested positive, the officials were told. The nursing home's kitchen was badly hit, with 6 out of 11 staff unavailable to work. Among the staff were married couples, and staff who shared accommodation, working across multiple units of the facility. 'As you know, all it takes is one,' the meeting was told.

The home was coping, but the meeting of the NPHET subgroup was told, 'We do not have enough cleaning, catering, carers and nursing staff to keep the infection from spreading to other units.' Tara Winthrop had sought cleaners from an employment agency, and were quoted double the standard rate. A planned delivery of 1,000 gowns had yielded just 100 and they would run out in two to three days. 'We need access to oxygen,' the manager said, 'we cannot get this.'

The reason, the home had been told by suppliers of oxygen and hand sanitiser, was because it was being made for the HSE. Residents in other units needed to be swabbed, but the department officials were told, 'We have no swabs. Our GP has no swabs.' Staff were anxious and burned out. It was a chaotic, fraught situation, and every new turn revealed more complicating factors; information about the virus being given to overseas staff from their home countries 'is incorrect and is being fed to them by family at home', the operator told the meeting.

If Ireland was slow to recognise the threat to nursing homes, it rapidly became clear in calls like this. After the meeting with Tara Winthrop, Kathleen MacLellan, the senior civil servant in the Social Care division of the Department of Health (the part of the department that looked after nursing home policy), and Niall Redmond, one of her deputies, sent frantic emails to HSE officials. It was 'imperative' that the HSE get support to the patients in Tara Winthrop over the weekend, MacLellan wrote. As it turned out, the home already was and would continue to be supported to a significant extent.

Redmond told the HSE that the situation in Tara Winthrop was immediate and pressing, but 'there is a much wider piece about preparedness of the sector to manage what is coming'. The call with the nursing home made the scale of the threat real for officials. But behind the scenes up to that point – and for some time after – the response was characterised by turf wars, PR battles and inertia.

—

The first battle was with Nursing Homes Ireland. At this time, Tadhg Daly had one setting: full speed ahead. He had been in overdrive for days, peppering the department with hundreds of emails, demanding that he be put on NPHET, insisting he get a meeting with Simon Harris. He had already seriously irked officials in Miesian Plaza when NHI advised that visits to nursing homes be suspended from 6 March, a move that NPHET branded 'unilateral' and that Tony Holohan publicly countermanded – before officially suspending visits just days later.

A native of Drimoleague in West Cork, Tadhg Daly was 'loud and boisterous' but 'clever enough not to burn his bridges', according to Jim Daly, the junior minister who oversaw the sector. Despite sharing a second name and hailing from the same part of Cork, the two were not related, although this did not stop some ministerial colleagues of Jim Daly remarking on the lobbyist's full-frontal assault on the government: 'Isn't Jim Daly's brother giving Simon Harris an awfully hard time?' one Cabinet minister recalled a colleague saying to them.

By the time he finally got a meeting with the officials – the meeting on 20 March, which heard the testimony from Tara Winthrop – many in the department and the wider political system deeply resented how Daly was at the centre of public discussions about nursing homes. He was a representative, not of patients or staff, but ultimately of owners, many of them multi-millionaires or lavishly financed international investors. The fact that the media in particular allowed him to hold forth as an authority on the situation in nursing homes, while in reality representing the interests of owners, fed resentment of Daly's style. In one email sent later in March, Niall Redmond bemoaned that 'much of the issue is being laid out by the sector representative, which is very unhelpful overall and counterproductive to the attempts of the state agencies to provide nursing homes with support'.

There were tensions, too, on the State side – specifically between the Department of Health and the HSE. The HSE view was that the department should, in effect, throw money at the problem. The department shot this down, stripping it from a plan that went to government. When the urgent emails landed in his inbox after the meeting with Tara Winthrop on 20 March, David Walsh, the HSE official directing the Covid response in nursing homes, wasn't slow to remind the department of this. In one email sent after midnight, he pointedly asked, 'Can you advise me of the actions the department intend taking to support this situation?' The HSE had asked for payments to the sector to be increased, he remonstrated. 'Unfortunately we are hamstrung by the deletion of such financial supports from the action plan that was sent to government.'

This was echoed by another HSE official, Michael Fitzgerald, who replied, 'It is clear that the sector will require an urgent financial support package [...] can this be expedited now? [...] It would appear that we would have far more centres running into these difficulties if they do not or cannot prepare for this upcoming surge.'

It was not surprising that the HSE's first instinct was to pitch in with more finance. Its connection to the private nursing home sector is tenuous and primarily financial, through the Fair Deal. But clinical oversight was non-existent, with a separate agency, HIQA, being responsible for regulation of the homes.

The HSE was also furious about how every plan the department cooked up seemed to involve them stepping up to manage a sector of which they had effectively zero knowledge. A NPHET subgroup was the source of considerable ire in the HSE, which felt it was a talking shop that was wasting precious time. 'Frankly, I think there are too many people on a very large group,' Fitzgerald wrote in one email to Redmond. 'Yesterday we ended up having a discussion on hearsay between HIQA and ourselves in relation to oxygen and we really cannot give time to such matters when there are pressing issues to be addressed.'

This sort of wrangling went on for days. On 27 March, MacLellan emailed Walsh from inside a NPHET meeting, with 'an indication of 9 nursing homes in the East with outbreaks. There is an urgency to support actions ASAP'. The HSE had been sending staff and equipment to homes, but in a response to MacLellan that day, Walsh again emphasised that there were limits to what the HSE could do. 'Operators must be resourced to do their side as HSE capacity must address multiple levels of the response to this disease,' he wrote. In another exchange, Walsh argued against draft plans for supporting the sector, which, he said, assumed that the HSE could support large swathes of the 85 per cent of nursing homes – those in private hands, with which it had a tenuous relationship – up to and including taking over those that were in extremely difficult situations, while at the same time managing its own problems.

Proposals for more funding went over and back; the HSE arguing for a plan that would cost around €60m. But Redmond told MacLellan that he couldn't back the plan. The timely development of a proposal was critical and 'cannot wait for a robust proposal from the HSE', Redmond wrote. In other words, the Department of Health was taking over. It would submit its own proposal to the health minister and onward to the Department of Public Expenditure and Reform (DPER).

After the initial funding plan finally collapsed, both Fitzgerald and Walsh separately sent impassioned emails. 'This group of people are the most vulnerable people in the country. A failure to protect them, as has happened in other countries, would be a matter of great public concern,' Walsh wrote to an official in the Department of Health, warning that he was going to escalate his concerns to HSE Chief Executive Paul Reid. 'This crisis is not in the future, it is happening now.'

Fitzgerald was similarly blunt in an email to the same official, referring to an outbreak ongoing as that week ended:

> This virus has a devastating effect in a nursing home when it gets into it, and we see even today how it can destabilise even a large one which is part of a chain and with unusually strong clinical resources. This weekend it teeters on the brink despite their best efforts and with strong supports from the HSE.
>
> We are concerned that this will become more widespread, feature in nursing homes that have less capability to manage it and happen in clusters.

A significant financial intervention 'would even now at this late stage [allow the sector] to boost its staffing, management oversight and infection control measures', he wrote.

—

As March drew to a close, the threat to nursing homes was becoming painfully clear. In the previous fortnight, much of the response had been planned through the Byzantine world of subgroups and working groups that existed under the umbrella of NPHET and that reported into the group. But on 29 and 30 March, Tony Holohan chaired two extraordinary NPHET meetings specifically on residential healthcare settings. The minutes of the meetings – which were never published on the section of the Department of Health website where NPHET records usually appear – show that the attendees recognised that 'more tailored, specific interventions were needed' and acknowledged the tinderbox in residential care, where large numbers of vulnerable people lived together in conditions that could see Covid-19 spread rapidly:

> It was noted that there are differences in the size, layout and staffing of different residential healthcare settings, and that their access to infection prevention control (IPC) measures may vary. It is likely that these residential healthcare settings vary in their capacity to respond and some may need targeted supports.

As understatements go, it was a big one.

In the weeks that followed, the State scrambled to make up for lost time. NPHET published a list of enhanced measures for nursing homes the day after Holohan's second emergency meeting. Tadhg Daly got his meeting with Simon Harris. The HSE was told to deploy integrated response teams across long-term residential care settings, while testing was prioritised for staff, and screening measures were introduced.

Weaknesses in existing policies, such as discharging from hospital, became painfully clear after the fact. During an extensive discussion on 8 April of asymptomatic and presymptomatic transmission of Covid-19, NPHET's Expert Advisory Group (EAG) noted that there was a risk of introducing infection into a nursing home by 'rushing the discharge of a potentially infectious patient'. On 18 April, a massive testing wave was launched across the entire sector to try to establish the true scale of infection. This was a precursor to the serial testing programme that would be launched during the summer, in which staff would undergo regular swabbing in an attempt to try to catch infection earlier.

As spring progressed, so did the crisis in nursing homes and other care facilities. There was no missing it, and it began to dominate the media and NPHET meetings alike. The virus was firmly embedded in homes. It continued to claim lives by the dozen across spring, including in Dealgan House, where 22 people died in April and May, and St Mary's in Dublin's Phoenix Park, where 24 residents died. Over the Easter bank holiday weekend alone, 9 people died in St Fintan's Hospital in Portlaoise.

However, some measures that would later seem obvious, like masking up when giving care in nursing homes, still lagged.

—

If the response failed nursing homes, the virus also found systemic weaknesses in the sector itself. Through March and April a steady stream of issues about how nursing homes were being challenged by the crisis were flagged with HIQA by third parties – sometimes staff, sometimes families or concerned citizens. These reports were sent into the regulator, often anonymously. While they are unverified, they paint a troubling picture of conditions being reported at the start of the pandemic.

In March, one concerned person contacted HIQA about 'the number of people attending wakes that are taking place in [the] nursing home putting residents and staff at risk of contracting Covid-19'. Another report in the same month detailed how '[a] resident absconded from the centre for a number of hours without staff being aware during the visitation lockdown. On their return no measures were put in place to isolate this resident from other residents in the centre. Risk of other residents now contracting Covid-19.'

Several communications outlined concerns about staff working patterns that could raise an infection risk, including 'staff working shifts both in an acute general hospital and a nursing home during the Covid-19 outbreak'. Dozens were related to precautions on social distancing, communication with families, access to PPE, or treatment of residents, including one where a resident was neglected by staff due to the Covid crisis. The person in question had been left in bed, was missing meals, 'has no clean clothes and has had a number of falls'. One report alleged a staff member had just returned to work after self-isolating for two weeks 'but did not have a Covid-19 test, [and] continues to have a cough'; another that staff were returning to work without quarantining after being abroad. Yet another alleged that symptomatic staff were not being prioritised for testing by the nursing home provider. Another complained that positive but asymptomatic staff had been asked to continue working rather than self-isolating.

As April wore on, there were warnings about how susceptible the nursing homes sector was to Covid. On 9 April, Mary Dunnion, the chief inspector with HIQA, wrote a note for NPHET about the structure of the sector. Just 23 per cent of nursing homes were fully compliant with regulations, and there was no nationally mandated staffing ratio for the sector, which meant that in a large number of private homes the number of staff, the skills mix and competencies were 'not commensurate' with being able to deal with residents' needs during an outbreak. Dunnion outlined how poor infrastructure, poor governance and management structures, inappropriate use of PPE and poor infection prevention control procedures all threatened the sector. Some 124 private and public nursing homes would need help in a context where the lack of a direct relationship with the HSE 'has highlighted a challenge to effectively project the specific needs of nursing homes during the Covid-19 outbreak'. HIQA would later tell the Oireachtas in a submission in June 2020 that many private nursing homes had 'a limited, if any, relationship with the HSE'. The health service did not even have an exhaustive list of where all the State's nursing homes were.

The structure of the nursing homes sector had been rapidly changing in the years prior to the pandemic. Smaller outfits were mopped up and big operators moved in, backed by overseas capital. In many ways, Tara

Winthrop, the nursing home whose testimony so alarmed department officials on 20 March, was typical of the big business, at-scale operations that had grown quickly in Ireland. It is owned by Grace Healthcare, which controls seven nursing homes across Dublin and Monaghan. Many of its shares are held by shell companies domiciled in Singapore or the Isle of Man.

Care of the elderly had become big business, to such an extent that HIQA had complained that consolidation was causing 'significant difficulties for regulators given the complex and changing ownership pattern'. Such was the speed of change that at times HIQA reported that it had 'experienced some difficulties in terms of identifying who is the responsible legal entity for providing a service'.

—

An unpublished report into outbreaks in ten nursing homes identified a litany of issues reported by departments of public health that contributed to the introduction or spread of Covid-19 in these homes, or made it more difficult to manage.

Early outbreaks saw staff and residents not being referred for testing because they didn't meet the 'specific and limited' criteria for who should be tested, the report found. Delays in obtaining tests, cancellations of tests and long wait times in March 'meant that outbreaks sometimes became established in the interim', while a 'culture of [staff] working through minor or major respiratory symptoms is prevalent and contributes to outbreak spread'.

The staffing crisis in the sector worsened by the day. The same unpublished report found that 'staff numbers were decimated and additional staffing was extremely difficult to get'. Senior nursing staff, including key decision-makers, were ill or excluded from work.

In mid-April, the HSE reached a deal with unions to redeploy staff to work in private nursing homes. Six days previously, it had made a formal request for Civil Defence assistance in nursing homes, but local authorities had said there were no volunteers to go into the homes. Even as the rest of the country prepared to reopen on a phased basis from mid-May, there were discussions in the EAG about drastic measures in nursing homes.

At one point, they considered whether Covid-positive staff could continue working if they weren't symptomatic, rather than risk manpower shortages. 'There may be more risk if the [residential care facility] is not able to operate safely due to staff absences than having asymptomatic staff with Covid-19 on site,' the minutes of a meeting on 22 April show. 'We could end up with unqualified staff looking after these patients and residents not being mobilised and socialised enough.' The minutes continue:

> Some members wondered if different rules should apply to nursing homes where Covid-19 transmission is already established and those with no cases of Covid 19 [...] there was a long discussion regarding whether staff can work if positive but asymptomatic.

The discussion went no further, but that allowing asymptomatic staff who had tested positive to work was even countenanced was indicative of how dire the situation was.

After the first wave, NPHET and the HSE commissioned a report into infection in healthcare workers by Professor Mary Codd of the UCD School of Public Health, who also ran the contact tracing centre on the university's Belfield campus. The authors interviewed over 400 healthcare workers who had been infected with Covid-19, which, they found, skewed disproportionately to those in long-term residential facilities such as nursing homes.

When a draft was submitted, it caused consternation in the HSE, and it was held back. It was never finalised or approved, and never sent to NPHET. The HSE's view was that many of the recommendations had already been put in place or would be impractical to implement. There were also concerns over the methodology used. It relied heavily on 'very negative' quotations, the HSE believed, to support criticism of issues not within the scope of infection prevention and control, or practices, which, if put in place, would not be appropriate. There were concerns, the health service argued in a note in late 2021 outlining why the report was never published, about participant bias with interviewees responding in a way to 'fit [their] perception of what they think [the] interviewer wants to hear or what shows themselves in the best light'. The HSE rejected two Freedom of Information requests for the document, which was eventually only released following an extensive appeal process.

But the concerns meant views from 400 healthcare workers never saw the light of day. The draft reveals a wide range of worries held by staff in hospitals and long-term residential facilities about what they feared drove Covid infection during the first wave.

It was detailed: interviews lasted, on average, more than an hour, and 90 per cent of those contacted were interviewed. This was a report from the frontline – 81 per cent were in direct contact with patients, and the same figure (81 per cent) had seen an outbreak of Covid in their workplace. More than half worked in residential facilities, with 40 per cent working in elder care.

In the course of their interviews, some were reticent: one 'became anxious' when asked about training in infection control, 'concerned that [their] employer would not want reporting to the HSE'. Respondents spoke not only about their difficulties accessing tests and living in fear of passing Covid on to family members but also about how testing was run in the workplace.

In many instances, compliance was high for self-isolation periods for infected staff, recommendations on PPE use, maintenance of isolation facilities and separate rosters for staffing Covid and non-Covid units. However, despite the headline figures, healthcare workers detailed many specific instances which left them distressed, frustrated or angry.

While almost all were given time off to self-isolate, some felt under pressure to be in work or return early. One was told they were expected to be back at work after eight days unless they had a temperature; another 'did not feel fully recovered but felt pressured to be back at work'. One felt that workers 'concealed the fact that they were symptomatic or Covid-positive in order to continue working and getting paid'. In one instance,

dismissive attitudes to PPE, with one saying they believed 'PPE is all a cod', while others said it was 'too hot'.

Speaking in August 2021, Mary Codd said she did not know why the report was never published by the HSE. 'There [were] certain things they didn't like about it, and then it went under the radar,' she said.

—

Just under one thousand deaths in nursing homes were linked to Covid-19 during the first wave of the pandemic. The human impact on the families of those left behind, as well as those who cared for them, cannot be measured easily.

While undoubtedly there were issues in some homes, staff in the sector continued to provide care in near-impossible circumstances. Those involved in the response felt the burden as well. People working across the HSE and the wider healthcare service burned out. David Walsh had to take an eight-week leave of absence after the first wave of infection.

There was no single set of criteria that determined whether a nursing home was hit. Research has found no statistical difference between public and private, and those involved in the response say some of the hardest-hit homes were among the ones they felt were best run.

But when Covid hit nursing homes, as with all aspects of society, it found and exploited weaknesses to devastating effect. And, in less than a year, it would do so again, with another one thousand lives lost in the third wave in January and February 2021.

Harris, who was health minister during the first wave, argued that the State stepped up – and it did provide millions of euros in support and untold working hours to the sector. 'We did it to protect those living and working in nursing homes. But there is no getting away from the fact that there is an urgent need for a new model of care for older people in our own country.'

—

In the second week of its Covid-19 outbreak, Glenaulin's second oxygen concentrator broke. The nursing home had set up an isolation area for positive patients, but more were becoming symptomatic. They couldn't get test results, so they couldn't be admitted to the isolation area, lest they be infected by residents who were confirmed for the virus.

But in the absence of a confirmation, managing symptomatic residents, especially those with dementia, brought its own issues. 'Staff were ground down,' Seamus McCormack, the owner of the home, said. 'I used to notice on their breaks they'd be within themselves. No jokes, no laughter.'

The HSE delivered more oxygen concentrators, which meant that sick and dying patients could get oxygen therapy, but staff, PPE and other materials were thin on the ground. McCormack, a former Air Corps pilot who flew the government jet, compared it to 'going to war without the proper weapons'.

Some staff – not many – walked off the job when Covid-19 landed; McCormack's teenage children worked shifts. In the absence of PPE, he bought painters' overalls for staff and wrote their names on the back. Masks were in such short supply that he bought ziplock bags so that staff could stow a disposable mask overnight for a second use – although it never quite came to that.

McCormack said the home had cancelled visits on 1 March, but they got a phone call from public health telling them to reopen, effectively overruling the decision they made on the ground. He also believes at least one Covid-19 case came into the home from a hospital; when readmitted to a hospital later, the resident tested positive.

Around sixty cases were ultimately confirmed in Glenaulin, between staff and residents, and seven Covid-linked deaths were recorded.

The first day he had Covid-19 test results confirmed, McCormack went into the home to set up the isolation area and returned home close to midnight. He remembers looking out of the back kitchen window and, 'I said to my wife, "God, what's next?"'

CHAPTER 8:

15,000 A DAY

22 March 2020
Cases: 906
Deaths: 4
Seven-day average of new cases: 105

On the penultimate Sunday in March, NPHET reported, in addition to 121 new cases and one death, that there was now at least one confirmed case of Covid-19 in every county in the country. The virus was taking hold, but how cases were detected had in the previous days become an increasingly fraught political issue.

Four days earlier, on 18 March, Leo Varadkar's BMW swept into the humble surroundings of the National Virus Reference Laboratory on the Belfield campus of University College Dublin. He was met at the drab entrance to the building by Simon Harris, a coterie of university officials and scientists, and Cillian De Gascun, the director of the NVRL and a member of NPHET. The media were also there. A former schools rugby star for Terenure College, and an Ireland schools international, De Gascun had trained in Trinity and UCD before working as a consultant virologist in the UK, and had been appointed director of the NVRL in 2013.

The country was at a low point, burdened with fear and anxiety, but Varadkar was at the start of a political upswing. The previous night, on

St Patrick's Day, he had addressed a nation stuck at home, unable to celebrate the national holiday. Aides had urged Varadkar to lean heavily on his personal ties to frontline medical workers. In the televised speech he described how his partner, his two sisters and both their husbands were working in healthcare in Ireland or the UK. 'Not all heroes wear capes, some wear scrubs and gowns,' he told a record-smashing audience of 1.6 million people.

He also leaned on colleagues, snaffling a line Simon Coveney had coined when the first restrictions were announced nearly a week earlier: that the government were asking people to 'come together as a nation by staying apart from each other'. Varadkar would later remark that he didn't think it was an especially good speech, but it landed with a frightened population and some of those around him felt it was an exhilarating high point. 'This is the calm before the storm. Before the surge. And when it comes – and it will come – never will so many ask so much from so few,' he told the nation, echoing Winston Churchill's commendation for the RAF during the Battle of Britain.

Now, in visiting the NVRL, he and Harris were doing the Covid-19 equivalent of visiting a wartime munitions factory. But in that building, evidence of a serious problem was emerging.

—

On 13 March, the criteria for getting a Covid-19 test were dramatically relaxed. People were now referred for testing only if they had symptoms, rather than having to be a close contact of a confirmed case or having a travel history to an area with presumed community transmission. The effect was immediate, and dramatic. The NVRL could typically process about 1,200–1,500 samples per day at maximum. Five more sites were processing tests, but they were hospitals, largely dealing with their own staff and patients.

Now tens of thousands of people were suddenly pouring into the system. On 16 March, an online referral portal for GPs went live, and almost immediately collapsed under the weight of numbers as doctors sought testing slots for their patients. The NVRL was already struggling massively with the pressure of incoming samples – some 6,000–8,000 swabs per day – that were stored in special buckets and left on corridors or wherever space could be found. Outwardly, Ireland's strategy was 'test, test, test', but in reality the State had no system to accommodate this.

The crunch point came as evidence mounted of the dreadful reality that the virus was spreading rapidly, invisibly and, as the early cases in Cork University Hospital and a cluster in County Clare had shown, could knock out healthcare facilities with terrifying speed. In Clare, a family had returned from an overseas holiday with Covid-19. The family members worked across a variety of healthcare and education environments, senior health sources later said.

The hospital emergency department in University Hospital Limerick almost had to close due to the number of positives or close contacts associated with the outbreak. This was particularly problematic because there was no alternative emergency department in the city; patients would have to go to Cork or Galway. Planned procedures had to be rescheduled and the flow of staff reduced almost overnight. 'It was kind of an almost perfect spreading event,' one senior source involved in managing the fallout from the cluster later recalled.

A major testing programme was needed to intercept and prevent these sorts of incidents. Even if Covid-19 did not overwhelm hospitals with patients it could still, if allowed to spread undetected, shut them down by putting hundreds of staff out of work; health staff absences ebbed and flowed throughout the pandemic, hitting as many as 15,000 in January 2022. But the tensions between finding cases and overwhelming the system were clear.

On 11 March, Professor Karina Butler, a paediatrician, warned NPHET's Expert Advisory Group that cases were being missed with the 'strict application of the current definition'; the meeting minutes noted the gap in knowledge about how much the virus was spreading in the community. The pressure was clear, but the testing target was, publicly at least, set rather unwittingly on that Wednesday morning, 18 March outside the NVRL.

Before going inside the building, Varadkar told the waiting media they were working towards ramping up to doing 15,000 tests a week. De Gascun interjected to say that 'it should be 15,000 tests a day, depending on how things go'. The Taoiseach was at that time instinctively drawn to the idea that testing, rather than lockdowns, could control the virus. To allies, he privately griped that there was no evidence that the harsh lockdowns in Italy were working better than testing-based approaches such as that of South Korea.

The following day, in an interview on RTÉ's *Today with Seán O'Rourke*, Simon Harris repeated the 15,000 tests per day figure, claiming that testing would be at that level 'in the next few days'. It was a political promise, an ambition dwarfing anything ever done before in the country. The NVRL would normally process around 15,000 influenza samples in an entire seven-month flu season, with a lower number done in some hospital labs. Now the system was going to have to do that every day, and it soon became an albatross around its neck.

—

The HSE could play fast and loose with public pronouncements on how many tests were being delivered: the figure of 5,000 per day was circulated in early April, but then that transpired to be the capacity to take swabs – samples – from people. Labs were still producing significantly fewer actual results. Capacity constraints and equipment shortages meant that at the start of April, only around 1,500 actual results were being produced per day by the labs – 10 per cent of the daily target.

The delays in both getting a test and then in obtaining results were causing stress and frustration among the public. Public health officials seemed nonplussed. Whether you were tested or not, the advice was to isolate if you developed symptoms. But that missed the point: testing was a visible part of the State's strategy to manage Covid-19 that appeared not to be working. Amid mounting pressure on the system, the criteria for testing was tightened again, reducing the flow of people into the system while shortages of a vital supply (reagent) prevented ramping up capacity, and labs fought to get new equipment up and running.

Testing was focused on priority groups, and swabs were flown to Germany to tackle the backlog. Sources recalled how at one stage thousands of people scheduled for tests were taken out of the system altogether and instead just told to isolate. In the background, the HSE told NPHET that it would hit capacity of around 16,000 per day, but not until May. With the structure under pressure, NPHET agreed that the HSE needed a single person overseeing what was becoming a sprawling system.

That person was Niamh O'Beirne, a senior partner with consultancy firm EY, who had been brought into the HSE in January 2020 to shake up its corporate structure. She had a long history as a private sector trouble-shooter working with public sector organisations. This had brought her into contact with Paul Reid, then a senior civil servant at the Department of Public Expenditure and Reform. She also pitched up at the Department of Justice, where she had been involved in reforming a department that had been beset by scandal and controversy related to an Garda Síochána. She had a reputation as being incredibly good at operational issues: 'A problem solver, indefatigable, a lean thinker,' recalled one person who worked with her during the pandemic. Usually, hiring a consultant – a senior partner – would cost an organisation a fee of hundreds of euros an hour, but O'Beirne came to the HSE for free. It did not hurt that her firm, where she is an equity partner, earned at least €17.7 million from the HSE alone for its work on the pandemic.

O'Beirne was chosen by Martin Fraser, the Department of the Taoiseach secretary general, and Reid, who plucked her from the HSE's management reform project and told her she would be running the system from the next day. 'I didn't know what test and tracing was,' she later admitted.

Her job was to mesh together parts of a disparate system that did not communicate with each other. When she arrived, there was no way for swabbers, logistics firms, labs and IT systems to talk to each other; there were no unique healthcare identifiers that might enable the HSE to tag a swab to a particular patient. Everything had to be built from scratch, and at pace, with Reid telling O'Beirne she had ten days to reduce waiting times for test results. 'Paul, in a very Paul way, gave me ten days to fix it and said, "In ten days, turn it to three days",' O'Beirne later recalled. It was taking 21 days for some test results to come back – and some never did at all.

The constant refrain of '15,000 tests a day' was a headache for someone who was just in the door, but it was about to get a whole lot worse.

—

The much-feared Department of Health press release with the latest Covid-19 case numbers and deaths dropped into inboxes at 6.01 p.m. on Friday, 17 April. Ireland was in the teeth of its first wave. Though it was not clear at the time, it would transpire that the peak of the surge in terms of hospitalisations had been reached two days earlier, on 15 April; the numbers in intensive care had also already peaked, on 10 April.

On that Friday evening, there were 44 new deaths, 597 new cases, plus 112 from the testing backlog in Germany. The overall number of cases of Covid-19 was now tipping towards 14,000. However, of all the numbers in the press release, only one stood out for Paul Reid – 100,000. NPHET had that day agreed to expand testing capacity to 100,000 tests per week. Testing would operate on a seven-day-week basis for a minimum of six months.

Reid later recalled that he 'lost the head' when he saw the announcement. He phoned Jim Breslin, the secretary general in the Department of Health. 'What's this?' he asked Breslin. 'This is completely outside of the process we agreed and that we were working on.' It was easy for Holohan to come up with targets, he railed, but it was down to the HSE and Reid to deliver them. Holohan's response was to point to the presence of several senior HSE officials on NPHET; how, he protested, could Reid have been blindsided?

The day before, Reid had told the Cabinet subcommittee on Covid-19 that the HSE was 'close' to running 10,000 tests per day, or 70,000 per week. Capacity was building in the system, but staffing would need to increase by between 500 and 600 to gather 15,000 swabs a day; it would require 30 labs working at full capacity; GPs would have to be briefed; test kits and PPE for swabbers would have to be found; reagent would have to be sourced. The entire logistical apparatus needed for this gear shift – increasing capacity by 50 per cent in one fell swoop – was clearly not ready for Holohan's announcement the following day. 'It's not that Tony was wrong, he was right. But the way he went about it was wrong,' Reid later said.

Niamh O'Beirne was equally frustrated. Holohan, she said later, does not think about how to operationalise a decision; 'He thinks of what he wants.' There was a familiar pattern to her exchanges with Holohan in her earliest days in the job. She would explain, 'Tony, I can't do that, because there is no IT system for me to do that.' However, the demand was unchanged. In the days after the 100,000 tests demand landed on her desk, O'Beirne told Holohan, '"Tony, how do you think I'm going to get to a hundred thousand? I have to find a lab, build a lab, procure the equipment, grow the lab, because in Ireland there are no labs that can do anything like that capacity." So you have to do a deal with somebody, they have to build it, then they have to hire the staff, and train them to be able to do the kind of volume you can do.'

One person later likened the testing demand to Holohan walking into a restaurant and ordering what he wanted, regardless of whether it was on the menu. 'Your man just said: "Well fuck that, I want beef, and lamb, and fish, and I want a load of desserts too."' But Holohan never accepted that his request was operationally impossible to achieve and would later feel vindicated. 'We set them out, and we were right and those [targets] were exceeded,' he said.

In the following days, Reid wrote to Breslin saying he was 'taken very much by surprise' by Holohan's 100,000 tests requirement and pointedly noting it had arrived on his desk via letter shortly before 9 p.m., three hours after the press release was issued. The letter, Reid wrote, was 'at odds' with a process agreed with the Cabinet subcommittee and in subsequent meetings with Martin Fraser. He went on to say, 'I'm at a loss as to why this direction from the NPHET to the HSE was given and publicly communicated without completing the jointly agreed processes and without regard to appropriate governance.' Ciarán Devane, the HSE chairman, wrote a similarly indignant letter to Simon Harris. Within days, Martin Wall revealed the thrust of the exchanges in the *Irish Times*.

Several days after the testing row first erupted, the two sides sat down for peace talks chaired by Simon Harris. Over Zoom, Harris, Breslin and his adviser Joanne Lonergan met with Devane, Reid and Anne O'Connor, the HSE's chief operations officer.

An unpublished memo of the exchange shows how an entire system was contrived at this stage to ensure there would be no surprises emanating from the NPHET meetings. Its language is largely emollient; there is talk of 'ongoing openness to strengthening processes'. Holohan's letters to the minister after NPHET meetings, detailing advice and decisions taken, would be shared with the HSE, and Reid would be briefed before the letters were sent. There would be a weekly call to 'ensure collective understanding'. The HSE was to see what was coming from NPHET, and to have time to react to it.

But there was also a clear message from Harris. 'The Minister said that NPHET is the singular mechanism for ensuring integrated and rapid response to the pandemic,' the memo stated. When it came to the pandemic, the HSE was the engine. But NPHET, and more specifically Holohan, was the power.

—

People who worked with both men felt the testing row cemented what was already a bad relationship between Reid and Holohan. 'Too similar,' a source who worked closely with them later said. 'Both are brilliant people, very committed public servants, both workaholics, both we owe a debt of gratitude to [...] but they're both really stubborn alpha males. They both like to be the boss.'

Turf wars played out everywhere. When Holohan asked Reid for the HSE's Anne O'Connor to join NPHET, Reid refused. Later, Holohan sought to have Niamh O'Beirne join NPHET, but Reid again refused.

He later explained, 'I was quite strong about it.' He felt strongly that the required representation already existed on NPHET in the form of senior figures like chief clinical officer Colm Henry and acute hospitals director Liam Woods. Reid believed there had to be a distinction between public health advice and the execution of it – and the execution was his job.

To Reid's mind, Holohan's preference was to control as much as he could and put his arms around everything. Ironically, Holohan felt that the people Reid didn't like to hear challenges from were those from the HSE who were from NPHET.

People who worked with both men felt their competitiveness sometimes descended to ridiculous levels: sniping at each other on calls over who had the most accurate number for hospitalised patients that morning, for example. Reid, for his part, said that while he 'fully respects' Holohan, 'we probably wouldn't be seen going for pints, put it that way'.

CHAPTER 9:

BONOS DÍAS

25 March 2020
Cases: 1,564
Deaths: 9
Seven-day average of new cases: 171

T he email Liam Casey had just received had an unusual subject line. 'Bonos días' it read. The email itself was equally eye-catching. 'Bono here. Is this still your email? and if so can I have a word in your shell-like? would love your advice on something important. hope you and yours are keeping safe. thanks. Bono.'

The U2 frontman wanted to help Ireland as it grappled with its first lockdown. The band had put aside $10m, but with the taps of global and State liquidity turned on, cash alone was of limited use. Product – specifically, PPE – was what was needed. So Bono got in touch with Liam Casey, the man known as 'Mr China'.

For 24 years, Casey's PCH International global product development and supply chain firm has been synonymous with business in the People's Republic. From his base in Shenzhen, Casey, the son of a County Cork dairy farmer, built a sourcing and logistics empire with revenues in the hundreds of millions of dollars. His business does one thing above all else: it navigates what can be a disorienting and opaque market.

Casey gets China, its people and its way of doing business. People think you have to speak Chinese to do business there; Casey has only a few words. They say you have to spend hours downing drinks at boozy banquets to get ahead; Casey doesn't drink. 'That's Westerners telling stories about China,' he said. 'Business in China is very much about the people […] you've got to interact with the people and engage with the people, build a relationship with them.'

In 2020 PCH added another product line to its business: PPE. In the middle of January, the company closed its Chinese facilities for the new year, and then found itself unable to reopen as Covid-19 took hold. While it initially focused on its own supplies of PPE, as the virus spread others began to come to Casey and his firm.

On 22 March, he received an email from Marc Andreessen, the legendary Silicon Valley entrepreneur and venture capitalist worth an estimated $1.7bn. Andreessen had co-authored the world's first web browser and went on to build and invest in myriad tech success stories. He wanted to introduce Casey to the head of the White House corona-virus taskforce. Casey, Andreessen said in his introductory email, was 'one of the top world experts on global supply chains, sourcing and distribution'. Three days later, the 'Bonos días' email dropped.

Bono had met Casey at a social event in Dublin in the early 2000s and they had kept in touch ever since. The rock star had introduced Casey to the American entrepreneur Jimmy Iovine, best known for co-founding Beats with rapper and producer Dr Dre, and PCH had helped launch the headphone company's products globally.

PCH's approach was to be on the ground, next to where the product was being manufactured. Counterfeit goods were everywhere. Casey later said he could have sent planeloads of PPE to Ireland without moving from his computer if quality wasn't an issue. PCH audited 60 factories but approved just 6. The company sent an Irish employee, nicknamed Marco Polo, criss-crossing the country to inspect facilities. It learned, counterintuitively, to stay away from medical factories where Chinese government officials and customs officers swarmed, instead finding tech facilities that could achieve volume and scale. Oversight from the State became even tighter when reports of counterfeit PPE began to circulate in Europe, with the Chinese authorities neurotic about protecting their reputation.

Companies were moving fast to adopt new product lines, as what had hitherto been a sleepy and predictable industry exploded. Casey knew of one firm that in February 2020 had never made a mask and by June was making 100 million of them a day. He and PCH executives read deeply into the area, scoping out different specifications of masks, examining what was being used in different jurisdictions, especially Asian countries. So did Bono, according to Casey: 'He was down into the detail, he wanted to know everything. He was doing it from a place of wanting to be informed. If he was going to do this, he wanted to do it right, he didn't want to bullshit.'

The pair spoke every morning for up to 45 minutes. Bono was interested in the raw materials, the manufacturing processes. He, like many others, became fixated on high-spec N95 respirators. But PCH and Casey had a different idea. They had identified a Type IIR mask which was plentiful, effective and cheaper than N95s. Ultimately, he convinced Bono that his money would go further invested in the Type IIRs – the disposable masks that became commonplace in Ireland across 2020 and 2021. Bono told Casey that he would talk to anyone, any time, if it would help secure the PPE he wanted.

Casey had already been talking with US multinational Salesforce, sourcing masks and PPE for its operations, and told the firm he could cut 30 per cent off its PPE costs. As the company hesitated, Casey tried to close the deal on a call with one of the company's executives in San Francisco. 'We have an opportunity here to partner with another organisation,' he told Salesforce, 'but I need you to fucking speak to someone. Hold there, I'm going to put Bono on the line.'

'Who?' came the reply from the Salesforce executive.

Casey rang the rock star, who joined the call. 'I'm telling you; it was the fastest closing I've ever seen!' he later recalled.

The Salesforce order was crucial. It gave PCH the volume it needed to open up factory gates in China and the orders from elsewhere started to flow. The fastidious Casey would not place Bono's order for PPE for

Irish healthcare workers without a signature from the HSE confirming it would accept it. That's where an ex-army captain came in.

—

Convivial and plain-speaking, Seán Bresnan left school to join the Defence Forces, where he spent nearly 15 years, including two tours to Lebanon, before getting into logistics with Bus Éireann and then the HSE. In November 2019 he was made national director of procurement at the HSE, and was in charge of a staff of around five hundred. Everything from the hand sanitisers at hospital entrances to highly sophisticated CAT scanners usually came through Bresnan's office.

Much like Liam Casey, the HSE had its own market intelligence from China. In February and March 2020, this information indicated that the market had been disrupted by plant closures and limited shipping channels due to port and airport closures. Demand for PPE was a hundred times the norm and prices were up to twenty times higher than normal. Export bans were imposed worldwide. The HSE would later identify 226 separate bans, restrictions, or state commandeering of products.

On 5 February, in the conference room of the Ashling Hotel, a five-minute walk across the River Liffey from Dr Steevens' Hospital, Bresnan met with thirty or so of the HSE's core suppliers and issued a call to arms. The HSE needed masks, gowns, gloves, face shields and goggles – as many of each as could be found. To underline the point, the last slide in his presentation that day showed a green jersey with the word 'Ireland' emblazoned across it.

But within weeks the market had become so disrupted that Bresnan asked Paul Reid to approve a plan he had drawn up to source and open up a primary supply line of PPE from China. The scale that was needed was beyond anything that Bono could help with, and beyond the parameters of normal deals for PPE. What was needed was a big bazooka. The State's industrial development authority, IDA Ireland, was called in. Its China director, Zhang Zhewei, recommended that only state-owned enterprises be approached. They had a better chance of a reliable supply line, and it would be easier to get the product out of China in what was becoming an increasingly volatile market, he argued. Within days, China Resources Pharmaceutical Group (CRPG) was identified.

By 12 March, as Leo Varadkar was announcing the first set of restrictions, Bresnan and senior officials from the Departments of Business and of Foreign Affairs as well as the IDA found themselves sitting with the Chinese ambassador to Ireland, He Xiangdong, at the embassy on Ailesbury Road, asking the ambassador for support in securing the manufacturing capacity of CRPG to produce millions of items of PPE for the Irish health service. By St Patrick's Day, Bresnan had concluded a deal with CRPG for around €208m, nearly 14 times the amount the State would typically spend on PPE per year.

It was unprecedented deal-making, moving at whirlwind speed. But for good reason. The day before, a confidential memo to ministers claimed that 'highly credible and highly reliable intelligence has emerged in the past number of hours suggesting that supply lines are tightening significantly'. There was, the memo warned, a need to include the transaction 'in the shortest possible timeframe' with the 'distinct likelihood' that the HSE would only be able to conduct one transaction with CRPG.

To that end, the HSE asked the government to more than double the order volumes. 'This estimate is in the absence of any detailed epidemiological modelling data and is based solely on commercial and inventory considerations,' the ministers were told. It was a frantic scramble for PPE, and Ireland was going to take whatever it could lay its hands on.

There was zero opportunity to haggle. In later correspondence to the Department of Health, Reid noted that prevailing market prices and increased demand had pushed up the cost of the original €208m deal by €48m. 'It has not been possible to negotiate downward pricing,' Reid told Jim Breslin. 'Any price speculation or market softening strategy on the part of the HSE was considered too high-risk.' In one example, a typical N2 face mask would cost 69 cent pre-Covid, but at the peak, the HSE was paying €11.20 for the same product.

In normal circumstances a deal of that scale would take a minimum of nine months, but by 29 March, Aer Lingus flight EI9019 arrived at

Dublin Airport from Beijing laden with the first consignment of PPE. Over the next 14 weeks, some 259 flights made the journey of over 8,000km from China to Dublin. One plane alone could carry 60,000 gowns, about enough to cover the health service for half a day at the peak of the pandemic. Casey would later say that the bilateral deal with China was 'the envy of every European country'.

It was needed. The HSE suddenly and without warning became the suppliers of first or last resort to private nursing homes, GPs and other health facilities across the country that would have typically sourced their own supplies. At its peak, the HSE delivered more than 15 million items of PPE per week (80 per cent of which were surgical masks and gloves) to over 3,800 separate locations.

This major logistical exercise was occasionally made more challenging by well-intentioned individuals making donations of products that did not meet regulatory standards. This included one instance of short-sleeved gowns being delivered to a hospital in the north-east of the country. Reid, who is five foot five, would later recall being teased by colleagues that he had ordered the short-sleeved gowns for himself.

—

The security of PPE supply into Ireland by April was in sharp contrast to horror stories being reported worldwide. Some governments were landing planes in locations only to see them take off empty because they could not secure a supply of PPE. In other cases, the HSE's own intelligence suggested officials from some governments were being sent to countries with bags of cash seeking to buy up any PPE at any price.

The HSE received other reports of planes landing in Budapest and Warsaw having products sold off the back of the cargo hold. Reid would later describe the market as being rife with 'modern-day piracy'.

While never falling victim to theft on the tarmac, in one instance the HSE provisionally agreed a deal for the supply of a million pairs of nitrile gloves before being told two days later that they had been outbid. The deal was gone. In another example of sharp practice, the HSE encountered document forgery. In order to conclude a transaction and activate a supply line, a supplier would typically provide what's known as a certificate of empowerment, a document signed by the health minister and given to the supplier by the HSE, proving their bona fides. But on one occasion in spring 2020, the HSE discovered, through one of its suppliers, a certificate supposedly signed by Simon Harris emanating from China. The document was discovered to be a forgery before it could be used nefariously.

Other deals that went awry landed the HSE in court. On 27 March, it struck a deal with Wicklow-based company Narooma for 350 ventilators at a cost of €7.5m with payment due three days later. A day later it all collapsed when the IDA told the HSE not to proceed; it had a number of concerns, based on intelligence from China, about Narooma's ability to deliver. Narooma later took the HSE to court over non-payment and also sued the IDA. In a High Court judgment some time later, Mr Justice David Barniville noted that Narooma had drawn up a contract using a template it sourced from a Google search.

When it came to ventilators, Bresnan and the HSE sometimes felt that their call to 'pull on the green jersey' was falling on deaf ears. Medtronic, a Galway-based pharmaceutical technology company, had in March and April 2020 made much of its ramping up of ventilator manufacturing at its facility in Mervue. It promised 400 ventilators a week by the end of April, 700 by the end of May and more than 1,000 by the end of June. The company even publicly shared the blueprints for one of its portable ventilator models so that other companies could make the devices.

But in mid-March, Medtronic became embroiled in what Paul Reid would later describe in a memo to the Department of Health as 'less than fruitful' discussions with the HSE over the supply of ventilators to the Irish health system. Medtronic asserted that its worldwide market needed to be supplied and that it had a general allocation principle that was based on the number of ICU beds per country. This hampered Ireland because before the pandemic the State had around 225 ICU beds, or 6 per 100,000 population – half the EU average. Even allowing for this, Medtronic also argued that Ireland was already receiving in excess of this principle with around a fifth of the company's European allocation remaining within Ireland.

Reid sought a political intervention and in mid-April, Taoiseach Leo Varadkar phoned Medtronic chief Geoff Martha to try to break the impasse. His message was blunt. 'I said if we did get into a serious situation where we didn't have vents in Ireland, and everyone knew that the vents were being made in the factory in Galway and the staff were going in and out of there every day to make ventilators for export, that we'd have a real problem,' he later recalled.

Varadkar hypothesised a situation where a relative of a staff member could be in hospital in Galway with no access to a ventilator, while a company just down the road was making and exporting them. 'We'd be the government and we'd be allowing them to do it and we would be under enormous pressure to do an export ban. It's a negotiation. I didn't threaten them or anything, it was just setting out the appalling vista,' the then Taoiseach would later say. It was a stark example of Ireland's decades-long open door to foreign direct investment suddenly coming into conflict with the urgent need for life-saving equipment for its citizens.

Medtronic's demands, according to a Department of Health memo later reported on in the *Irish Examiner*, included that the company be deemed an essential operator, which would allow it to operate during lockdowns, and that it would be prioritised for PPE, as well as testing and contact tracing in the event that one of its employees contracted Covid-19. The Department of Health memo described these 'as difficult, if not impossible, for a government to provide'. In the end the HSE maintained its ask at that time was never fully met, despite Varadkar's intervention.

Medtronic later claimed it had 'positive communications' with the government and the HSE, including letters of thanks. 'As our supply increased, we made provision for additional ventilators for Ireland if necessary and thankfully the HSE did not require all of this allocation,' the company said in a statement.

—

On 21 April 2020, NPHET issued a directive that all healthcare workers should wear surgical face masks in health settings. Suddenly, and without prior warning, the HSE needed 1.2 million masks per day – five times the number being used every day at that point. The Chinese market was flooded, but South Korea had approximately 250 certified face mask manufacturing facilities and a capacity to produce 10 to 12 million masks per day.

The IDA, through its Korean director on the ground William Kim, identified DOBU MASK, the second largest manufacturer of N95 masks in the country. But there was one major problem: South Korea had issued an export ban that meant that manufacturers were required to supply 80 per cent of their production to the government for distribution to the general public, health workers and other frontline staff. To get around this, the Department of Foreign Affairs set up a call between the Taoiseach and South Korean president Moon Jae-in. Leo Varadkar made the case that Ireland should get a temporary exemption from the export ban on humanitarian grounds and found sympathetic ears.

The supply line was unlocked and a €120m deal for some 120 million masks was done. But it was complicated by DOBU having to ramp up its manufacturing capacity and a delay in the actual lifting of the export ban. The HSE had expected this would happen in early May 2020 but in the end the first delivery from Seoul did not arrive until 22 July.

In the interim, Paul Reid turned to Bono, his fellow Dublin northsider. Both Finglas born and bred, Reid used to slag Bono that he was from the posh part of the north Dublin suburb whereas the HSE boss was from what he considered 'the real part'.

By this stage, PCH had already shipped around six planeloads of U2 donations, including masks, gowns and other items of PPE. It was all welcome, but Reid explained to Bono the sudden predicament the HSE found itself in – needing millions of masks at short notice because of NPHET's new directive.

Bono contacted Casey and told him the HSE was interested in securing millions more of the Type IIR masks that the PCH boss had mentioned to him weeks earlier. Eventually, via Bono, Casey linked up with Seán

Bresnan, and on 10 May PCH delivered the first shipment of Type IIR masks into Dublin. Millions more followed across the month of May and right into June.

Casey later recalled how Chinese airports and logistics were a waking nightmare at the time – days-long tailbacks snaked along approach roads where aircraft were juggled between two-hour windows. Almost everything was going out on empty passenger planes, which meant that kit couldn't be loaded on to pallets. Shipping PPE on aircraft seats needed everything from regulatory dispensations to precise engineering knowledge about how to balance out the weight on an aircraft using sandbags. 'It was crazy intense,' Casey said.

—

The cost of all this was enormous and the HSE's policy in such a volatile market was 'pay now, answer questions later'. In total the HSE would spend close to €1bn on PPE in 2020. A KPMG audit of spending, which did not emerge until July 2021, unsurprisingly suggested that traditional procurement rules were not always followed and due diligence was not always carried out.

'There was little or no epidemiological data available to conduct robust and detailed demand planning exercises,' Reid later admitted in a letter to Jim Breslin in the Department of Health. 'The PPE sourcing effort was being conducted against the background of increasing cases and mortality rates across Europe and in particular the emerging scenes in Italy.'

Once again the scenes from Bergamo were conditioning the State's early response and few things brought this grim reality home more than the sourcing of body bags. Typically the HSE would hold between 1,000 and 1,200 body bags in stock, well short of what might be needed if the virus was allowed to spread uncontrolled – which could result in tens of thousands of deaths. The HSE ordered an extra 5,000 body bags at the start of the crisis and within weeks found itself co-ordinating funeral directors who were reporting difficulties securing supplies. Around the same time, NPHET's subgroup on acute hospitals was discussing what extra refrigeration requirements might be needed.

It wasn't just a logistical concern. At the very highest levels of government and officialdom, they knew how the sight of overwhelmed morgues would shred public confidence in the State's capacity to handle the crisis. A group was set up between the Department of the Taoiseach and the Department of Housing to plan, and the nuts and bolts fell to the HSE.

That sobering task fell to Ciarán Browne, one of the HSE's lead officials on emergency management planning. Pre-Covid, Browne was typically focused on planning for mass casualty situations – a terrorist attack, a building collapse, a plane crash. Browne's concern was not so much a bomb going off in O'Connell Street – there are five major hospitals in the area – but what if a bomb went off at the Rose of Tralee? Helicopters would have to be used to transport victims to Dublin.

Confronted with the startling mortality projections, Browne at one point found himself placing an order to reserve 10 refrigerated storage units for dead bodies that could be placed adjacent to existing mortuaries. Of the 10 four-metre-long steel containers, 7 were eventually deployed across the country's five cities. 'It was one of the most awful decisions of my working life,' Browne later recalled. 'The day I rang to place the order for these units, I really couldn't believe what we had just done. This was now very real.'

Confidential records from the group planning to handle mortality show it discussed 'possible re-interment of deceased remains due to expediency requirement'. The group believed that, if deaths exceeded the capacity of local authorities or funeral directors to handle remains, there could be exceptional circumstances in which bodies would have to be buried where space could be found in cemeteries, and later dug up to be reburied in family plots.

A temporary mortuary was also erected in Kilmainham – a massive tent with rows and rows of planking ready to receive the remains of up to 600 people. Anyone going in to inspect the facility had their mobile phones taken from them by Department of Health staff. It was obvious why. Browne would later describe the scene inside:

When you see it in real life, the size of it, and you imagine it with hundreds and hundreds of remains, you stop. You only see this stuff in movies, you never really believe it's going to happen in your country. I thought to myself, 'My God, if this thing is full up, what is our nation facing?'

CHAPTER 10:

THE UNKNOWN MAN

26 March 2020
Cases: 1,819
Deaths: 19
Seven-day average of new cases: 180

A t 8 p.m. people all across Ireland stopped and stood to applaud frontline healthcare workers – a gesture of solidarity and support. It was no different in the socially distanced Dáil. But Simon Coveney stood at the back of the chamber, away from the cameras. The Tánaiste and Minister for Foreign Affairs was on the phone to his Peruvian counterpart, Gustavo Adolfo Meza-Cuadra Velásquez: 'We have people trapped in your country, we want to get them out, and it'll be quick.'

Peru was just one part of an unprecedented mobilisation to bring home thousands of Irish citizens stranded across the globe as the pandemic hit, and it was particularly tricky. The country had closed its borders on 16 March and imposed a strict 15-day national lockdown. Coveney would later recall how local populations had effectively turned against Europeans, 'blaming them for bringing Covid, which was this sort of plague-like disease that no one really understood but were very frightened of, to South America'.

Based in Santiago, Chile, Paul Gleeson was Ireland's first resident ambassador. A graduate of Trinity and the London School of Economics, he had been Coveney's political director for two years. Now barely a year into his Latin America posting, Gleeson and his small team had to negotiate with bus operators in Peru, over three thousand kilometres away, to organise the collection of those Irish stranded across remote and mountainous regions. They then had to appeal to Peruvian police to let the buses through multiple roadblocks. In the end, around 135 Irish tourists left Peru on a British Airways flight arranged through Aer Lingus's parent company, IAG. By 2 April 2020 some five thousand people had been flown home from around the globe.

The dramatic closure of schools, universities and crèches had been followed by a drip feed of further regulations: first, pubs and restaurants were closed on 15 March, then non-essential retail was shuttered on 24 March, as income supports were ratcheted up from €205 per week to €350 per week. As the country shut down, the State was stepping up in extraordinary ways.

On 16 March, Leo Varadkar held a meeting in the private dining room next to his office. Twelve other men crowded around the table. One of them recalled afterwards, 'I was kind of looking around the room and thinking it was a super-spreader event.' They included Varadkar's two advisers, Brian Murphy and John Carroll, Paschal Donohoe and his adviser Ed Brophy, as well as Simon Harris. On the civil service side were Martin Fraser, Robert Watt from the Department of Public Expenditure, Jim Breslin and Paul Bolger from Health, and Derek Moran from Finance. The HSE's Paul Reid and Colm Henry were there too.

Varadkar asked that all options for further hospital capacity be examined, 'including the possibility of purchasing hospital staff if that proved necessary', according to Fraser's note of the meeting. The State had 18 private hospitals with 1,900 beds and 100 ICU beds – capacity equal to a fifth of the public health system – and the Taoiseach wanted to buy it all up. 'I was up for CPO-ing [compulsory purchase order] them, either buying them or the threat of CPO,' he later recalled. 'One, it would be a quick way of increasing hospital capacity and two, it would be a permanent way to increase hospital capacity.'

These were now effectively the most powerful people (all men) in the State, collectively spending hundreds of millions at the drop of a hat, unencumbered by the usual political or budgetary constraints, spit-balling ideas like buying up a few hospitals. It was deadly serious, but one participant recalled how there was a near swagger to it at times.

It was a remarkable proposal but one that, to the Taoiseach's mind, would help to achieve the government's policy of ending the two-tier health system. 'Never waste a good crisis,' Varadkar would say privately around this time. A document drawn up for the meeting was less ambi-tious, outlining instead a cost-only arrangement in which the State would agree to pay a peppercorn rent but cover all the operational costs of the facilities.

Watt told the meeting that the government would negotiate a robust deal with the private hospitals. It was so robust, in fact, that Harris later recalled threatening one particular individual in the sector who, he claimed, was resisting the plan. 'I'm going on the *Six One News* tonight and I'm naming the hospitals that wouldn't help Ireland, and that had ventilators when our citizens were left gasping for breath,' he said he told this person, whom he declined to name.

It took two weeks – a lifetime in a pandemic – to agree the deal with the Private Hospitals Association, and at a cost of nearly €300m it would prove controversial, but it was done at a time when no one knew what was coming. In the end, the main issue with the deal was the consultants, who hated it. One politician recalled countless rough meetings with consultants who viewed them as 'communist or something'.

The consultants were the best-remunerated doctors in the State, and some viewed the deal as a threat, a costly one that would curtail their most lucrative work. Their usual earnings were worlds apart from what they would get under the deal. One senior HSE official recalled how, among the consultants, anyone on less than a half million euros per annum was the equivalent of 'living in caravans'.

It was a loveless and expensive marriage, and the deal was not extended beyond the end of June 2020. A successor deal took some six months to negotiate, with private hospitals eventually agreeing to provide up to 30 per cent of their capacity depending on the incidence of the virus with scope to provide more if required.

The government also gave itself extensive powers via the Emergency Measures in the Public Interest Act. This included banning evictions and rent increases, a policy intervention that housing minister Eoghan Murphy had for years insisted was not possible. The Department of Housing was terrified that the homelessness crisis would be exacerbated by the pandemic, or, as one person involved put it, there would be 'a situation where you were taking two or three bodies off O'Connell Street after they died of Covid'. A huge push was made to lease short-term lets so that family hubs and other emergency accommodation didn't end up harbouring clusters of the virus.

In the Department of Justice, Charlie Flanagan was being forced to countenance the release of hundreds of prisoners in order to free up space to allow for social distancing. For the party of law and order, this was uncomfortable territory. 'How do you pick them and who do you release?' Flanagan asked. Later, in consultation with victims of crime, the Prison Service and the Probation Service, some six hundred prisoners would be released. It raised eyebrows at Cabinet, Flanagan later recalled, but, he said, 'it worked because it had to work'.

—

Change at this scale relied on normal people behaving in abnormal ways – staying at home, staying away from each other. Martin Fraser believed this needed to be communicated clearly. You couldn't risk having some line minister going off message and confusing the public. The weekend after Leo Varadkar announced the first public health restrictions, Fraser called communications guru John Concannon.

Two years earlier, Fraser had written a report recommending that Concannon be put out of a job as head of the Strategic Communications Unit (SCU) over newspaper advertisements promoting government spending plans which, the opposition claimed, were more about promoting Varadkar and Fine Gael. Micheál Martin in particular was apoplectic, describing the SCU as 'dangerous'. Fraser needed the leader of Fianna Fáil's approval, or at least his acquiescence, to bring Concannon back into Government Buildings. He called Deirdre Gillane, Martin's most senior adviser, to run the proposal past her and approval was forthcoming.

The spin doctor planned a full-scale communications barrage. Daily press conferences and themed events would be run on a tight roster. There would be 'close collaboration' with RTÉ in particular, which would be 'critical to informing the public and helping in the national effort to respond', a communications plan stated.

Simon Coveney bought in to the plan. He later made a conscious effort to appeal to RTÉ to 'just understand the importance of national cohesion' while holding the government to account. He would stress this message to producers and presenters after interviews. The role of the national broadcaster in covering the pandemic would at times generate disquiet among some commentators who felt it was too closely aligned with government messaging.

That messaging was delivered in a variety of ways, but perhaps most unusually by Liz Canavan, one of Fraser's key deputies in the Department of the Taoiseach. Canavan would, in the early days of the pandemic, hold a daily press conference at 11 a.m. It was an effort to depoliticise communications. Canavan was sufficiently unknown and, as one insider later recalled, 'a bit like Denmark', in that she would be viewed as inoffensive and competent to those watching at home. But away from the media, she was a pivotal figure whom Fraser considered his most important appointment when he asked her to chair the Covid-19 senior officials group in February 2020. Canavan and her team were responsible for pulling together Covid-19 memos and detailed communications plans at short notice as well as navigating the complexities of pandemic policy-making. In late March 2020, as Ireland entered a total lockdown, it was left to Canavan, Fraser and another department assistant secretary, John Shaw, to spend a weekend working out what could be classed as an essential retail outlet. Four years of planning for Brexit had made it easier for them to determine which outlets had to remain open to ensure the continuity of critical supply chains. As an ex-Department of Health official,

Canavan was well placed to lead the national response and she was, one adviser later recalled, viewed as Fraser's 'eyes and ears'.

Concannon's plan also succeeded in annoying many of the constituent parts of government, some of whom saw him as an unwelcome presence. Press statements had to be cleared centrally, which meant logjams developed – to the frustration of ministers and their advisers, who privately bitched among themselves that it was all the fault of Concannon and his 'spin unit'. One of them later recalled contacting Concannon directly, suggesting that he send an email to all ministers' press advisers outlining how the new structures would work. Concannon never responded.

There was another thread to the disgruntlement. Many in government felt that, in the face of a threat unlike any other the State had ever faced, power was being sucked into what those working outside Government Buildings refer to as 'the centre' – a handful of top civil servants, the Taoiseach, his staff, some senior members of the Cabinet, and Martin Fraser.

By its design and nature, the role of secretary general to the Department of the Taoiseach is an immensely powerful position. The secretary general's most obvious function is to be a gatekeeper to the Taoiseach, providing advice and guidance on a near-constant basis. The best can, in time, anticipate what their boss is thinking. But they also dictate the unseen rhythms of government, planning the business of the administration of the day, troubleshooting problems and knocking heads together when needed. Varadkar believed the role was akin to that of a chief of staff in the White House.

Fraser carried at least that authority during the pandemic. 'To me, this whole story is about Martin,' a senior official later recalled. Another described him as 'the hero of the story'. A career civil servant since he was 16, Fraser is lauded by many as a strategic genius with a deep understanding of the inner workings of the Irish State.

He knew how to land ideas and policies effectively and which people to lean upon to get things done. His direct approach could be mistaken for a Malcolm Tucker-like bluntness – a reference to the volatile spin doctor in the BBC political comedy *The Thick of It* – but those who work with Fraser say that's a disservice; his style is more nuanced, and he is more convivial. But he does have teeth, and is not afraid to bare them often; and, like the BBC character, he is at the centre of everything.

'He is the big figure,' Varadkar later said. 'I think Shane Ross described him as the sixteenth member of Cabinet or something. That would be an accurate description.' But Ross would go further than that: 'I think I'd go as far as to say he had more influence than the Taoiseach.' This view, shared privately by others who worked in government during the first wave of the pandemic, made some uneasy, not least the Cabinet ministers who were not centrally involved in Covid decision-making, even though they liked and respected Fraser. During their most insecure moments, they wondered whether the new power dynamics were undemocratic.

Simon Coveney, Varadkar's Tánaiste, is unapologetic about how things were done. 'This was a national emergency, we needed the most experienced people that we had managing from the centre,' he said. Central though he may have been, few outside the chattering classes of politics and the civil service knew Fraser's name. He was low-profile and liked it that way. During the talks on Northern Ireland in 2014, *The Guardian* ran a picture of UK Prime Minister David Cameron addressing the media. In it he is being watched by a group of men that included Ulster Unionists Michael McGimpsey and Danny Kennedy, and Mark Kennelly, Enda Kenny's chief of staff, each captioned by name. A fourth watching figure was billed as 'an unknown man' – that was Fraser.

Fraser found it funny. What greater achievement was there for the career civil servant to be at the right hand of power for a political generation or more, to wield huge power yourself, and yet be totally unrecognisable? It belied his true role as an architect of strategy, down to the tone and tenor of engagements, right down to the location. When Donald Trump came to Ireland, Fraser was among those arguing that Varadkar should meet him on neutral ground, not travel to his Doonbeg hotel where he was holding court.

He was also key to the plan to hold Brexit negotiations with Boris

Johnson in Wirral, outside Liverpool, a city with strong Irish connections, and a long way from London. Fraser knew how to wield power effectively. One person who was deep in the Brexit trenches recalled a particular pinch point in negotiations, when both Brussels and London were desperate to get a read from Dublin on a particular point. The phones in the Taoiseach's department were ringing incessantly, but a takeaway had just been delivered. 'Let that ring,' Fraser said. 'We'll call back after our dinner.'

—

In mid-March, Robert Watt, the secretary general of the Department of Public Expenditure, walked into Paschal Donohoe's office. 'We think six hundred thousand people will be approaching our Intreo offices this weekend and we don't have the systems or the ability to cope with that many people,' Watt told him. 'There will be a tsunami of people on the dole here.'

The Department of Social Protection had begun to feel the strain. Pubs and restaurants were closed, and tens of thousands of people were presenting at Intreo offices across the country. There were queues down the street. The restrictions would soon mean that these offices would have to close as well, but before that even happened a Covid-19 outbreak in the Swords Intreo office forced it to close, while two dole offices in Donegal were also shuttered when cases emerged.

Some ministers, including Donohoe and Regina Doherty, the outgoing social protection minister who had lost her Dáil seat, thought that the government policy triggered an obligation to support people. But figuring out how was another thing entirely. A fly in the ointment came on Friday, 20 March, when British Chancellor Rishi Sunak announced a furlough scheme that would see the government pay the wages of millions of workers across the UK to keep them in jobs, rather than have their employers lay them off.

It was an eye-catching measure aimed at shoring up a locked-down British economy, but Donohoe and his officials, who were mulling over a similar scheme, were curious to figure out how it would work, and conscious that any Irish effort would have to match it. So they phoned the UK Treasury. 'What are you doing? How are you going to do it?' one senior official asked their British counterpart. 'We have no idea,' came the response, according to two sources with knowledge of the call. When the Irish official pointed out that the announcement had gazumped the government in Dublin, the Treasury official responded: '1–1 for your bank guarantee', a reference to Ireland's dramatic decision to issue a blanket guarantee to its banking system in September 2008, a decision that caught the Treasury on the hop and that many in Whitehall resented.

Watt and Fraser were part of a group of senior civil servants who were tempered in the fires of the financial crisis and then Brexit. 'They do crisis management,' Eamon Ryan would later observe. 'They grew up in it.' A forceful figure in the public service, Watt was appointed to head up the newly created Department of Public Expenditure and Reform in 2011, making him one of the youngest people ever to lead a department. DPER was responsible for making sure the wild excesses of the pre-collapse budgets never returned; taking the punch bowl away just as the party was getting started … or making sure it was never put out.

Inevitably this meant that Watt, who swears like a sailor, could antagonise colleagues for adopting a hard-line stance in budget negoti-ations. This was not helped by his tendency to pop up in the media. To his detractors he shamelessly courted the limelight, but Watt believed that civil servants should not be faceless mandarins. In 2014, at the MacGill Summer School in Glenties, County Donegal, he did an impromptu doorstep with journalists and talked about the need for a debate on making it easier to sack civil servants. He could also clash with his polit-ical masters. In 2019, Watt argued trenchantly against a €3bn plan for the State to deliver high-speed broadband to every home in the coun-try, claiming that it did not represent value for money for the taxpayer. Donohoe was annoyed about Watt's opposition and the fact that it had become public knowledge before the decision was made. The government ended up pursuing the plan and their relationship never recovered.

Equally, Watt was annoyed that his efforts to become governor of the Central Bank were thwarted. He had gone for the job in 2015, losing out to Philip Lane, and later told friends he felt then finance minister Michael Noonan could have handled it better. Four years later, Watt felt much the same when the government appointed New Zealander Gabriel Makhlouf instead, believing he [Watt] was the wrong man for the job. Still, Watt was fond of Donohoe, despite what he confided in colleagues was 'the bullshit' with the Central Bank job.

In spring 2020, Watt, along with the likes of Derek Moran in the Department of Finance, was part of a group of public servants clustered around Donohoe – who was determined that this crisis would be different from what had happened a decade earlier when the State had ceded its sovereignty over its affairs to the EU and the International Monetary Fund. 'If the country or broader economy begins to think that this building – the Department of Finance – doesn't have a plan – and that happened once before – it has consequences,' Donohoe later said.

Confidence and authority had to be projected outwards, even if Donohoe felt inwardly that Ireland was again staring into the abyss. The weekend after the UK furlough scheme was announced, officials in Merrion Street scrambled to devise their own scheme. Niall Cody, the head of the Revenue Commissioners, told Donohoe they could reverse-engineer their systems so that, rather than collecting tax, it would pay employers to keep their employees on the books. 'I will do it,' Cody told the minister, 'if you give me the weekend.'

This memo was still warm from the printer when Donohoe carried it into the Cabinet room the following Tuesday. The Temporary Wage Subsidy Scheme (TWSS) would refund employers up to a maximum of €410 per week and would run for 12 weeks. Eventually it was revised and recast as the Employment Wage Subsidy Scheme, and it lasted well into 2022. This was not how the government was supposed to function. Mammoth open-ended schemes would normally take months, if not years, to devise and agree. But in March 2020 it was all happening within days, with no certainty of how long it would last, or how much it would cost the exchequer. By the middle of January 2022, tens of thousands of firms and hundreds of thousands of workers had been supported by the two schemes at a combined cost of almost €10bn. More than €700m was spent through another scheme, the Covid Restrictions Support Scheme, and hundreds of millions more was warehoused in tax liabilities or paid out through other programmes. More than €9bn was also spent on the Pandemic Unemployment Payment (PUP), an unconditional payment paid to those laid off as a result of the restrictions. The details of the PUP had been hammered out that same weekend in the Whitaker Room of the Department of Finance, where Regina Doherty made the case for paying it at a rate of €350, or €147 more than the standard jobseeker's payment. 'Lads, if you really want these people to stay at home, you have to replace their income,' Doherty told them, 'this is a no-brainer.' Earlier in the crisis, Doherty and Watt had sharp exchanges on the design of a scheme, but those fell away.

One proposal on the table was to pay a weekly rate of €400, but the €350 proposal was seen as the most equitable – it would fully cover the incomes of the vast majority of laid-off workers. Some of those laid off would inevitably earn much more than their weekly wage, with students working part-time jobs among those to benefit. Donohoe queried whether there was a way to differentiate the payments: could it be done on a sliding scale? No, Doherty responded, because that would involve creating an entirely new IT system. 'We do it, we've just gotta do it,' Donohoe conceded.

Within about ten days of its inception, PUP would become a reality. The only checks carried out on those applying were with Revenue to see if their employers were already availing of the TWSS. Anyone paid by both schemes had their PUP rescinded. But otherwise there wasn't any enforcement taken by the Department of Social Protection, and though the vast majority of payments were legitimate, inevitably some scammed the system. Employers later complained that PUP disincentivised people from returning to work when the economy reopened. Closer supervision and enforcement followed, but in spring 2020, Regina Doherty later said, 'The mantra was "close your eyes and authorise."'

—

The unprecedented fiscal response by the Irish State was made possible in large part because the EU decided on a co-ordinated approach.

By May, plans were afoot for the EU to raise a €500bn bond to fund the recovery from Covid-19. Fiscal rules had already been suspended, meaning that member states' borrowing limits were lifted. The pandemic prompted a radically different approach from the response to the 2008 financial crisis – countries would be able to borrow and spend to fund recovery.

In Dublin, it was more succinctly summed up by Fraser after one official expressed concerns about massive spending denting Ireland's credit rating in the bond markets. 'I don't give a fuck about that,' Fraser bluntly responded, according to that official. A new paradigm was in place. Worries about bond yields and spreads would not supersede the need to fund the State's spending response.

Pre-pandemic, the prospect of such massive intervention would have been unthinkable amid fears in Brussels and in larger EU capitals about the moral hazard that could arise. But as Donohoe, who became president of the Eurogroup in July 2020, would later say, 'The moral hazard concerns about a centralised fiscal response in the euro area had to be set aside when you've dead people being moved around in army trucks.'

CHAPTER 11:

THE ARMY COUNCIL

3 April 2020
Cases: 4,273
Deaths: 120
Seven-day average of new cases: 307

From his generous period home on the edge of picturesque Enniskerry, County Wicklow, Shane Ross, then aged 70, was cocooning, dialling into a meeting of the Cabinet subcommittee on Covid-19, as the government, civil service and health service tried to grapple with the pandemic.

The estate of the stockbroker turned journalist turned politician is at the end of a short, tree-fringed drive, shielded from the view of the public road, and is completed by two acres of gardens, upon which also sits a two-storey, two-bedroom mews coach house.

The main house has many period features, including an intricately carved oak staircase, and a modern glazed kitchen extension that had been renovated in the 1990s. It boasts four bedrooms, three with good-sized bathrooms, and six reception rooms, including a drawing room with a marble Victorian mantelpiece. It has a sunroom, office, shower room, store rooms, wine rooms and a tennis court. French doors give access to gardens 'flowing away behind' the house and, in the inimitable phrasing of the *Irish Times* property supplement, which advertised it for sale in 2005, it is a 'manageable family home' – with potential to develop more properties on its lands, naturally.

Like any old house, it creaks and groans. Specifically, the door to Shane Ross' study squeaks, and on 3 April, the squeak was annoying Leo Varadkar. In the Sycamore Room of Government Buildings in Dublin were Tony Holohan and Paul Reid, joined by senior Cabinet ministers, including Paschal Donohoe, Heather Humphreys and Simon Harris, and senior civil servants including Martin Fraser. Varadkar was complaining that too many people were waiting on the results of Covid tests – the backlog was climbing into the tens of thousands – but interrupted himself to curtly ask Ross to close the door.

Some time later, the subcommittee was interrupted again by Ross's wife, Ruth Buchanan, bringing him a cup of tea. Fraser would later tell Ross that he remembered Buchanan from *Poparama*, the 1980s youth programme she hosted on RTÉ Radio 2 – and jokingly asked the minister if he should put her tea-ferrying appearance into the official government minutes of the meeting. At other meetings, as spring turned to summer, participants were treated to the sight of Ross in his straw hat.

At another meeting during this period, Varadkar teased Robert Watt over his choice of velvet curtains hanging behind him. The Tánaiste would later recall that the senior civil servant's backdrop was 'like a boudoir'. Watt told Varadkar that there had been similar comments from the last person he had been on a call with. Varadkar shot back at Watt, 'I look forward to reading that in the *Irish Independent*.' Some politicians suspected that, for a civil servant, Watt spoke with journalists a lot.

These were rare moments of humour during an otherwise grim period for the Covid-19 decision-makers. The Cabinet meetings themselves were highly unusual in that a third of ministers had either lost their seats or not run again. Charlie Flanagan, the justice minister, who did have a mandate, would later admit it was 'unsatisfactory and certainly shouldn't happen again'. Constitutionally, they were still the government, but all the air had gone out of the Cabinet room. The energy was different.

Colleagues observed that Varadkar was very down after Fine Gael's electoral shellacking. The blistering rows over judicial appointments that once frayed relations between Fine Gael ministers and their colleagues in the Independent Alliance – or more specifically Shane Ross – were no more. With the Cabinet split between different rooms to ensure social distancing, Varadkar would 'do the rounds', and Finian McGrath, the Minister for Disability Issues, who had not run in the February election, sensed that the Taoiseach spent more time in rooms with fewer Fine Gael ministers in them. 'I got the impression he wanted to get away from his own guys, who were kicking his ass because he did badly in the election,' he later said.

Others felt there was a pecking order, with the senior and more powerful ministers in one room with Varadkar and Fraser (Fraser and Attorney General Seamus Woulfe were the only non-politicians allowed to attend Cabinet meetings). Harris, Donohoe, Flanagan, Humphreys and Regina Doherty all had big, heavy-spending departments with multi-faceted interactions with pandemic policy. But the rest were relegated to the Italian Room in the Department of the Taoiseach, and only brought into discussions periodically. 'If you weren't directly involved in, or your department wasn't directly involved in, the decision, it was nothing to do with you,' Doherty, who had lost her seat in the general election, would later recall.

Compliance with Covid-19 protocols could make things awkward, challenging and occasionally farcical. At times, only a certain number of ministers could be at the table, so others would sit around the edges, balancing on their laps Cabinet papers detailing the spending of billions and the radical suspension of civil liberties. Infractions were observed – ministers standing too close to each other on the margins of the meetings, none of them wearing masks, which NPHET had not yet advised for widespread use in indoor settings.

Varadkar got into his stride – lifted by the pandemic, firmly in the public eye and, most important, unbelievably buoyant in the polls, he fully bought into the public health restrictions. By mid-June 2020, an Ipsos MRBI poll for the *Irish Times* had his popularity at an eye-popping 75 per cent – up 45 points. The government was up 51 points to 72 per cent; 88 per cent of respondents thought the government was doing a good job in the pandemic. Fine Gael itself was up 17 points to 37 per cent. It was the stuff political dreams were made of. 'Varadkar was fighting for his political life, they said they were going into opposition, Covid arrives and it was manna from heaven for them: he suddenly becomes the statesman,' Shane Ross said later.

Ever the doctor, Varadkar asked challenging questions that only someone with a medical degree could ask when Simon Harris was briefing Cabinet. He was very keen to remind colleagues of adherence to public health guidelines; he would get up and leave the room after the two-hour limit for meetings was hit. At one stage, the government chief whip Seán Kyne, who had lost his Dáil seat but was appointed to the Seanad, coughed into his hand. 'Cough into your elbow – I saw that, Senator Kyne,' Varadkar chided. 'But I'm here by myself!' Kyne remonstrated – he had been attending the meeting remotely.

In a time of unprecedented crisis, huge decisions were made with little consultation across government. Many of the other ministers at Cabinet felt they were relegated to a second tier in terms of power and influence, as well as being physically in a different room. 'Broadly irrelevant,' recalled one senior official later, before deciding more firmly, 'actually, totally and utterly irrelevant.' One of these ministers, Finian McGrath, decided early on to kowtow to most Cabinet decisions, and to focus on his area – disability services. But he never lost his sense of fun. 'I used to say, "Jesus, it's like the army council here; you lads come in and tell us what to do."' He also had a nickname for the ever-serious chief medical officer: 'Father Tony'. Holohan's 'preachy tone used to remind me of a priest', McGrath later said. 'This ethical sincerity used to get up our noses.'

Agriculture minister Michael Creed and rural affairs minister Michael Ring were less cheerful. Colleagues thought both of them were probably beginning to realise they would be out of Cabinet when a new government was formed. Creed did not think his exclusion from decision-making was deliberate, but nonetheless found it frustrating that he would hear things in the media that would normally be briefed to ministers beforehand.

Ring, on the other hand, tended to be more assertive, sticking to an article of faith that had served him for decades: that rural Ireland was being screwed at the expense of urban elites. He tackled civil servants if he felt they were trying to trammel him. 'What constituency did you get elected to and what vote did you get?' he would demand. To Ring, a bare-knuckle political boxer, most things in politics could be distilled down to that doctrine.

McGrath would later recall Ring at one meeting shouting up at the Taoiseach 'like something you do in the middle of an election campaign at the back of a lorry, or at a trade union rally down at Liberty Hall'. He enjoyed winding Ring up. During one impassioned contribution from the Fine Gael minister about the poor people of his native Westport, a vibrant tourist town, McGrath mischievously chipped in, 'Whatever about Westport, what about Darndale?' – a reference to the deeply deprived part of his Dublin Bay North constituency. 'He'd go fucking mad then,' McGrath later recalled, gleefully. 'He'd go worse.'

Ring would shoot back at McGrath, needling him over the deep-seated impression held by some in Cabinet and across government that McGrath was an enthusiastic briefer of the media. One week after McGrath missed a meeting due to illness, Ring told him, 'Jaysus, Finian, I got no coverage since you left.'

—

Early on in the pandemic, Minister for Children and Youth Affairs Katherine Zappone was desperately trying to secure a childcare scheme for frontline workers. It was predicated on the idea that crèche workers or childminders could come into workers' homes to care for their children. But across government there was resistance – it was feared that such a scheme would run contrary to public health advice, a fear shared by NPHET, whose endorsement was lukewarm at best.

Zappone, however, was in a bind, and the government was under immense pressure. The previous attempts to solve the childcare conundrum for frontline workers involved encouraging employers to let spouses work from home, and use up annual leave. This was woefully inadequate, and as if the government did know it already, the public sector unions let them know with both barrels across the airwaves and in print.

The situation crystallised the brittle realities of pandemic politics. While spending constraints were gone, room for compromise was also erased. The normal palette of fudges, trade-offs and constructive ambiguities that were the stock in trade of political deal-making were not available. A special deal would open the door to a range of demands for similar carve-outs from restrictions for other sectors, create inconsistencies, expose contradictions in the rules, and risk undermining the all-important public health effort.

Nonetheless, Zappone, a Seattle native with an American accent straight from central casting, who had carved out a life and a political career in Ireland, pursued her goal with gusto. After one meeting, she went so far as to follow Paschal Donohoe into his office, arguing the case for the childcare scheme. Donohoe shot back, 'Katherine, this is a really bad idea, it won't work.'

In the view of both Donohoe and those advising him, the idea of telling the entire country to stay at home, but simultaneously saying that certain people could actually go into the homes of strangers to care for their children behind closed doors was a disaster waiting to happen. 'It won't work. People won't want to do it,' the Fine Gael minister told Zappone.

But the tenacious Independent TD, who was widely admired for her campaigning on issues like same-sex marriage and abortion, was insistent that it would. The scheme was signed off on 6 May, at a cost of €4.7m. It collapsed a week later as insurers refused to provide cover and just six providers signed up.

—

As the weeks of lockdown wore on, agitation among ministers grew; it was the seed of something that would develop across the pandemic. Ring and Creed were to the fore. At one meeting, Ring, who was becoming increasingly frustrated with the power he perceived Holohan had, asked, 'Who is the Taoiseach? Who is running the country?' He and Creed were consistent in their view that the lockdown was crushing and cruel for older people, who needed a break. But Charlie Flanagan was also growing agitated and concerned at the idea of ministers ticking boxes for Holohan. Ross, although supportive of restrictions, was less pleased about Cabinet agendas and memos arriving late, sometimes just before meetings began, and about the number of incorporeal meetings in which massive decisions were being waved through after ministers had been contacted by a civil servant and asked to agree to the proposition put to them.

While the harsh lockdown was beginning to chafe at political level, it was working. The crude public health measures and the compliance of the public were beginning to bend the curve of new infections downwards. In fact, the first signs of hopeful progress were seen before the 'stay at home' order, initially planned to run until 12 April, was extended to 5 May.

But in recommending the extension, Tony Holohan told Simon Harris that there were 'encouraging signs' that measures were having an impact which 'may allow for a reduction in the intensity of measures over time'. It was cautious and heavily caveated, but it was clear that minds were turning towards the next phase. A week later, hospital and ICU admissions were plateauing.

In the days that followed, NPHET began to discuss how measures might be eased. The political system began to gear up. On 16 April, the Cabinet Covid-19 subcommittee, which was now the nerve centre for pandemic policy, sat down to consider what reopening might look like. A confidential paper circulated to the meeting noted that there would be 'increasing expectation among citizens and businesses that at least some of the current restrictions will begin to be lifted after 5 May' and outlined in detail how lockdowns hammered everyone in the same way.

But peeling back the restrictions would be harder. 'The next phase has the potential to be far more divisive as the reality of the long-term implications sinks in,' stated the paper. 'This includes unemployment, reduced income, increased debt, closure of businesses, reduced educational opportunities, restrictions on movement and social inter-actions, and ultimately the loss of loved ones.'

It was inevitable, the memo warned, that 'different individuals and groups will be affected differently' and 'this will be even more difficult and potentially divisive, as people find themselves being treated differently to others by government as restrictions are lifted, even if that is for clear public health reasons'. The virus would be an 'ever-present threat well into 2021 and quite possibly beyond that,' and the potential of Ireland facing a 'disastrous second wave of the disease is very real'.

It sketched out a future fraught with risk, where health resilience had to be maintained alongside complex negotiations with unions and employers. The way ahead involved unpicking a whole host of overlapping issues, including the future use of new Garda powers, the modification of pandemic payments, travel, the border, the formation of a new government. All these had to be dealt with while 'managing people's expectations, and not creating hopes that are then dashed', the memo said. The *Irish Times*'s Fiach Kelly reported that government sources thought the content was 'jaw-dropping'.

A full Cabinet meeting got the same message several days later, as hopes to begin reopening on 5 May were redrafted, despite the improving situation. Data showed that the public remained accepting of their freedoms being curtailed, but were still troubled. The public found the extension of restrictions 'unsurprising yet unsettling', the Cabinet memo said, and the 5 May date pegged for reopening to commence was 'not expected to be an end point; we will be living in a new reality for a long period.' The message to Cabinet was that the Irish people were beginning to feel worn out. 'Fatigue may creep in,' the memo said. However, the government hoped that a mix of duty and opprobrium might keep people in line: 'We may lapse but our sense of collective responsibility and fear of social disapproval will enable us to maintain our resolve.'

There was still widespread support for interventions and for Garda strategy, but there was also trepidation about reopening. The message from field research was distilled for the ministers: 'We want this to be over but not at any cost.' The author of the memo was Martin Fraser, who was now encountering an increasing appetite among the politicians to get the country open again.

—

Towards the end of April, some ministers were growing increasingly frustrated at finding it next to impossible to get access to people on NPHET. At one meeting, Ring slammed his hand on the Cabinet table. 'This is ridiculous, you're asking us to make decisions and we haven't got answers to questions!' he roared. It was unsustainable: the ministers might have been irrelevant in some people's eyes, but they were still ministers. They had to be mollified.

A briefing with senior NPHET members, including Holohan, was arranged for 30 April. The meeting would be chaired by Simon Coveney. The Tánaiste was chosen because of what colleagues saw as his pacifying and diplomatic capabilities. There was a view among ministers that some of their number were 'going to eat these medics alive'. It was another vintage Ring performance: he compared living with the 2km travel restriction to living in a police state, he bemoaned the huge impact on people's mental and physical health from the lockdown. People had to be given hope or they'd be on the street, he told Holohan. Creed again raised concerns about the over-70s, a view echoed by McGrath, who was later reported to have given the CMO 'a hard time'.

While Holohan held the line, the most telling intervention came from Fraser. He laid it on the line for the ministers. This disease can restart, he said. There was no treatment and no vaccine. This was not over, and it could get out of control at any time – it would not be cured on that day or the following day and it would likely be with the country through 2021.

The roadmap for reopening would be set by NPHET, Fraser told the meeting, with the safe stuff first. It would all be guided by assessments from the Department of Health and the capacity of the healthcare system. In other words, NPHET were setting the pace – and they had Fraser's backing. 'I remember it. I thought he was great on that,' Simon Coveney would later recall. 'This [was] an extraordinary challenge for the State, and that's the context in which we [were] having this conversation with the CMO – and I think it did hit home with people.'

To Coveney it was the job of the politicians to reflect what their constituents were feeling, and that was the purpose of the meeting: ministers venting at the man responsible for the harsh restrictions. But, Coveney said, for the likes of Holohan and Fraser it was 'their job [...] to say the unpopular stuff all the time'. It created tensions, he admitted, but that was part of Fraser's job: to manage the tension.

But it also did something else. It underlined why Fraser, an unelected civil servant, was in many ways more important than those ministers griping about the public health restrictions. This was not just the private view of some ministers who observed the situation at the time; it was a view that Coveney himself articulated in late October 2021. 'In many ways, I think he was more important than a member of Cabinet,' he said. 'He has to deliver the whole time. Every time we make a decision, Martin's got to operationalise it, and we make mistakes, and he has to try and manage that.'

—

The crisis, and the centralisation of power, was also disrupting long-held relationships at a senior level in the civil service. While Robert Watt and DPER were closely involved in designing the first economic responses to the pandemic, Watt became a more marginal figure during the first wave, confiding in colleagues that he had been more or less told to mind his own business.

As far as he was concerned, the decision-making process had been designed by Fraser to exclude other departments, though he still felt that DPER was running the show when it came to economics. 'We represent the taxpayer and public – no open-ended bailouts or guarantees for shareholders or bondholders this time!!!!' Watt wrote in one email to fellow secretaries general in late March as he sought their views on what supports their sectors were likely to push for.

The pandemic threw all the budgetary dogmas out of the window. If it was seen to be workable, more or less every single spending request was waved through as the State stepped up unprecedented interventions. In this context, DPER was without a mission. Watt appreciated the seriousness of the pandemic and knew it required an unprecedented response, but he wasn't always happy about it.

At one point he clashed with Fraser, who had accused him of not co-operating with a spending demand that the Department of the Taoiseach had made of DPER. Heated words were exchanged. Colleagues observed that Watt was unhappy and feeling marginalised; he even claimed to one that he felt Fraser was going to sack him. But Watt did not really believe he would be sacked – and it wasn't possible anyway. The truth was that he and Fraser had been through many battles together over the previous decade, the bailout and Brexit among them, and they were never going to fall out permanently. One senior figure likened them to '[Gerry] Adams and [Martin] McGuinness' – a reference to Sinn Féin's former leadership team.

Nonetheless, there was a clear divergence of views between the two northside Dubliners when it came to the lockdown and the pace of reopening. As lockdown ebbed, a more complicated future sparked battles everywhere.

CHAPTER 12:

CANCELLED

1 May 2020
Cases: 20,833
Deaths: 1,265
Seven-day average of new cases: 378

Leo Varadkar shuffled awkwardly on *The Late Late Show* couch and patted his pockets before pulling a folded A3 sheet from his right trouser pocket. 'I haven't actually learned it off yet, but I will one of these days,' Varadkar breezily admitted, unfolding the plan to gradually reopen society following two months of severe restrictions. It was a bizarre moment in an otherwise upbeat interview with Ryan Tubridy. For the first time, the government was talking about opening up, not shutting down.

While there had been little surprise, or opposition, when NPHET asked the government to extend the lockdown again until 18 May, the pill was sweetened with the prospect of eased restrictions. A five-stage plan that would culminate with pubs reopening for indoor drinking on 10 August was published on the Friday Varadkar appeared on *The Late Late Show*. The resumption of indoor drinking and something resembling pub culture would become the benchmark for Ireland's pandemic. As long as the pubs were closed, it was clear that the new normal would be uncomfortably dissimilar to the old normal.

There were some concessions that would come sooner than the first reopening date: the 2km exercise limit would be relaxed to 5km and 'cocooners' could leave their homes, under strict conditions. It was, in truth, a crumb of relaxation and no more. But what mattered was that the journey out of lockdown was under way.

As Varadkar talked Tubridy through the plan, he was asked about the Leaving Certificate. The exam occupies a unique space in Irish culture, embedded in the psyche of almost anyone who has been through the State education system. Even if they don't remember exactly how many points they received, most people can recall the trauma of sitting in a sweaty exam hall in June. It also attracts a huge amount of media attention every year, a set piece with guaranteed coverage of the national picture, the college points race and the inevitable human interest stories, usually involving students scoring over six hundred points.

At the start of April, Varadkar had insisted that plans were being drawn up for the immutable exam to go ahead 'by hook or by crook' and the position was the same that Friday night: exams would start on 29 July. The government would be guided by public health advice, and alternatives such as predictive marking were being explored, Varadkar said, but that was not perfect either. However, unbeknownst to the audience, the plan to cancel the exam was already being finalised.

Earlier that day, Minister for Education Joe McHugh had met with the education partners – teachers' unions, parents' groups and student organisations – as part of a consultative forum his department had set up at the start of the pandemic. It was one of the only in-person meetings taking place during the lockdown, with sufficient space in the department's Clock Tower for the thirty or so attendees to be socially distanced. In that meeting it became clear that the exam could not go ahead.

McHugh had wanted to make sure that teachers were on board with the alternative, but the following day Fianna Fáil, through its education spokesperson Thomas Byrne, went public with its demand for the exam to be cancelled. With no support from the main opposition that had propped up the minority government for four years, the jig was up.

McHugh, a soft-spoken Donegal man who taught geography and

maths at a secondary school in Letterkenny and, later, A-level economics in Dubai, was politically close to Varadkar. His wife, Olwyn Enright, herself a former Fine Gael TD, worked in public relations and was among those advising Varadkar's campaign for the Fine Gael leadership in 2017. As education minister, he had earned a reputation among some media commentators and government colleagues as having been captured by officials in the department, which was known for its institutional power that marked it out even among other branches of the civil service. The perception among some in government is that the department is always concerned about the vested interests, in particular the powerful teachers' unions.

On several occasions McHugh challenged them to implement policies they initially resisted, including one that allowed Leaving Cert students to defer exams if they suffered a bereavement. When it came to the question of running the Leaving Cert in the middle of a pandemic, McHugh wanted to do it and was deeply resistant to any predicted grades system. He had spoken to Mike Ryan and came away with the distinct impression that the Irishman in the WHO was of the view there was no reason it could not go ahead.

But at a meeting in Government Buildings on the night of Wednesday, 6 May, the opposition of senior civil servants to the Leaving Cert going ahead hardened, much to Varadkar's annoyance. 'It was clear that the teachers' unions and the department itself wasn't overly keen on [the exam going ahead], and they had all the reasons as to why it was wrong,' he later said. But the meeting that night was a chance to challenge the officials, to make them justify their position that it should be cancelled. 'I wanted to look them in the whites of their eyes,' Varadkar said.

Around the Sycamore Room's oval table sat McHugh, Varadkar, Martin Fraser, Liz Canavan, the Department of Education's Secretary General Seán Ó Foghlú and Assistant General Secretary Dalton Tatton, Chief Inspector of Schools Harold Hislop, the department's communications chief Cliodhna O'Neill, McHugh's advisers Ed Carty and Mark O'Doherty, Varadkar's advisers Brian Murphy and Philip O'Callaghan, and Attorney General Seamus Woulfe.

Varadkar said he had not read any medical advice to the effect that the exam could not go ahead. He asked how it was that countries like Portugal, Germany and Italy were able to run exams and that schools would be opening there in a matter of weeks. How was it that the plan was to have schools – which had been closed since 12 March – reopen in September and, in the meantime, theatres and cinemas would reopen in July but the Leaving Cert could not go ahead?

Ó Foghlú pointed to advice drawn up by the National Educational Psychological Service (NEPS), which had evaluated running the exam against a system of calculated grades, and had concluded that running the exam would pose 'significantly greater risk to the wellbeing and mental health of the majority of students at this time' than using calculated grades. That system, with 'its rationale of fairness, inclusivity, reliability and validity', was, in the circumstances, the one that 'better promotes for most, a sense of efficacy, resilience and wellbeing'.

Hislop briefed on how calculated grades would work. It was complex, but he impressed Varadkar, who later remarked that the chief inspector 'knew his stuff'. Nonetheless his concern and that of Brian Murphy, his chief adviser, and others in the room was grade inflation; that such a system would be unfair on students who had done their exams pre-pandemic and that it would devalue the Leaving Cert in comparison with exams in other jurisdictions. Some of those in the meeting later recalled Varadkar comparing scrapping the exam with 'cancelling the Olympics and giving everyone a gold medal for trying' and pointing out that 89 per cent of students would receive an A, B or C in Irish in the Leaving Cert when 'half of them couldn't even order a bag of chips in Irish'. Varadkar later said he didn't remember these comments.

For McHugh, it was a question of fairness. 'I couldn't see the fairness of the model that was being presented to me,' he said later. 'In the space of a few weeks you went from ninety-five years doing a Leaving Cert, which you could argue was fair or unfair, to moving to introduce a completely new system with different teachers and different data and no baseline. My worry with calculated grades the whole time was fairness.'

McHugh had been back and forth with Philip Nolan, NPHET's modelling chief, in the weeks running up to the meeting and believed there was a landing zone for getting the exam going ahead that summer. Nolan later recalled that the tone of the conversation was that it was 'really hard to assess the risk' of it taking place: 'On the one hand, you're saying it's the potential for being a controlled environment, distanced, so it could be run as a relatively low-risk, high-priority activity when everything else is locked down. On the other hand, it puts enormous pressure on a symptomatic student to stay away from their examination.'

As the meeting dragged on that night, Martin Fraser intervened, saying that the CMO had been asked several times if the Leaving Cert could be done, but that the conditions he had set out under which the exam could take place made it impossible. Students would have to avoid public transport, social distancing would have to be maintained before, during and after the exams, with desks socially distanced in exam halls. The exams themselves would have to be reduced in length and there could be only one exam per day. 'The Leaving Cert we are talking about is absolutely undoable,' Fraser said.

The meeting had been a probing affair, with Varadkar leading the charge. There was a great political desire to run the Leaving Cert but within the ranks of officialdom there was, as one senior official put it, 'truculence' and a firm belief that the exam was not doable. There would be only one winner and, on this occasion, it would not be the politicians. But while it was, at times, tense, it had allowed the politicians in the room to arm themselves ahead of the backlash from their ministerial colleagues that would probably follow. Varadkar and McHugh knew it would be hard to sell to the full Cabinet later that week.

Two days later the Cabinet met to, in effect, rubber-stamp a decision already taken at the highest levels of government. 'How in the name of God can't we hold the exams when everything else will be open?' Michael Creed asked. Charlie Flanagan spoke for many in the room when he said he was 'uneasy' with what was being asked of ministers, but insisted that 'everybody must back Joe'. Creed, Flanagan and Ring – the Cabinet's awkward squad – were all aligned. 'This won't go away too handily,' Ring said.

Others were, surprisingly, more militant. Culture minister Josepha Madigan bluntly stated that 'in good conscience' she could not support the decision. She asked for the public health advice and questioned how teachers carrying out the calculated grading could be completely subjective if they were coming under external pressure from parents. Ultimately, Madigan, like others, had little option but to approve the decision. There would be little point in resigning from a government that had just weeks to run.

But Varadkar's annoyance over the whole affair lingered. Four days later, he emailed Fraser, Murphy and Canavan about an item on the reopening of schools across Europe, including Germany and Norway, on RTÉ's *Drivetime* the previous day. It had included a primary school principal from Cork expressing the view that it would be very difficult for schools to reopen in their entirety in September. 'Worth a listen,' Varadkar wrote, before somewhat provocatively adding, 'Could Ireland be one of the last education systems in Europe to reopen its schools – would not reflect well on the education partners.'

But at the same time, he knew that there was no going back on the cancellation decision. On 21 May, Fraser emailed Varadkar seeking approval to hold an incorporeal Cabinet meeting to sign off on an indemnity for teachers and schools involved in the calculated grades process, noting that he understood McHugh had already spoken to him. 'He did. Very briefly en passant during a phone call yesterday. He seemed to think I had been briefed about it already,' a slightly irked Varadkar wrote back. 'Anyway, that doesn't matter. It's appropriate and necessary so proceed.'

The Leaving Cert as it was known was dead. Across government, unimaginable changes were taking place at breakneck speed.

CHAPTER 13:

SUPPRESSED

11 May 2020
Cases: 23,135
Deaths: 1,467
Seven-day average of new cases: 195

The email to Martin Fraser and Brian Murphy dropped just before lunchtime. 'Personal service – especially hair,' read the subject line. Leo Varadkar hadn't had a haircut in months.

He felt he had spotted a hole in the government's reopening plan, which would see people able to mix indoors in their homes from 8 June. 'It's almost certain that loads of people will have their hairdresser or barber over as a friend – grey economy/public health risk. Would be much better to have a protocol in place for safe opening by then,' he wrote.

The email was typical of Varadkar. As his three-year spell as Taoiseach drew to a close, he was anxious to get as much open as possible. 'People needed to get back to work, and we needed to get the economy going again,' he would later say. 'It wasn't just about macroeconomics and balancing the budget, it was businesses surviving.'

From NPHET's perspective, the transition out of harsh restrictions could be considered partly because the disease was coming under control. By early May, the risk of hospitals being overwhelmed was well gone.

April's war over testing had ended and the HSE was telling Holohan it expected to hit 15,000 tests per day by the middle of the month.

Ireland stepped into the first phase of unlocking on 18 May, when thousands of shops, businesses and construction sites reopened. But the appetite to move faster intensified around the Cabinet table with particular focus on the two-metre social distancing rule – the benchmark for determining when someone was a close contact of a Covid-19 case.

On 22 May, both the *Irish Independent* and the *Irish Examiner* reported on a push by ministers to cut the social distancing rule to one metre. The *Examiner* went as far as to say that Leo Varadkar would be requesting an urgent meeting with NPHET 'after nearly half the Cabinet demanded a relaxation of the 2m social distancing rule'. In fact, it was a mere handful of ministers, most notably Finian McGrath and Minister for Higher Education Mary Mitchell O'Connor, whose names appeared in the press.

Far from seeking an urgent summit with NPHET – which had already ruled out slashing the two-metre rule – Varadkar was furious about the leaks from Cabinet. He angrily reprimanded his ministers in an email the next day. The post-leak note sent by his private secretary, Nick Reddy, was titled, 'Grateful if you can bring the email below from the Taoiseach to members of Cabinet to your ministers' attention'.

> Dear Colleague,
> I am writing to you to express my distress at the fact that one or more members of the Cabinet told others about our discussion on physical distancing rules.

After a reminder that government operates on two principles – collective responsibility and Cabinet confidentiality – he continued:

> These principles exist so that everyone at the Cabinet can be trusted with the confidential information needed to make important decisions. Once made, it is a duty that we all support and stand over those decisions so that stakeholders and citizens can

have confidence that the decision is final and implementation can begin.

On this occasion, it isn't just a case of a breach of loyalty to me and to each other, it undermines the work of everyone battling the virus including those on the frontline. It is spectacularly unfair to business people planning to open their businesses in a few weeks to [*sic*] time, to teachers and lecturers planning to reopen schools and colleges in the autumn and citizens who are carefully adhering to the guidelines.

If any change is made to 2m rule, it should be made based on solid advice, in an orderly way and communicated properly not flagged to the media by Ministers so ashamed at their actions that they hide their faces and do not own up to their actions.

I really hope this will be the last time this happens. There's only a few weeks left in this Government. Please let us finish well.

Ironically, Varadkar would end up dealing with a leak controversy of his own later that year after he passed a confidential document to a friend. But his anger over leaks did not weaken his appetite to move as fast through the phases of reopening as the public health advice would allow – and it was an aim shared across the system.

—

In the Department of Public Expenditure, Robert Watt was counting the cost of the lockdown daily and sending distress signals.

On 25 May, Watt wrote an email to Martin Fraser, Orlaigh Quinn in the Department of Enterprise and Derek Moran in the Department of Finance:

The fiscal costs are mounting weekly and the long-term damage to the economy will be significant if we continue with this approach to the social restrictions. We have got to accelerate this roadmap. It is too slow, given the number of cases we have, the lessons we are learning from other countries and the enormous damage being done to the country.

Most retail shops should be opened that week, he said:

It makes no sense that I can go to Woodies and not to Ikea or Arnotts. It could be argued that the approach is more dangerous given the crowds turning up at a limited number of retail outlets.

The following week, Watt argued, restaurants, bars and coffee shops with outdoor facilities should be open:

The current restrictions have no sound policy basis. I also fear that people will start ignoring even the basic public health advice, given the erosion of support for the current approach.

Recording his strident views in an email was classic Watt. It was also far from a one-off during that period. Watt emailed Fraser again on 3 June, copying Jim Breslin in the Department of Health, with a copy of a Davy Research note on the Irish economy which, he said, showed Ireland 'has the slowest recovery from the lockdown of all the countries surveyed'. Ireland was 'projected to be four to six weeks behind other countries, I would be interested in seeing the rationale behind this?'

Watt's concerns gave voice to a wide range of emerging pressures on the government. Despite the billions in spending, the reality was that firms and State bodies were just not able to sustain themselves for ever in suspended animation. Months of subsidies could slow down the crumbling of the economy, but they couldn't prevent it.

The threat to Bus Éireann, sketched out in a memo drawn up for government in June, was an example. Public transport companies, both State-controlled and private operators, had been nearly obliterated by lockdown, with 90 per cent of private companies ceasing operation and passenger volumes on the public and commercial routes that remained dwindling to almost nothing, the memo outlined. The risk presented by the difficulties Bus Éireann faced were much more complex, and more politically toxic. The commercial part of the business, the Expressway service, had been hobbled by Covid-19. The other parts of Bus Éireann's operations – school transport and publicly subsidised routes – were prevented from making any profit, so they could not be subsidised. 'Expressway's weekly losses since the beginning of this crisis have been steadily depleting Bus Éireann's financial reserves, such that the company is now within days of having its reserves completely exhausted, thus making it insolvent,' the memo stated.

The implications of this were grave: the immolation of jobs at a commercial semi-state company could undermine confidence in the State's capacity to handle the crisis. There was also the very tangible threat of what would happen to the workforce. The government was warned that Bus Éireann was considering closure, which would have meant 400 job losses. Even more crucially, its cash problems meant this would be done on basic terms – it would pay those made redundant only what it had to under the law. 'This would be an extremely severe measure in employment terms and has not happened in a State company since the mid-1980s,' the memo said. Politically, a threat to 'safe' jobs like this was clearly toxic.

The industrial relations fallout could be contagious. The memo warned that closing the service 'may result in "wildcat" action in other CIÉ companies'. The prospect of such action being tabled, even if it were ultimately avoided, would 'be extremely likely to provoke deeply negative industrial relations reaction within Bus Éireann and very probably negative reaction more widely'.

Extra support was needed across the sector, at an estimated cost of between €80m and €100m. In the end, a decision was made to buy time. But the wider question posed by this was whether the State could continually step into the gap. How long could lockdowns be sustained before the old normal simply evaporated?

—

Just seven days into the first phase of the reopening plan, Tony Holohan declared that the data from the previous week 'indicates that we have suppressed Covid-19 as a country'. On the same day, the *Irish Times* reported that Varadkar was mulling over making an announcement in early June on easing aspects of the lockdown measures.

The wider economy was proving to be more robust than had been feared in March and April. Extraordinary actions by the European Central Bank, and a common affirmation by the markets and EU governments that the Covid crisis would be financed by debt and deficit spending, had opened the doors to massive intervention by the State. Economic collapse wasn't threatening to suck the entire country down the plughole, and one of the main reasons to stop spending – the threat of wider fiscal oblivion – wasn't materialising. It was a complex moment. As the disease receded, there was no fiscal signal from the markets to stop the massive spending. Life under lockdown would clearly warp and damage the economy and the workforce, but seemingly endless spending could keep them in a sort of suspended animation. Nonetheless, it couldn't last for ever.

The Economic and Social Research Institute (ESRI) warned that plummeting consumer spending could reduce indirect taxes by more than a fifth; and the State's spending watchdog, the Irish Fiscal Advisory Council, warned that the incoming government might be faced with a whopping bill once the party was over.

Against this emerging backdrop, Varadkar and Donohoe issued none-too-subtle messages that it might all be coming to an end. There is 'no such thing as free money', the Taoiseach told the Dáil on 21 May. Fine Gael's predisposition to fiscal rigour was given at least rhetorical prominence – this could be the end of the acute phase of Covid, and it was time to signal changes.

'I was convinced that it would be a one-quarter event and I thought it would be fine,' Varadkar would later say. 'I do wonder what decisions would we have made differently – more conservative decisions potentially – if we had known it would go on for so long. We took the view that it was a one-quarter event and "open the taps".' However, as far back as

9 March – the first time the Cabinet's Covid-19 subcommittee met – there had been warnings that the duration of the economic shock would not be short. A memo on possible economic and budgetary implications of Covid-19 for ministers explicitly warned, 'It will not be confined to the first quarter of this year.'

CHAPTER 14:

REOPENING AND REPLACING

11 June 2020
Cases: 25,238
Deaths: 1,703
Seven-day average of new cases: 14

Just before midday, Martin Fraser emailed Leo Varadkar, copying in Brian Murphy, with details of a government memo to approve an extra €25m for the stricken arts sector. A medium-term plan would be needed 'in an era where mass gatherings are unique and will be problematic for quite a while', Fraser wrote.

Fraser's emails and texts to the Taoiseach in this period, the final days and weeks of Varadkar's reign, were carefully constructed, conveying caution at a time when the political system was both keen to open up and anxious to dole out money to sectors hit badly by the lockdown. 'Any chance we can get the sports package done for Cabinet this week?' Varadkar texted Fraser on 16 June. 'It's my former parish as you know. Lot of them on to me. They want to be planning to open now and not wait until July.'

Some things could be done; others could not. Five days earlier, Fraser had responded to a request from Varadkar for information on the cost and implications of introducing a new household broadcasting charge. Any change to the licence fee would require legislation and was therefore 'not feasible in the current context', Fraser wrote.

The government was on the way out and unable to legislate anyway owing to the lack of a fully constituted Seanad. 'I do think it could be done quickly under a new government if that was decided,' Fraser wrote. 'So RTÉ's financial issues arising from the Covid-19 crisis will have to be dealt with along with those other semi-states.'

Fraser knocked back other Varadkar ideas in June, but none more important than a proposal to replace NPHET. 'We were talking about replacing NPHET with a new body like other countries had done, kind of a reopening body rather than a closing body,' Varadkar later recalled. 'Belgium and other countries had set up groups of people that weren't just healthcare professionals and public health people, they included people from wider society in the private sector and so on to plan their reopening.'

To Varadkar the logic was simple. The new body would contain a mix of business groups and unions, as well as the medical and scientific people. But Fraser's view – ultimately supported by the outgoing Taoiseach – was that if any decision like that was to be taken, it had to be one for the next government.

There had been a clamour among some politicians to restructure or even replace NPHET in the summer of 2020. Stephen Donnelly, the Fianna Fáil health spokesman, argued for 'a separate group of people with economic, commerce and psychology backgrounds' to advise the government. Within Cabinet, the outgoing housing minister, Eoghan Murphy, had for months been discussing with colleagues and Varadkar the possibility of using the National Emergency Coordination Group, a body run out of the Department of Housing, that had successfully responded to a series of extreme weather events in recent years.

But Varadkar's failed attempt to replace NPHET that summer was significant for far more fundamental reasons, reasons that go some way to explain why the relationship between the politicians and NPHET would become more complex and, at times, fraught as the pandemic year wore on.

By the summer of 2020, the outgoing Taoiseach had come to the view that the way NPHET functioned was, as he would later say, 'suboptimal'.

He had discovered that it had been established without even a submission to the health minister, never mind one to the Cabinet for decision, and that its membership had increased substantially without any political oversight. 'I thought it was too big,' he said in November 2021, 'I did think that there should have been political involvement in the composition of it and there wasn't. I still don't know for sure who decided who were members of NPHET.'

What's more, he would later say, it was his understanding that 'it was essentially Tony who decided who was on NPHET'. The criticism was not necessarily that Holohan was too powerful, Varadkar stressed, but he believed that for any decision-making body it was important to make sure that decisions are properly scrutinised and challenged. 'Certainly what was said to me by others – not going to say [who] – that he comm-anded enough respect and authority to carry the meeting.'

And yet, while he harboured these strong views in the summer of 2020, Varadkar never pushed for NPHET's overhaul once the new coa-lition was formed. But he believes it should have happened. 'I am not going to blame anyone for it because I didn't particularly push it,' he later admitted.

—

Any desire to overhaul NPHET would perhaps have been tempered by the fact that the health advisers were telling Varadkar and others what they wanted to hear. Twice in his last three weeks as Taoiseach, he accelerated the country out of lockdown measures, with the backing of NPHET, which had signed off on condensing the remaining three phases of the original five-phase reopening plan into two.

Varadkar was only too happy to go along with this, but rejected suggestions that he had put pressure on NPHET to bring about that outcome: 'Did I want to end on a high with the virus suppressed and the economy reopening? Yeah, of course I did, and that's entirely normal, I would have thought. Did I try to pressurise or engineer that advice from NPHET? No.'

Holohan was of the same view: 'I saw an opportunity to accelerate and I am sure society was impatient and I am sure I was myself, everybody was – who wanted to be in economic and social restrictions for any longer than was needed in public health terms?'

The memo to Cabinet on the day the final acceleration was announced, Friday 19 June, was a reopening charter. The economy was being clattered by restrictions that had already been lifted elsewhere in Europe; 220,000 jobs were gone, unemployment was going to reach 25 per cent, and GDP was projected to decline by 10 per cent in 2020. And the government had other things to worry about: 'The heightened risk of a hard Brexit at the end of 2020 could exacerbate the difficulties facing the economy and recovery prospects,' the memo warned.

It suggested that parts of the economy that had reopened were being held back by ongoing closures, and the interdependence of sectors meant that as long as many of them remained either closed or restricted 'there may be consequential restraints on other areas of the economy'. Impacts on mental health, education and minority groups were detailed at length, as was the increase in domestic abuse and the risk of online bullying and grooming of children. People's vulnerabilities, Cabinet was told, were being exacerbated by the restrictions, 'with an increased risk of violence and abuse at a time when there are fewer people entering the home to provide care and safeguarding'.

Relaxation of the penal restrictions prohibiting people from leaving their homes unless for essential reasons was also mapped out, with hints from the Garda Commissioner that the tough policing approach was becoming increasingly unenforceable. The memo outlined Drew Harris's concerns about 'the extent to which effective practical enforcement can be given to revised penal regulations' when people could leave their home at will.

In his final address to the nation from behind a podium on a warm June evening at Government Buildings, Varadkar outlined a reopening plan that would be overseen, ultimately, by a different Taoiseach. With the cover of NPHET advice, the new plan outlined how almost everything, with the exception of very large gatherings, wet pubs, night-clubs and casinos, would reopen before the end of the month.

—

With less than a week left in office, Varadkar pushed for more. On Sunday 21 June he texted Fraser: 'Think plan has been well received. Only back-lash seems to be around very large indoor venues – churches/ballrooms/arenas. Have we given any consideration to max per sq metre rule or something like that?'

Fraser's response was telling:

> We just received and then followed NPHET advice on mass gath-erings. Obviously indoor activity is more dangerous, and mixing with alcohol more dangerous again. Also issues re close contact entering and exiting in large venues. Hence hotels, ballrooms, arenas are problematic.

Fraser relayed that he was meeting MCD managing director Denis Desmond the following day along with the Arts Council to discuss venues, noting that the issue would not be solved quickly, and adding that he would see if better guidance could be obtained from NPHET in the week that followed.

Varadkar wrote back: 'You think I/we could ask them to? Had impression from Archbishop's comments that they had made proposals and had expected more.'

Fraser responded that he believed more could be done and that he would check it out, but he again injected a note of caution, this time about the vulnerability of churchgoers:

> If you're in contact with CMO no harm to ask him. I didn't get the impression NPHET had thought about churches specifically as mass gatherings to be honest I don't think it occurred to any of us either. That said the demographics of church goers always a concern.

Four days later, at 8.33 on the morning of Thursday, 25 June, in one of his last emails to Varadkar as Taoiseach, Fraser updated him on the communications on the penultimate phase of reopening, due to be signed off by the Cabinet at its final meeting that day, before coming into effect the following Monday. Noting that there were plans to have visible monitoring of pubs and restaurants for compliance with new guidelines, Fraser concluded:

> I'm quite worried that people might relax too much at exactly the same time that we have a big increase in movement and activity, including riskier social activities.
>
> There's increasing evidence worldwide about a rise in cases where lockdown lifted – not just the US and the UK, which have different approaches, but also successful countries such as Germany, Australia and Israel (who had approx 1000 cases in the last two days).
>
> There's also evidence that younger people are getting infected more, which as we know will have more of an impact (lagged) via community transmission to vulnerable groups than on the infected younger people themselves.
>
> I just wanted to mention these concerns this morning as you're thinking about what you say later.

Varadkar responded, 'that all sounds about right', and queried whether a decision had been made on plans for an RTÉ Comic Relief event. Varadkar would later observe that Fraser was someone who 'might have been more cautious and more conservative' as the pandemic progressed, having been 'on the liberal side at the start'. There's no doubt that as Varadkar left office, the tone of Fraser's correspondence to him was one of caution.

He was not the only one who fretted over the impact of relaxing restrictions; the wider debate would become politically charged as parts of society sought ongoing protection from the virus. At the final meeting of the Fine Gael–Independent minority government that day, Seán Kyne, the outgoing Gaeltacht minister, was troubled by the plan to accelerate the reopening of offshore islands. The original roadmap had envisaged them reopening no earlier than 10 August.

Two Aran islands, Inis Oírr and Inis Mór, had already held surveys that overwhelmingly rejected an early reopening and there were concerns about the impact on elderly islanders, Kyne told colleagues. But the memo to Cabinet was clear: 'Given there is no public health reason to restrict movement to and from the islands, there is no legal basis to make any special arrangements in respect of islands.' Having failed to win the argument, and finding no support from the outgoing Taoiseach, Kyne was annoyed and frustrated. At six foot seven, the newly elected senator was an imposing figure as he got up from the table and stormed out of the Cabinet meeting.

It was a bizarre postscript for a government that was mere hours from being replaced.

—

As the focus of the political system shifted towards the imminent change in government, the shake-up of departments and, more important, the ministers in them, something else, imperceptible even to expert eyes, was also starting.

Ronan Glynn, Holohan's deputy, would soon have to step up. Much later, he would observe how a troubling pattern in the disease began to emerge in June. 'If you look back at the data in retrospect [cases of Covid-19] grew 3 per cent a day, day on day, from June, but obviously it was growing from a very low level. Lots of people think the disease got low and nothing happened until August; in absolute terms that's true, but in terms of a trend, you can see that where we ended up in October, started at the end of June.'

While Ireland had effectively emerged from lockdown, the country was already quietly being stalked once again by Covid-19.

CHAPTER 15:

'THIS IS GOING TO BE COMPLICATED'

27 June 2020
Cases: 25,437
Deaths: 1,734
Seven-day average of new cases: 9

The formation of a new government after the uncertain outcome of the February election took a backseat to the Covid-19 crisis throughout the spring of 2020, but as summer approached, the need for a new administration became more pressing. The lack of a fully constituted Seanad (because it did not have 11 senators nominated by a Taoiseach elected by the new Dáil) meant that legislation could not be passed.

It was an inconvenient truth, and one that Martin Fraser was not shy about reminding the caretaker government about. While it had almost all the powers of the Constitution available to it, the minority administration no longer had the ability to legislate. If a government cannot legislate, it can barely govern. Fraser's view, frequently aired in meetings, was that it had become unsustainable and a new government had to be formed – and soon.

As the first lockdown set in in March, Green Party leader Eamon

Ryan called for a national unity government involving all parties, with Leo Varadkar, Simon Harris and Simon Coveney all remaining in their posts. While Varadkar later admitted that he was, for good reason, 'not entirely hostile to that idea', he knew it would never fly with Fianna Fáil or Sinn Féin, who had each won more votes and more seats than Fine Gael.

Ryan was the subject of some ridicule during the first wave when he called on Irish people to grow salads on south-facing windowsills so that 'we'll have our salads ready to go' if there was a food supply chain crisis. Just as amusing to TDs was when Ryan fell asleep in the Dáil just a few weeks after the Greens entered government in July 2020.

Still, the Dundrum native and graduate of Gonzaga College and UCD is a canny political operator. A veteran of the ill-fated Fianna Fáil–Green coalition a decade earlier, he had been the Greens' point man on the financial crisis. His father, Bob, had worked all his life in banking, eventually ending up with AIB. Ryan junior, meanwhile, had a good rapport with the late Brian Lenihan and bought into Fianna Fáil's approach to the crisis.

In spring 2020, Ryan privately believed that if the national unity government proposal floundered – and it quickly did – a coalition with the two Civil War parties could not be ruled out. What's more, he believed that Green Party members would back the idea despite an influx of new members who were inherently hostile to the traditional 'big two' parties.

Fianna Fáil and Fine Gael had already agreed to enter exploratory talks to form a government two days before the first public health restrictions were imposed, their leaders later agreeing without much debate that Martin would get first go at being Taoiseach, reflecting the fact that Fianna Fáil had won more seats in the election. A slow dance continued for weeks until formal talks got under way between the three parties at the start of May.

By mid-June, their respective negotiating teams had broken the back of a draft programme for government, but as they gathered to finalise the document on Saturday, 13 June, a problem emerged. The Greens were insistent that any new government should put a major focus on public transport projects all across the country, and their Fingal TD Joe O'Brien felt that Fine Gael's proposals on the issue were quite a distance from what had been discussed. In effect, the Fine Gael transport plan would not pass muster with the Greens' grassroots.

O'Brien, who grew up on a farm in Grenagh, County Cork, is usually a pleasant, mild-mannered type, but that day, he lost it. 'This is too much for me, this is too much,' he told the room, raising his voice and swearing. 'He threw a complete strop,' one eyewitness recalled. Eventually, O'Brien led the Greens out of the room, believing that continuing the talks gave Fine Gael more credit for their proposals than was deserved.

It was one of a number of walkouts that day. At one stage finance and public expenditure minister Paschal Donohoe led the Fine Gael team out of the room, saying, 'We're clearly not on the same page.' The transport issue was not easily resolved. While some involved never felt it threatened to collapse the whole process, others were taken aback by O'Brien's aggression and anger; at one point he sat in the Green delegation's room with his head in his hands. 'They're not happy,' he said of the Fine Gael team. Eamon Ryan was on the other end of the phone telling his man to hold the line.

Barry Cowen came into the Greens' room to make peace. Cowen, brother of former Taoiseach Brian Cowen, was known for his forthright manner. Of pure Fianna Fáil stock, he emerged as a genuine big beast as the party wandered the post-financial collapse wilderness. He was as close to a nailed-on certainty for a Cabinet position as existed within Fianna Fáil, and recognised when common cause had to be found to keep the negotiations on track. 'We can figure something out here, come in and we can sort it out,' he told O'Brien. The other two parties sensed that Fianna Fáil were desperate for a deal to enter government and would be all over any threat – perceived or real – that the talks might collapse. Discussions resumed and the Greens got concessions on local bus services. Roads and public transport would remain a source of tension throughout the coalition's first two years in office, but that night a deal could be done.

A nearly-16-hour session concluded at 3.54 a.m. on Sunday, 14 June. Donohoe took a picture of a giant electronic clock on the wall for posterity. A programme for government document was more or less agreed, save for a number of outstanding issues that were ironed out by the three party leaders in the days that followed. Once their memberships had voted on the deal via postal ballot, with all three parties securing strong majorities, Micheál Martin was elected Taoiseach in the Convention Centre on Saturday, 27 June. Due to Covid-19 restrictions on travel, not even his wife could attend.

—

The division of Cabinet ministers was a delicate balancing act. Martin would have five spots, as would Varadkar, with Ryan given two. Each leader would be able to appoint a minister of state to sit at Cabinet but with no voting rights – although Cabinet rarely, if ever, holds votes. Varadkar's task was made all the more difficult by the fact that he would be forced to drop more than half a dozen Cabinet ministers. One by one, Michael Ring, Richard Bruton, Charlie Flanagan, Joe McHugh, Paul Kehoe and Josepha Madigan were all told there was no room. After the ministerial cull, Varadkar confided in colleagues how awful he felt at having to let go not just ministers, but their staff too.

For Martin, meanwhile, it was a more businesslike affair. He had put many of those hankering after ministerial office on his negotiating team and then told them to go off and sell the deal to party members. The brutal reality was that he was not going to have enough jobs. Dara Calleary, who had led Fianna Fáil's negotiating team, thought he would be in Cabinet, as did the rest of the political world. But, the affable Mayo TD later recalled, instead he sat in his Leinster House office that Saturday afternoon after Martin had been elected, scrolling through Twitter: 'X was going, Y was going, Z was going, and I'm still in the office.' It dawned on him, 'This is going to be complicated.'

He eventually got the call and found himself sitting in Government Buildings beside Norma Foley waiting to go in to see the Taoiseach. Foley thought Calleary knew what job she was going to be offered; the reality was that Calleary knew nothing but was fearing the worst. Foley was brought in and offered the job of Minister for Education. It was as much a shock to her – she was a secondary school teacher from Kerry who had just been elected to the Dáil four months earlier and had no previous national legislative or political experience – as it was to the rest of the Fianna Fáil parliamentary party.

Calleary was next in. 'This is very difficult, but you're the chief whip,' Martin told him. To Calleary it was a kick in the gut, a very public humiliation that neither he nor his supporters nor his family expected. He was deputy leader of the party. Martin attempted to assuage the anger and disappointment, telling Calleary he wished he had more places to offer but saying he wanted to ensure continuity between those who had shadowed ministers and were now taking up ministerial posts.

Darragh O'Brien was one of those; after marking outgoing housing minister Eoghan Murphy for the previous two years he was going straight into the Custom House where, Martin felt, he could hit the ground running. Another was Stephen Donnelly, who had shadowed Simon Harris since March 2018 and whom Martin had brought into the party. The idea of changing a health minister mid-pandemic was borne out of the fact that 'it was kind of made clear to us that Fine Gael were not looking for Health', Martin later claimed. Donnelly, the Taoiseach said, 'had done a lot of work as opposition spokesperson', but his appointment was still a surprise to many in Fianna Fáil, given that the Wicklow TD had for six years, both as an Independent and co-leader of the Social Democrats, lambasted the party during its long winter in opposition.

'Take a look at Fianna Fáil policies for the past fifteen years and tell me you don't see serious incompetence,' Donnelly wrote on Twitter in 2011. Three years before he joined the party, he railed against the Fianna Fáil culture 'of jobs for the boys, bonuses for the boys, lack of accountability and two fingers to the Dáil'. When the column that he wrote for the Sunday Independent was quoted back to him on the day he joined Fianna Fáil in February 2017, Donnelly claimed, 'I don't believe I wrote those words. It doesn't sound like the kind of language I use.' But they were his words, as was his statement a year earlier that 'the stale cartel of Irish Civil War politics' must be challenged.

Donnelly had enough self-awareness to know that there were people who had been in Fianna Fáil a lot longer than him who would not be happy that he was being elevated to Cabinet. But he also had enough self-confidence to approach Martin directly in the weeks before the government was formed to tell him he wanted the health minister's job. He wasn't the only one to offer himself, which was a 'big cultural change', Martin later observed, from when he himself had been elevated to Cabinet 23 years earlier.

Fast forward to that last weekend in June and Donnelly was sitting in his office in Leinster House watching Netflix when the phone rang. Deirdre Gillane, Martin's closest adviser and his soon-to-be chief of staff, asked him to come and see the Taoiseach. Donnelly was thrilled and shocked in equal measure when he was offered the job as health minister in a coalition of the two parties he had castigated for years.

—

The Taoiseach's first week in office was far from ideal. His new chief whip, Calleary, was disgruntled and not shy about informing his local radio station of his anger and annoyance. 'I had to be [pissed off on radio], I wasn't going to be walked over, was I? But then you couldn't dwell on it, you had to get on with it,' Calleary later recalled.

The geographical make-up of Martin's Cabinet was the subject of sharp criticism across the media, where it was tagged the 'Cromwell Cabinet', due to the lack of any ministers from the west of Ireland. Martin's selection of junior ministers went down equally badly. A gobsmacked Michael Moynihan, Martin's loyal party whip for nearly ten years, gave the Taoiseach both barrels over the phone after being told there was no job for him.

But any difficulties Martin had that week with geographical imbalance or old allies with whom he had sundered relations were relegated to minor inconveniences by that Friday afternoon, 3 July, when a phone call came in from Barry Cowen, now installed as agriculture minister. He had difficult news for the Taoiseach.

CHAPTER 16:

TWO DRINKS, ONE DINNER

30 June 2020
Cases: 25,473
Deaths: 1,736
Seven-day average of new cases: 12

The rumours had circulated in political circles for years that Barry Cowen had been arrested for drink-driving. At least one Fine Gael TD briefed the story to the media and included an allegation that Cowen had made a U-turn away from the Garda checkpoint – a claim the Offaly TD would strenuously deny.

On the first Friday in July 2020, Fionnán Sheahan, the *Irish Independent's* Ireland editor, was preparing to break the story he had managed to confirm. Micheál Martin had known nothing of the rumours that had swirled around Leinster House, and it was his position that he first learned of the story when his chief of staff, Deirdre Gillane, took a call from Sheahan, who told her about the U-turn allegation.

Cowen also rang the Taoiseach himself to explain what had happened. On the evening of 18 September 2016, he had been stopped at a Garda checkpoint on his way home with a friend from the All-Ireland football final and had failed a breathalyser. He had had two drinks before the match and a light meal afterwards.

Despite driving for over twenty years, Cowen did not have a full licence, which, he later admitted, was bad practice. He received a fixed charge penalty notice, a €200 fine, and because he did not have a full licence, he was disqualified from driving for three months. Cowen spent the next few days after the story broke publicly apologising for an 'appalling lapse of judgement', culminating in a contrite statement in the Dáil the following Tuesday.

The next day, Wednesday, 8 July, Cowen took a call from an official in the Taoiseach's office who told him that the Department of Justice had been in contact and had noted that his Dáil statement did not refer to the narrative on the Garda record that said Cowen had attempted to evade the checkpoint. Cowen told the official that he had already made the Taoiseach aware of this claim during their call the previous Friday (though the Taoiseach, through a spokesman, later disputed this) and that he was rejecting it completely. He also told the official the information should not have been in either their possession or that of the Department of Justice as it was confidential to the Garda file.

The development disturbed Cowen. It appeared to him that unelected officials in two major government departments, Taoiseach and Justice, were discussing the confidential Garda record of a member of the Cabinet. He later referred the phone call from the official in the Taoiseach's office to an investigation by the Garda Ombudsman (GSOC) to adjudicate on.

While he had hoped to put the saga behind him after his Dáil statement, that weekend the *Sunday Times* reported that Cowen was challenging the official Garda record of his arrest for drink-driving, which, the story claimed, said he 'was pursued by gardaí after doing a U-turn as he approached a checkpoint'. Cowen, through his solicitor, denied to the *Sunday Times* that he attempted to drive away from the checkpoint. According to Micheál Martin's spokesman, the newspaper story was the first the Taoiseach knew of the Garda report that Cowen had turned away. But Sheahan had told his chief of staff on 3 July, and the Dáil record from 14 July shows the Taoiseach confirming that, on that weekend that the story first broke, Cowen 'adamantly denied any suggestion or implication that he would have evaded or attempted to avoid a checkpoint' when Martin spoke to him.

But this U-turn allegation was now public and Cowen, who had obtained the Garda record and was challenging its accuracy, faced new questions. Early that Sunday morning he drafted a statement describing the newspaper report as a 'flagrant breach of the criminal law and my rights under data protection law' and that he would be 'instructing my lawyers to take all necessary steps to vindicate my good name and data protection rights'. He denied that he had evaded or attempted to evade Gardaí.

He asked Fianna Fáil to issue the statement on his behalf, but was told the party would not be doing so. Cowen was on his own. He emailed the statement to journalists from his wife's personal Gmail account just after 9 a.m. that Sunday. By that afternoon, Gardaí had referred the matter to GSOC. Cowen believed the Garda Ombudsman was the most appropriate way of vindicating his rights and clearing his name.

But the political reality was that the wind was against him and he was becoming increasingly isolated. That much became clear in the Taoiseach's office that Monday evening, 13 July, when Micheál Martin sat behind his desk taking copious longhand notes as Cowen explained himself. Martin impressed upon Cowen that he needed to go into the Dáil. Cowen did not agree, insisting he wanted GSOC to adjudicate on the facts and make a report. Going before TDs would make him 'a sitting duck to the amateur lawyers and amateur dramatics in the Dáil chamber', he told Martin that night. 'If you are not prepared to go into the Dáil you need to reflect on your position,' the Taoiseach told him.

Cowen concluded from this that he had been brought into Martin's office to be got rid of. He drove home to Offaly that night to retrieve the file of details Gardaí held on him, which Martin had asked to see. Cowen had been able to access the file in the days previous under data protection law. He took a picture and sent a copy to Martin the following morning, Tuesday, 14 July. Martin again asked Cowen to go into the Dáil and take questions. That afternoon the Taoiseach was quizzed on the debacle by Sinn Féin's Mary Lou McDonald and Labour's Alan Kelly. Martin defended Cowen, insisting that the Garda record of the incident was 'not quite as portrayed' in the media. The opposition attempted to reorder

Dáil business and haul Cowen into the house, but with its majority, the government was able to vote down the move.

As he left the Dáil chamber that afternoon, the Taoiseach rang Cowen and again asked him to go into the Dáil.

'I told you last night, I told you this morning, I am telling you again, no, and I don't think much of the fact you are asking me that having defended me and won a vote in the Dáil an hour or two ago,' Cowen forcefully told his boss.

But Martin argued that the story would not go away. 'You should have to face the Dáil,' Martin said. The minister was unmoved. Driving home that evening, at around 7.30 p.m., Cowen's phone rang. It was the Taoiseach again.

'Are you still not going into the Dáil?' Martin asked.

'No, I am not,' Cowen responded.

'Well, I am going to have to do something about it.'

'Well, you do whatever you have to do … So are you sacking me? Is that what you are trying to say to me?'

'Yes.'

'At least give me an hour to tell my family.'

Cowen pulled into a service station in Kinnegad and rang his wife. 'I've been sacked for standing my ground,' he told her.

Cowen later said that the Taoiseach voting down moves to make him answer Dáil questions while privately imploring him to do just that was 'not a great character trait'.

'I had no issue with my wrongdoing, for that I will be eternally remorseful, but to be hung, drawn and quartered without adequate recourse to a proper assessment by GSOC still dominates my thoughts every day of the week,' he said in August 2021.

But responding to this in November 2021, Martin said, 'The key point that Barry needs to answer is a very simple one: go into the Dáil, give a clear breast of it, tell the full story. That's to me – and I've seen ministers do it in the past and it works – far better and I think it went too legalistic.'

Back in Dublin that night, 14 July, there was a scramble to inform President Michael D. Higgins of Cowen's removal from office. 'I need you to suspend the business of the house, I'm sacking Barry,' Martin told Dara Calleary, who had been summoned to the Taoiseach's office.

'What the fuck?' the chief whip responded. After Martin explained what had happened, Calleary put arrangements in place for the Taoiseach to go into the Dáil just before 9 p.m.

Announcing the sacking of a man he had appointed to Cabinet just 17 days earlier, Martin stressed that nothing could disrupt the nascent coalition's war on Covid-19. 'It is in everyone's interest that the government not be distracted in any way from doing what is necessary to protect public health and our efforts to rebuild our society and economy,' he told a near-empty chamber.

The following morning, Martin rang Calleary and told him he was appointing him Minister for Agriculture. 'Off we went again,' Calleary later remarked. '[It was a] bit of a shitstorm.'

———

Micheál Martin had enough problems in his own ranks without having to deal with what observers detected was an increasingly unhappy Tánaiste and Minister for Enterprise.

Leo Varadkar had become the first former Taoiseach to serve in a lower office of government. At one point, Eamon Ryan noticed Varadkar leaving the Sycamore Room and turning right to go to his old office instead of left to his new one. 'It must have been tricky for Leo,' the environment minister later observed.

'Nobody's ever done it before,' Varadkar would later reflect. 'It wasn't easy at first, going from number one in an organisation to number two in a three-party coalition, but that's life.'

The Fine Gael leader was anxious to get the country as open as possible, but Covid-19 case numbers were rising. The date to reopen wet pubs was pushed into August, while efforts to kickstart international travel were hampered by confused messaging, caution from public health officials and the Taoiseach's office.

Varadkar wanted to let people go on holiday, telling the Dáil in mid-July that a proposed travel green list would include countries where you would be no more likely to get Covid-19 than if you went on a weekend to Dublin or Killarney. But the list that was eventually published contained just 15 countries, some of them holiday destinations, but with the official government advice still encouraging people not to travel.

In early July, the coalition leaders gave tentative consideration to establishing green zones, parts of the country where more could open up, including wet pubs. Varadkar was keen, so much so that, even as case numbers increased, the Fine Gael leader saw the imposition of local lockdowns, when they came, as a point where the Rubicon had been crossed. To him, it meant that local measures could apply to opening up just as they would to locking down. But the virus was hampering the self-confessed Covid-optimist's hopes.

His mood soured. In late July, Varadkar showed up for a meeting in the Sycamore Room and, it was observed by some, was annoyed that it had been rescheduled at short notice because of an issue with the Taoiseach's diary. Running on someone else's time was not something Varadkar had been used to over the previous three years. Nor was he used to the new Taoiseach's style. He would later observe that Micheál Martin was 'less likely to stick to a schedule' and 'less insistent than I would be on papers being available well in advance of a meeting'.

Mounting tensions came to a head at a meeting of the Cabinet on 18 August. Ministers were to discuss reintroducing some restrictions, including limiting indoor gatherings to just six people. Varadkar dialled in from his holidays, icily telling the meeting, 'If you keep doing business like this, we won't be doing business much longer.' It was a remark typical of Varadkar when he was angry: cutting, brief, and primed for leaking – which it duly was.

It frustrated some of his own party colleagues and, across government, many felt it made things awkward, overly political, and conflict-driven. But the real problems at the Cabinet meeting that day went beyond barbed comments. Ministers and their staff were increasingly frustrated with the Department of Health, specifically with the new minister, Stephen Donnelly, and his team. Material was coming across late, or not at all.

The talent and smarts of Donnelly's team were not in doubt, but their capacity to master the rigours of government was. Some colleagues felt they lacked experience working in the front line of government. This meant grasping the intricacies of how to land an idea, as well as devise it, and to tend to relationships across the ranks of officialdom, advisers and fellow ministers. In short, the issue diagnosed with Donnelly's camp was not necessarily policy – it was their understanding of the idiosyncrasies of moving ideas through the different levels of the civil service and the political machine. 'The process definitely broke down as to how Health interacted with the centre, interacted with the Cabinet,' a minister later recalled.

The memo that came to Cabinet that day was a perfect example of this. It was badly constructed, and it carried bad news. Cabinet colleagues felt it simply reproduced advice given by NPHET to Donnelly, with little thought for the political or practical realities of implementing it. It was edited and extensively rewritten at the Cabinet table, which one minister said was extraordinary: 'I have never been at Cabinet at any matter where Cabinet memos were rewritten.'

August is traditionally a month when politicians are rarely seen or heard from, escaping to their constituencies and taking a couple of weeks' holiday. But here they were in the middle of summer, announcing that the country was going backwards in its fight against Covid-19. It made for a bad atmosphere.

At a subsequent press conference, the Taoiseach was visibly irked by journalists' questions about how the new measures would work, with acting chief medical officer Ronan Glynn forced to step in to provide clarity where he could. That evening Calleary, who had been in post in Agriculture for just over a month, was sent out to deliver the bad news. Outlining the rationale for curtailing indoor gatherings, he told RTÉ's *Six One News* from the Leinster House car park that 'Covid loves to party.'

It was a line that would haunt him within days.

—

On Wednesday, 19 August, Calleary rang the president of the Oireachtas Golf Society, former Fianna Fáil senator Donie Cassidy, to check that the society's planned dinner at the Station House Hotel in Clifden, County Galway was still going ahead that evening. The function had been organised to honour the late Mark Killilea Jr, a former Fianna Fáil MEP and family friend of Calleary's. Cassidy told him the event, on the margins of the society's annual golf outing, was going ahead and that it would be in compliance with the public health guidelines, which had for several weeks allowed for indoor gatherings of up to 50. The previous day, however, Cabinet had agreed to reduce the numbers allowed to just 6. But the minister thought no more of it.

In the days leading up to the Clifden dinner, Calleary's officials had been grappling with an invitation to an informal meeting of EU agriculture ministers that would be hosted by his German counterpart, Julia Klöckner, in Koblenz on the banks of the Rhine in early September. The decision was eventually taken, in consultation with Liz Canavan in the Taoiseach's office, that Calleary was unlikely to go amid fears over how it might look for an Irish minister to be travelling to such an event during a pandemic.

But no such concerns arose when Calleary walked into the Clifden Hotel on the evening of the event. The first thing the Mayo TD noticed was how busy it seemed – and not just because of the golf dinner he was there for. 'It was my first time out and I was thinking, "Jeez, there's a lot of people here."' The golf society dinner was split across two rooms, separated by a moveable partition, with fewer than 50 people in each. The organisers had satisfied themselves that this was allowed as neither the regulations nor the Fáilte Ireland guidelines for the hospitality sector had, at that stage, been updated to reflect the new 6-person rule agreed by Cabinet earlier that week. Calleary and his wife were led to their table, where he sat down beside Phil Hogan, the EU Trade Commissioner, who had played golf that day.

Over a dinner of Connemara lamb and Atlantic salmon, Calleary saw an opportunity: 'Phil Hogan and myself spent the whole evening talking about fishing and CAP [Common Agricultural Policy]. This was my opportunity to download from the outgoing agriculture commissioner, the trade commissioner, the senior man in the commission. And I took it,' he later recalled. 'He was brilliant. Everything he predicted in terms of CAP, in terms of Brexit, in terms of fishing subsequently happened.' Calleary delivered his tribute to Killilea, whose family were among the audience. It was close to midnight before it ended. Calleary drove home that night, thinking nothing of what had just happened. Within days, both of the men who had chewed the fat on substantial EU affairs would be gone from their posts.

The following day, Calleary got a call from Aoife-Grace Moore at the *Irish Examiner*. Within hours the *Examiner* broke the news of one of the biggest political controversies in years. Up to eighty people, including Calleary and several current and former TDs and senators, had attended an Oireachtas Golf Society dinner a day after the Cabinet agreed to introduce new rules and regulations that would limit such indoor gatherings to six. Later that evening, the *Irish Independent* reported online the attendance of two other high-profile figures, Phil Hogan and RTÉ's Seán O'Rourke.

This was dynamite stuff to a public weary of Covid restrictions. Although a court would later find no laws were broken, people across the country reacted viscerally. Emails began pouring into Calleary's inbox from members of the public who were deeply upset at what appeared such a flagrant breach of the rules by the very man who was part of a government setting those rules. He texted Ronan Glynn, the deputy chief medical officer to apologise. Glynn acknowledged the text.

Others Calleary texted that night included Green Party deputy leader and tourism minister Catherine Martin, and Varadkar, whose own party was caught up in the scandal. The Fine Gael leader was texting the senators who were reported to be at the dinner. He was not happy, reportedly sending sweary text messages. A Fianna Fáil senator who was at the dinner reportedly screened calls from the Taoiseach. By contrast Calleary phoned his boss to inform him of the impending storm. 'This is the last thing we need,' Micheál Martin, who was trudging around the flood-damaged West Cork town of Skibbereen when he took the call, told his latest agriculture minister. The pair spoke again later that night. 'We both knew where it was going,' Calleary later recalled. 'In fairness to him, he didn't hold a gun to my head.'

Calleary told colleagues that the controversy in Northern Ireland over senior Sinn Féin figures' attendance at the funeral of former IRA member Bobby Storey – and the fact that there had been no resignations – only served to undermine public confidence in the public health messaging. There could be no such situation in the South. The Taoiseach told him to sleep on it, but Calleary had already made up his mind. He would resign. He sat alone at his kitchen table in Ballina at 3.30 that Thursday morning typing his resignation letter, as the rain poured outside.

At 6 a.m. he texted the Taoiseach to see if he was awake and got his press adviser Adam Ledwith to cancel scheduled appearances on RTÉ's *Morning Ireland* and on Newstalk. Calleary spoke to the Taoiseach just before 7 a.m. to confirm that he was resigning and then texted Norma Foley, the education minister, who was due on *Morning Ireland*, to apologise for landing her in it. Foley had to grapple with awkward questions on behalf of the government, which now feared that its public messaging would be undermined by the fiasco fast becoming known as Golfgate.

That afternoon the arcane rules governing Cabinet resignations meant that Calleary's resignation letter had to be printed, signed by him, and then collected by his private secretary, who drove over 235km to Calleary's home in Ballina, had a cup of tea, collected the letter and then drove back to Dublin with the document, which was conveyed to the President – the second Cabinet departure in 54 days of the new government. The final ignominy for Calleary came the following day when the Taoiseach rang to say that journalists had queried his position as deputy leader of Fianna Fáil. 'I might as well resign from that as well,' Calleary told Martin. He duly did that Friday afternoon.

With Calleary gone, the focus switched to Phil Hogan, who was now facing a barrage of questions about his travels around Ireland in the days leading up to the Clifden dinner. A defiant Hogan insisted he had done nothing wrong, but the coalition leaders took a different view and on Saturday, 22 August told Hogan to 'consider his position'.

Despite a very public fight-back, Hogan was forced to resign within days, the story of his movements having become a mess of contradictions. The fallout from his departure would last for months. The coalition leaders felt they had no choice, but their detractors felt they had, in effect, taken out Ireland's strongest ally in Brussels at a time when Brexit talks were at a crunch phase.

The united front presented by Martin, Varadkar and Ryan at least engendered good relations between the three coalition leaders, who had endured a rocky start politically. But as the challenges unfolded in that first pandemic autumn, the truth was that the government was reeling, without a sense of common purpose, and lacking any political momentum.

CHAPTER 17:

GOBSHITERY ON SPEED

2 July 2020
Cases: 25,489
Deaths: 1,738
Seven-day average of new cases: 12

I n a government department, the secretary general is effectively the chief executive – and then some. They run the administration, but also handle politically sensitive issues, provide policy advice, and help the political side of the house navigate sometimes choppy and treacherous waters. Jim Breslin had been the Department of Health's secretary general for almost six years, fielding the countless blows – from CervicalCheck to the overspend at the National Children's Hospital – that go with heading up the most politically volatile government department.

A few days after Stephen Donnelly was appointed the new health minister, Breslin told him he was leaving the department to become the secretary general of the newly created Department of Higher and Further Education, ironically the new home of Simon Harris, Donnelly's predecessor and constituency rival. Breslin, an incredibly resilient character, had, in the view of those to whom he spoke about his departure, run his race in Health.

Donnelly was shellshocked. Here he was, a new minister with no experience of government or a department, and the country was in the middle of a pandemic. Senior political figures thought Breslin's move should not have been allowed to happen, and in time, Donnelly came to that conclusion too. 'It would be reasonable to say that was probably a mistake, Jim [Breslin] moving at the start of the new government,' he later said.

Colm O'Reardon was appointed acting secretary general. A former economist with the ESRI, consultancy firm Indecon and the OECD, O'Reardon was also a grizzled political veteran, having served as a senior adviser to Eamon Gilmore, the former Labour leader, when he was Tánaiste. If you were looking for a steady hand, he was the obvious choice, and, what's more, Martin Fraser asked him to go in.

But whatever the shock caused by Breslin's departure, it was, in that same week, superseded by an even more disorienting blow for Donnelly. Tony Holohan announced on Thursday, 2 July that he was taking a leave of absence. His wife, Dr Emer Feely, had been diagnosed with multiple myeloma, a form of blood cancer, in 2012, and now her condition was deteriorating rapidly. She had been moved to palliative care the previous Saturday.

Given the nature of her terminal disease, this had always been a possibility – 'ever-present', in the words of one senior official. Holohan had spent time out of work the previous summer, and, as Covid-19 hit, there was a conscious effort in the department to ensure that Ronan Glynn knew everything that Holohan knew in case the CMO had to leave again at short notice.

Glynn grew up in Lydican, Oranmore, County Galway, and initially qualified as a physiotherapist before getting his medical degree and becoming a civil servant. He was just a few months past 40 as he entered a leadership role, and his public profile grew as one part of NPHET's public faces. It was a deliberate strategy to get Glynn in front of the media to get him used to the scrutiny and to ensure the media and, most crucially, the public were used to him.

Glynn was good at it, even though he hated it. He was a consumer of news, interested in politics and had an awareness of how the business worked through his wife Carla O'Brien, a journalist with RTÉ. Yet he saw every press conference as a stressor, a risk, a potential for trouble. Like most senior NPHET members, he would commit his share of cardinal media sins before the end of the pandemic, but he was, in essence, a good communicator, methodical and calm. Although he wasn't particularly magnetic, he had a humanity and an earnestness that travelled well.

Glynn only found out on the day Holohan announced his departure that he was to take over as acting CMO. The level of trust in Glynn's capabilities was high, but it was still, inevitably, a risk. 'Daunting,' he later described it. 'You have to sit down with yourself and say, look, this is the situation now, you can sink or swim.'

Managing the absence of Holohan in particular presented a whole range of challenges. Officials were feeling the pace. People went off sick, or were given leave, having in some cases not had a day off since Christmas. The CMO's division had, over time, become the largest in the department, responsible for a whole swathe of issues from alcohol and tobacco to screening programmes, and now pandemic policy. It was logical, but it was also a function of Holohan himself who, a senior figure later said, was 'an unbelievable bureaucratic empire builder'.

Over the summer the department was streamlined and reorganised, a process that had begun while Breslin and Holohan were still there. Glynn's role was to be more narrowly focused on Covid-19 policy and public health leadership, with a new principal officer, Laura Casey, overseeing that function. Fergal Goodman, one of the most senior officials in the department, was given responsibility for many of the new and emerging functions, which cleared Glynn's decks – to some extent.

No amount of reorganisation, however, could change the fact that the political backdrop was beginning to shift as the situation with the disease deteriorated again.

—

In mid-May 2020, Michael Errity, a senior civil servant in the Houses of the Oireachtas, and his team were busy preparing for the resumption of political action in Leinster House. The Dáil had sat in a constrained format during the first wave; now the establishment of a special committee on Covid-19 earlier that month meant that parliament could begin probing the State's response to the pandemic.

But shortly before midnight on 18 May, Errity received an email threatening all that. Martin Cormican, the HSE's infection prevention and control expert, said he had spoken with colleagues in public health and it was his view that a two-hour limit on witnesses' testimony had to be imposed. It was a dramatic U-turn given that a day earlier, he had told the committee clerk, 'I do not understand the limitation on being in the chamber or committee room for no more than two hours.' Now witnesses had to be in and out in under 120 minutes.

This last-minute wobble was compounded by the unwillingness of some of the witnesses to attend together for more than one two-hour session, members were told. These witnesses included Tony Holohan, Jim Breslin and Paul Reid – the three most senior officials involved in the Covid-19 response. Michael McNamara, the chair of the new committee, was told the session couldn't go ahead.

But the Clare TD, formerly a rebellious Labour deputy who had just regained his Dáil seat as an Independent, resolved the issue by splitting the day into three sessions, with witnesses split between the Dáil chamber, where the committee was sitting, and a committee room elsewhere in Leinster House, from where their testimony was beamed in to the committee. The bouffant-haired barrister and farmer from Scarriff was not about to see the committee denied its star witnesses. There were signs that officialdom had started to feel jumpy about the inevitable reckoning with decisions taken during the first wave. Like death and taxes, post-crisis inquiries are a certainty, and they are dreaded by officials, who see them often as a hunt for a scapegoat. In mid-May, the Senior Civil Service Association wrote to Ceann Comhairle Seán Ó Feargháil reminding him that their members had to be treated in a way that ensured 'fair procedure and appropriate redress mechanisms [...] No matter what redress might be offered after appearing before a committee, damage that may be done to a person's reputation and health cannot be undone.' They also referenced the Supreme Court's judgment in the case of former Rehab chief executive Angela Kerins, which found that the Public Accounts Committee had acted outside its remit when questioning her in 2014. Robert Watt also brought up the ruling in a letter to the clerk of the special committee, pointing out that the constitutional and legal rights of civil servants had to be respected, and warning about leaks of briefing materials from committees to the media. The Kerins judgment had cast a shadow over how committees operated; the letters were a clear shot across the bows of the Oireachtas.

McNamara is against lockdowns and was sceptical about the State's decision to shut society down, especially the manner in which it imposed criminal sanctions on people. He was uneasy with how quickly regulations were signed and given the weight of law. As a politician, he was frustrated that laws were being rammed through the Oireachtas, and had already resolved that the committee would provide a full and proper examination of the State's response, both political and in relation to public health. The truth was, McNamara saw little difference between them. 'The hope was to hold the government to account, and in this instance, it was quite clear the government was NPHET,' he later said.

While examining in detail what had happened during the first wave and the contemporary issues of that summer as the Covid-19 situation began to deteriorate, committee sessions also embraced a contrarian streak. Members questioned whether the State should be more worried about hospitalisations than about rising case numbers; if too wide a net was being cast in counting Covid-19 deaths; and asked whether it was any worse than a bad flu season. It explored whether Ireland could do the same as Sweden, which had deployed a controversial herd immunity policy in the first wave.

Some sessions raised already high blood pressure in the Department of Health and irked some NPHET members who saw it both as evidence of, and an accelerant to, a weakening consensus around the public health response. 'From late summer 2020 on, there started to be multiple messages,' Ronan Glynn later said, 'and I think it became more difficult for people to know what the best advice was, which made it harder to get the core public health message across.' Donnelly, who sat on the committee before being appointed health minister, later said, '[I was] taken aback by some of the stuff I began to hear the chair of the committee say.' One senior official later fumed that the committee was 'gobshitery on speed'. Asked about this criticism over a year later, McNamara coolly quipped, 'I've never taken speed.'

NPHET's leadership also felt its message wasn't landing with the political system, not helped by a series of leaks from within, or briefings about the team's work. They struggled to locate exactly where the leaks were coming from, or identify precisely who was briefing against them, but the message was crystal clear: the politics was changing. Two senior colleagues on NPHET later said that, eventually, as 2020 wore on, Glynn felt undermined by the Tánaiste in particular.

—

The new Taoiseach was determined to do something about confusing public health guidance on face masks. Micheál Martin's phone had for months been buzzing with texts from his sister-in-law in Singapore. 'Masks, masks, masks,' she told him.

In April, Tony Holohan told a press briefing there were risks and unintended consequences from masks; that they would give their users a 'false sense of security'. The concern across the health system was that the public, in effect, could not be trusted with face masks. It was evidence, Martin would later state, of 'an element of paternalism' in public health that is almost part of the discipline itself.

There were terse debates among medics on NPHET's Expert Advisory Group over mask use, even among healthcare workers, during the first wave. Having voted down advice two days previously that masks should be used in nursing homes, there were sharp exchanges at an EAG meeting on 10 April. Supply was an issue; at the time, the State had only a ten-day stockpile. Martin Cormican told the group, 'if there is a benefit, it is very small', and that 'widespread mask use also rapidly degenerates into poor practice, which could increase the risk of Covid-19 transmission'. It was, in fact, the second time in a matter of days that the EAG had debated masks. As Covid ripped through nursing homes, the group had been unable to reach a consensus on the use of masks when providing direct patient care within two metres in the facilities.

Colman O'Loughlin, an intensive care doctor from the Mater, said it wasn't clear whether masks would reduce presymptomatic transmission, while others on the group argued staff in critical care could run out of masks if they were more widely mandated. Others said they had seen poor practices in acute hospitals.

But paediatrician Karina Butler, who would later come to prominence as chair of the National Immunisation Advisory Committee (NIAC), pointed to evidence from Beijing and Hong Kong on the efficacy of masks. 'We can't assume people won't wear the masks properly,' she told the meeting. 'They have a strong reason and motivation to do this properly in the current context.' Following a vote, the decision to advise widespread masking among healthcare workers was approved, but even then, one member dismissed the ballot as 'based on sentiment rather than evidence'.

The indecision over masks went on for months afterwards, especially over the wider mandating of masks in society, and it frustrated Martin. 'Look, what's the story with masks?' he asked Tony Holohan and Ronan Glynn when he took over as Taoiseach. He later said, 'I think public health were slow on masks, in my view it was a mistake.' Within weeks of his inquisition of the public health team, the NPHET recommendation was that masks should be mandatory across retail and other indoor settings. 'Sign the regulation,' the Taoiseach recalled telling Stephen Donnelly, the new minister. 'It'll enforce itself.'

—

The new coalition picked up an old habit from its predecessor: spending. The scale of the fiscal response had been and would continue to be unprecedented. There were, in effect, multiple budgets across 2020 and 2021; two 'official' budgets and a third in the form of the July Jobs Stimulus, which injected another €5.2bn into the economy, way in excess of recent budgetary packages. On top of that, each round of restrictions saw the various pandemic support schemes either recharged or extended, while there were numerous 'below the line' measures in addition to direct cash payments: rates holidays, tax warehousing, loan guarantees. It was unparalleled and unconstrained. By November 2020 Irish cash payments to businesses were equivalent to 16 per cent of gross national income (GNI*, a measure of economic activity and growth that strips out the distorting effects of Ireland's large multinational sector), outstripping almost all other advanced economies. The traditionally hawkish Departments of Finance and Public Expenditure had removed the barriers to spending.

The Cabinet memo outlining the stimulus package noted that spending had, at that stage, increased by nearly a third – €19bn in a year. There would be another €700m for the pandemic unemployment payment across 2020 and 2021; €1.9bn for the extended wage subsidy scheme in the same period; €300m for restart grants; and €150m for a range of schemes operated by Leo Varadkar's Department of Enterprise. There was €100m here for training, €200m there for labour market activation.

The only disagreements were on how to spend the money. Fine Gael wanted to cut capital gains tax, which Varadkar saw as a necessary stimulus. It was also a pro-business measure that delivered for his party's core vote. But it ran into serious opposition from the Greens, who drew up a research note arguing that it would accrue to high income earners, who would likely save it up, and windfall gains realised by selling assets would not be reinvested.

There was a political argument against it as well – if and when PUP and other supports were cut, it could be viewed as especially regressive. The cost was high – an estimated €585m – and the payoff dubious. The compromise was a VAT cut, costing €440m. It held no political gain as voters would be unlikely to notice it.

Another stimulus measure, the 'Stay and Spend' tax relief scheme for hospitality, worth a putative €270m, proved convoluted and, in any case, pointless; by the time spending became eligible for the relief, much of the economy was closed or closing as Covid-19 came roaring back.

The stimulus package had been an early road test of the new relationships in the coalition, and it came together fairly well, perhaps not surprisingly, seeing as tough choices were few and far between. But not all of the relationships were that new. Micheál Martin's chief of staff, Deirdre Gillane, and her counterpart in Varadkar's office, Brian Murphy, had worked closely together for four years under the confidence and supply deal. There was frequent contact to flag what was coming up or troubleshoot disputes over policy.

A towering figure, Murphy was Varadkar's trusted lieutenant and a veteran of three departments before his boss became Taoiseach in 2017. But he did not have to teach Gillane anything about the mechanics of government. The straight-talking Cork native had worked for Brian Cowen when he was Taoiseach and had been an adviser to Martin when he was health minister. A former trade union official, Gillane is a commanding presence behind the scenes in Fianna Fáil. Given that she is unelected, some TDs resent this, but at the same time there is a grudging respect for her political astuteness, her grasp of the detail and her stubbornness in negotiations. 'When you see the phone ring [with Gillane's number] you're terrified,' confided one adviser. 'You kind of presume you have done something wrong. She's the trusted lieutenant, the mudguard, the rollbar, the enforcer.' Above all else she is fiercely loyal to Martin. One senior coalition figure described Murphy and Gillane as 'the non-elected axis of government'.

On the elected side of the coalition, Paschal Donohoe and Michael McGrath enjoyed a similarly strong working partnership, the latter slipping seamlessly into his new ministerial role and impressing veterans of government.

Of course, it helped that McGrath was doling out cash. One of the most underappreciated but remarkable aspects of the first two years of the Covid-19 crisis was the new paradigm in spending. Some worry that this has engendered a cavalier outlook among ministers who have operated for their entire tenure without any brakes on spending. 'It's an entirely new experience for everyone – there's no fucking constraints any more,' one coalition adviser observed later.

But in July 2020 nobody stood in the way of such spending. It was hoped that Ireland was on the way out of the pandemic. But three weeks into the new government's term the reality was very different. On the day the stimulus was launched, 23 July 2020, a total of 25,826 cases of Covid-19 had been diagnosed in the State. It was only slightly more than two per cent of the total number of cases that would be diagnosed by the time Holohan advised that NPHET be stood down, in February 2022. In the first days of 2022, there would be single days where as many cases were diagnosed as across the entire first wave, which had convulsed the political, economic and social life of the country. In reality, much of the hard slog lay ahead of the government.

CHAPTER 18:

LIVING WITH COVID

3 August 2020
Cases: 26,208
Deaths: 1,763
Seven-day average of new cases: 45

N iamh O'Beirne, the HSE's lead on testing and tracing, and her team had spent much of the summer preparing for September, when they expected a resurgence in Covid-19 cases. 'Everyone had been thinking nothing would happen in August and that it would rise when the schools returned,' O'Beirne later recalled.

But then came the August bank holiday weekend and within days GPs reported a large increase in the number of patients seeking a test. It became apparent after that weekend, O'Beirne said, that 'this was going to move, and it was going to be a problem'.

Ronan Glynn, the acting chief medical officer who was barely a month into the job, was delivering gloomier forecasts to the government. Over the course of July, the situation with the disease had deteriorated more rapidly than expected. It was no surprise when the date to reopen wet pubs was pushed back and, on 4 August, the move to phase four of the government's reopening plan was delayed.

The political mood shifted. O'Beirne recalled some 'difficult meetings in August' with Stephen Donnelly, who was particularly anxious to know how many contact tracers the HSE had. The health minister had looked at international evidence and told O'Beirne, 'We're going to need a lot more contact tracers.' He wanted 150 contact tracers at first, growing quickly to 250. Donnelly told Paul Reid he wanted the HSE to up its testing capacity from 100,000 per week to 150,000.

The virus was beginning to get a foothold, most visibly in meat plants, which were a perfect breeding ground. Many of the workers were non-Irish nationals, sharing accommodation and transport, insulated by language and cultural barriers from wider public health messaging. They worked at close quarters in chilled environments where there was a lot of noise, which meant they had to shout at each other. They were poorly paid, with bad terms and conditions, and in the absence of sick pay arrangements, they were often forced to work when they were sick in order to send money home or support themselves. While Covid-positive workers would have been entitled to enhanced illness benefit, there were doubts in government as to whether this was widely known within the communities many workers lived in.

All of these issues were clear right at the top of the Department of Agriculture, where Dara Calleary had been installed. He believed language and cultural barriers were a 'major issue'. Brazilians, for example, would be working, commuting, living and socialising together, and often consuming Brazilian media, laden with bogus messages from the country's president, Jair Bolsonaro, a Covid-19 denier.

There were reports of the lengths workers would go to to get a day's pay: sitting together in cars with the air-conditioning on before work, munching paracetamol to get their temperature down before going into a factory. The veracity of these reports was never fully established, but Calleary was hearing it from people he trusted, and he believed it. 'People were desperate to work, desperate to get a wage, sending money home to people in the most appalling conditions, so they were going to take that chance,' he later said.

Covid-19 outbreaks in the Midlands were initially driven by four big outbreaks in meat plants. Briefing documents drawn up for Donnelly in early August identified them as Kildare Dog Food, Kildare Chilling (the largest, with 160 linked cases), O'Brien's and Carroll's. The same documents also show there was a clear awareness at the highest levels of government about the conditions workers were living and working in. A note dated 26 August refers to 'linked clusters in direct provision centres'. Potential contributory factors included language barriers, but also 'socioeconomic challenges which workers may encounter as a result of not working' and, most important, 'workplace policies which disincentivise reporting of symptoms'. These warnings were repeated to Donnelly across August and September.

The battle to control Covid-19 in meat plants was being waged amid the broad patchwork of rules and agencies that regulated the sector. There were 149 'approved meat premises' in the country, but the Department of Agriculture only had a presence in 49 – premises where animals were killed. And that presence was a vet, sometimes co-funded by the plant itself, who had no function in relation to infection control or employee welfare.

The HSE's public health teams had responsibility for outbreaks, as well as testing and tracing, but had no powers of inspection or enforcement in the plants. Internal documents outline how the Health and Safety Authority was responsible for inspecting employee-related issues and standards in the plants, but there were concerns over how frequently they visited, and the notice of inspections given to meat plants. Meanwhile, the Department of Justice was responsible for direct provision, while the Health Protection Surveillance Centre set requirements for infection prevention and control. A total of five government departments or bodies were involved.

Calleary sensed his own department was being overtaken by events in early August. He was also frustrated with the institutional attitude towards the sector within the department, and its approach. 'In Ag, their view on the meat factories was a view which I fundamentally disagree with, which was that their duty was to keep them open – keep the farmers open, we have to mind the farmers,' he later said, criticising the siloed approach.

Some in government also privately felt the relationship between the meat industry and the department was too close. There had been long-standing concerns over the appointment of a former senior civil servant in the department as chair of Meat Industry Ireland just months after his retirement in 2015.

Meat plants were the perfect breeding ground for Covid. As with nursing homes, the virus found a weak point, and ruthlessly took advantage.

—

While the meat plants and the associated infections in the Midlands were challenging, they were ultimately brought under control through localised lockdowns in Laois, Offaly and Kildare in early August. 'Myself, Eamon and Leo,' Micheál Martin later recalled, 'just convened a meeting one Sunday morning in August and we said there's a problem and we took decisions.' Ronan Glynn had briefed them and later recalled the measure was to stop the virus 'getting out into the community'. But even as the meat plants were brought under control, a much more complex problem began to emerge: Dublin.

Construction sites in the capital had been among the first places to see Covid flare-ups during summer 2020 and while these outbreaks had been brought under control, the disease was still growing. Unlike in the Midlands, the increase in cases could not be narrowed down to a handful of factories that might be driving it. It was across multiple settings, in many parts of the city. By early September, NPHET estimated that the reproductive rate of the virus was significantly higher in Dublin than in the rest of the country. The virus was growing by four per cent per day.

At its meeting on 10 September, NPHET considered moving Dublin to Level 3 of what was then a draft of a plan for Covid-19 restrictions. The Department of Health had, over the summer, been tinkering with this plan, which eventually evolved from a yellow–orange–green–blue framework to five levels. Much of this was informed by the experience of the local lockdowns.

The draft plan was to become the five-level *Living with Covid* document, which, after a fraught summer for the coalition, would be published in mid-September, just as the Dáil returned from its summer recess. It was intended to be a significant political moment. Officials involved in producing the plan believe that Martin Fraser recognised the unifying potential of having a single Covid-19 document that, in theory, would lay out a coherent approach to managing the disease.

In tandem with the plan, Fraser would chair a new Covid Oversight Group of senior officials involved in the pandemic response, separate from the politicians. 'It was Martin trying to get his input and get his arms around it all,' Paul Reid would later recall. It was also recognition of an inalienable truth: politicians love plans because they are something to anchor themselves to. Programmes for government, budgets, manifestoes – they're all plans that provide a footing for wider political projects. But the first outing of *Living with Covid* was anything but steady.

On 11 September, Glynn told Donnelly that Dublin could remain at Level 2, but with extra measures. The situation was of 'grave concern', so household visits were to be restricted, and wet pubs should not be allowed to open on 21 September, while visits to nursing homes were to be restricted. However, when that recommendation landed, there was pushback from government. How could the capital go to an enhanced version of Level 2 of a plan that hadn't even been published yet?

Senior NPHET officials took the view that the politicians were concerned that acting on the advice at that point, 11 September, would scupper the plan's launch. It would be four days before Dublin's extra restrictions were announced. The delay sparked an angry backlash from some. Simon Harris, the former health minister, was especially annoyed. 'We have lost five days in the fight against the virus because they didn't move and he's really not happy about it,' a source close to Harris told the *Irish Independent* at the time.

Speaking in 2021, Harris acknowledged his concerns: 'I think there were warning signs highlighted by our public health experts in relation to Dublin in 2020. No decision in relation to Covid is easy but it is well known I was always of the Mike Ryan school of thought that speed trumps perfection.' However, Donnelly would later defend the decision to delay: 'You're trying to have the biggest impact possible, and obviously it's really important that there's a coherent message for that.' Waiting for the new framework, he argued, was important to secure the public's buy-in.

The launch of the plan itself was an unmitigated fiasco. Elements were still being finessed at that morning's Cabinet meeting, participants later recalled. At a press conference to announce it, the Taoiseach haltingly tried to explain how every county had been put on Level 2, but Dublin was simultaneously 'effectively on Level 2 with some modifications'.

Afterwards, Donnelly, who had sounded hoarse during the briefing, returned to the Department of Health, where he began to feel unwell and developed Covid-19 symptoms – some reports at the time said a cough, and Donnelly remembered it as a 'mild headache'. He was attended to by Glynn, who advised him to take a test. Because he had been in the Cabinet room, the entire government then had to self-isolate. There was panic in Leinster House, where Helen McEntee, the justice minister, was in RTÉ's basement-level studio being confronted with the news on live radio. In the Dáil, Ceann Comhairle Seán Ó Fearghái abruptly adjourned the day's proceedings until further notice. The entire day had now turned into a shambles for the coalition.

Behind closed doors in the Department of Health things were not any better. Four sources who were in the department that day later said that, by being there while symptomatic, Donnelly had upset and alarmed members of staff, including junior civil servants, working on the same floor as him. One source recalled how staff on the sixth floor, where the minister's office is located, were 'furious'.

They had been coming into Miesian Plaza for the best part of the last six months, even as the thousands of workers across the public and private sector were at home. 'I think everyone was incredibly angry with him. I think he really lost the department after that,' the source recalled. Another source said there was 'uneasiness' about it – 'a bit around the office of "for fuck's sake"'. A third source said that staff 'said to one another, "Well, why was he in the building at all?"' A fourth, who had been working on the floor below, said, 'things had gone into a mental panic upstairs because the minister might have Covid'. A spokesperson for Donnelly later said he followed all public health guidelines, isolating and working from home.

—

It had already been an inauspicious start for Donnelly. He had been rocked by the departures of Jim Breslin and Tony Holohan, and had spent his first weeks attempting to get a handle on his new department. He met his assistant secretaries, talked to Ronan Glynn and got to know Paul Reid and the HSE board. He believed the pandemic was not remotely over and, in fact, by the end of August he was warning that a surge in cases was 'close to having us lock down the country again'. The comments took some by surprise given there were no such explicit warnings from NPHET.

Donnelly had a simple strategy for healthcare that he would lay out in early meetings through the use of a Venn diagram. In one circle was Covid-19, in the other was universal healthcare and the intersection was the nascent winter plan, a major €600m initiative to prepare the health service for a challenging winter ahead. 'This is the strategy,' Donnelly would tell senior health officials as he proudly presented his Venn diagram. 'I wanted to keep things simple,' he said later. It was classic management consultancy from the ex-McKinsey executive, an attempt to peel back layers of complexity and inertia, to cut through to the essence of a problem. But health policy is inherently, unavoidably complex and requires balancing multiple interdependent factors and competing priorities.

Paul Reid later recalled Donnelly being a particularly strong ally in the push to get as much funding as possible for the HSE's winter plan. But while the minister was supportive of the HSE at the start, Reid also recalled that, on occasion, Donnelly conveyed a view to some of the HSE team that, 'You're not doing this right, you didn't do that right.' Reid would push back: 'Hold on a second now,' he told Donnelly.

Reid later said there were 'a couple of challenging early discussions – very challenging – but that would be expected'. Donnelly, he said, would raise matters you would expect a new minister to raise, but 'there was a style about how he went about that at first' which 'could have been perceived as being a little dismissive, not respectful, that would have got my team riled up quite a bit'.

Within the department, there were raised eyebrows when Donnelly sometimes appeared concerned with trivial matters. On the evening of Thursday, 8 September, Matthew O'Gorman, Donnelly's private secretary – the gatekeeper of his diary and correspondence – emailed the department's corporate services team in Miesian Plaza:

> Colleagues
> The Minister has asked for the following
>
> - He is requesting that access to the 8th floor/roof be granted;
> - He has requested that the gym be reopened for Department staff.
> - He would like a Surface Pro so he can see how it shapes up compared to an iPad which will have compatibility issues.
> - The Driver has requested clarity re the swipe for eCharging points – does it work on any eCharging spot or just those on site.
>
> Grateful if you would look into these matters.

Donnelly would, on occasion, raise the gym issue with O'Gorman in meetings. In one instance, according to one official who witnessed the exchange, he asked his private secretary, 'Did you get the gym open yet? I need somewhere to let off steam.'

O'Gorman was told in response to his email that the gym in Miesian Plaza was a landlord-provided facility that had closed as a result of the department's guidelines issued earlier in the pandemic. The landlord was now considering reopening the gym with reduced capacity in light of latest public health advice. As for the roof, access was not possible for tenant staff.

O'Gorman did not work for Donnelly for long, and by early October he was transferred out of the minister's office. His departure was the talk of the department. The role of private secretary is often given to civil servants on an upward career trajectory. Many in the department believed there had been compatibility problems owing in part to the fact that O'Gorman had worked with Simon Harris. But others insisted it was entirely normal for a private secretary to move on after a period of time working in what can be a high-pressure job.

Donnelly also had early problems with the media. In opposition he was frequently leaned on by journalists for comment and reaction to the latest government controversies. Before he joined Fianna Fáil, he drove the agenda on vulture funds and the complex legal structures they used. But in government his every word was scrutinised and analysed; there is no hiding place for a minister. Get a statement half-wrong and it could be the lead item on *Morning Ireland* the next day.

Donnelly spent weeks attempting unsuccessfully to hire a press adviser. Eventually, Susan Mitchell, the former health editor of the *Business Post*, whom the minister had recruited as a policy adviser, approached Colette Sexton, her former colleague at the newspaper, who had since forged a career in public relations with Edelman. Sexton agreed to come on board, but immediately problems emerged.

In one of his first TV interviews as minister, with Virgin Media's Zara King, Donnelly compared the risk of children catching Covid-19 to jumping on a trampoline: it was 'an inherently risky thing to do', he told a bemused King. She interjected, 'But are we comparing that, Minister, to a global pandemic, to a virus that kills people? It's not the same as sports really, is it?' A wide-eyed Donnelly nodded, conveying that it was the same: 'Well, driving cars … people die on the roads, lots of people die on the roads.'

The interview caught fire on social media and not in a good way. Sexton later told colleagues that Donnelly had told her she should not have let him sit down with King and thus give the impression to the viewer that it was an extended sit-down interview. The furious minister is said to have told his new press adviser she should have stopped King from asking him those types of questions. Asked about this later, Donnelly's spokesperson asserted the minister never told Sexton she should have dictated the types of questions that should be asked – but didn't address whether she was told she should have intervened to prevent the questioning.

Relationships with certain journalists and outlets could be frosty, and sometimes rocky. Coverage from some reporters rankled in Donnelly's camp. He avoided sit-down interviews with newspapers and colleagues believed he did his best to avoid RTÉ broadcaster Claire Byrne after a poor performance in a pre-election debate on her TV show.

He wanted to target invites to press conferences; Sexton was told to invite specific journalists, but she aligned with the department's press office, which sent invites simultaneously and allocated spaces on a first come, first served basis, as is the norm. Donnelly denied through a spokesman ever suggesting 'specific named journalists' should be invited, saying he asked his advisers to ensure health reporters were briefed as much as political correspondents. This was the justification given for excluding some journalists from a press conference in mid-February 2021 – including from papers who didn't have a health correspondent. Among them was Craig Hughes, political correspondent with the *Irish Daily Mail*, who had been needling Donnelly over changes to the vaccine programme. The journalists were shut out until RTÉ's Fergal Bowers intervened. During the vaccine rollout, Donnelly also confided to some his annoyance at analysis by the *Irish Examiner*'s deputy political editor Elaine Loughlin.

Occasionally Donnelly could see the funny side of his bad press. When the *Sunday Independent* revealed that Donnelly had texted a thumbs up emoji in response to a text from Holohan about the rising reproductive rate in Dublin, he was mocked on social media, with Twitter users replying with thumbs up emojis to his every tweet. Donnelly brought Holohan into his office one day and showed him the stream of thumbs up emojis. The two men laughed about it.

But that September, with Holohan still on leave, Ireland's first winter with Covid was around the corner. The omens were not good and the increasingly prickly relationship between the government and its public health advisers was about to go into meltdown.

CHAPTER 19:

OCTOBER SURPRISE

2 October 2020
Cases: 37,063
Deaths: 1,801
Seven-day average of new cases: 393

On the first Friday of October, Tony Holohan was back in the Department of Health. He was three days early, having told Ronan Glynn he would return the following Monday. Word got around that the CMO was returning after a three-month absence; most assumed it was because his wife's condition had stabilised.

It was true that Emer Feely's health had improved. Holohan weighed up whether he should return to work or not. He would either go back properly or not at all. He could also see that the situation with Covid-19 had begun to turn. As winter approached, most of western Europe was seeing an increase in cases, and Ireland was no different. 'I could see that things were sliding, it didn't take much to figure out what was happening,' Holohan later said.

The seven- and fourteen-day incidence rates, numbers in hospital, ICU admissions and deaths were all increasing. The disease was growing at between 4 and 5 per cent per day. NPHET had met the previous day, 1 October. Dublin and Donegal were already in Level 3 restrictions, with limits on household mixing and the closure of restaurants and cafés for all but takeaway and a limited outdoor service.

The team discussed the possibility of moving the country to Level 3 but decided against it. However, in his letter to Stephen Donnelly, Glynn recommended that Level 2 measures be extended for three weeks, with an added restriction, carved out from Level 3: no more than two households should meet at any given time. Glynn was warning the government that lockdown was a distinct possibility, but he was not recommending it – yet.

In the Department of Health that Friday, Glynn ran Holohan through a presentation he had prepared in advance of his return. It showed the very latest data and Holohan formed a clear view, which he articulated at that meeting: 'Level 3 isn't going to do it.' He wanted to hold a NPHET meeting as soon as possible.

The following morning Holohan spent a couple of hours poring over more data and holding a series of conversations with colleagues. He rang Colm O'Reardon, the acting secretary general of the Department of Health, to tell him he was so concerned that he would be calling a meeting for Sunday. He also rang a number of NPHET members to get their take on matters, including close allies like Glynn, Philip Nolan and Cillian De Gascun. He had two fundamental questions for each of them: 'What's your sense of things? And is there more we can do?'

It was clear to many of those he spoke to that morning that Holohan was coming back to work with a more alarming perspective on matters. 'Part of me does wonder if Tony came back after three months and thought, what are you at?' De Gascun would later admit. 'If you're looking at 4 per cent growth per day on a weekly/fortnightly basis – as NPHET would have been – it might not seem that significant […] we were perhaps not taking that step back and looking at the larger trend, whereas Tony comes in after some time away and says, "Look at the whole graph."'

Holohan also reached out beyond his close-knit NPHET inner circle. He rang Kevin Kelleher, the HSE's assistant national director of public health, who was roaming around Limerick Milk Market. Kelleher told the CMO directly that he would have introduced a heightened level of restrictions weeks earlier.

Holohan also phoned Colm Henry in the HSE. 'I am kind of worried about this. I think it's going badly, and I am ringing to see what you think,' he told the HSE man. Henry, who was at his Cork home, told Holohan it was important to recognise Glynn's role over the previous months, while he had been on leave. A tightening of restrictions, when Glynn had recommended staying at Level 2 just two days earlier, would, almost by definition, appear to undermine the deputy chief medical officer.

But for all the phone calls made that Saturday, Holohan did not speak to Stephen Donnelly. Instead, at 12.40 p.m., Holohan picked up his phone and composed a text:

> Minister, Tony H here. Sorry to cut into your Saturday. I'm going to call a meeting of NPHET tomorrow at 12. Case numbers today exceed 600. Likely to be even higher tomorrow. I'll keep apprised.

Donnelly texted back:

> Hi Tony. Welcome back. Looking forward to catching up with you, lots to discuss. Thanks for the heads up.

Holohan responded:

> Thanks, Minister. Looking forward to working with you. Regards Tony.

From the text exchange, Donnelly did not appear overly concerned about what might arise out of the meeting suddenly arranged for the following day. From the health minister's perspective, it was not abnormal for Holohan to call a meeting of his team following a long absence. He did not sense a change was in the offing. 'It was only thirty-six hours since we'd had formal advice from NPHET so I wasn't expecting an outcome of the meeting to be any significant change to that advice,' Donnelly said later.

The minister texted the Taoiseach to update him. Micheál Martin in turn relayed the development to his own team, including his chef de cabinet, Deirdre Gillane, who told some ministers. The coalition party leaders were also told. Eamon Ryan was due to appear on RTÉ's *The Week in Politics* the following day.

There was little indication of any panic in government. The Taoiseach was not aware that Saturday that the chief medical officer was concerned and about to recommend escalating public health advice on restrictions. Ryan would later pinpoint the key difference as Holohan's return. 'There was a sense that Tony would be slightly more upfront, Ronan would be sort of diplomatic,' the Green Party leader said. 'Tony's coming back in with both guns coming out of the holsters, bullets flying in every direction.'

Holohan had expected to get a call from Donnelly, but it did not come until the following morning, Sunday, 4 October. At 9.39 a.m., Donnelly decided that he probably should talk to Holohan and texted the CMO:

> Morning Tony. Could you let me know when NPHET is meeting today? Also, could you give me a call beforehand to get your thoughts. Thanks.

Holohan told Donnelly the meeting would be at midday. 'I'm free whenever suits you,' he wrote back.

Donnelly rang and the pair spoke for 20 minutes. 'Should I have called him on Saturday afternoon rather than Sunday morning?,' Donnelly mused, in the autumn of 2021. 'In fairness, if it happened now, I'd pick up the phone.' Holohan told him he was worried and explained why. 'I told him that I didn't think Level 3 was going to cut it,' he said later. 'I told him we were going to have to do something as a whole country but I didn't get drawn – and he didn't ask me – as to whether it was going [to] Level 4 or Level 5.'

However Donnelly's version of the phone call, which he would later explain in the Dáil, was that they discussed the current situation and the possibility of moving to Level 4. 'I conveyed my belief that it was important that NPHET adhere to the parameters set out in the framework for each level,' Donnelly told TDs. By this he meant that NPHET could not pick specific public health measures from different levels, it should stick to the framework in the *Living with Covid* plan.

Speaking a year later, Holohan said that at no point did Donnelly set parameters for the discussion which would take place at NPHET that day. 'I just wouldn't have accepted that,' he said. 'What he can't do is tell me the parameters of the advice that I have given. What he's entirely free to do is take the advice or not.'

As NPHET met that Sunday at midday there was no clear sense across government as to how urgent Holohan viewed the situation as being. The Taoiseach later recalled 'something [was] in the ether' that morning. But what was it? Level 4? Level 5? Eamon Ryan did not express much alarm when he popped up on the couch of RTÉ's *The Week in Politics*.

Asked directly by host Áine Lawlor, 'Are we looking at Level 4 restrictions?', Ryan responded, 'I hope we can avoid that, I think we're going to have to do everything to avoid that.' He said no circuit breaker lockdown was being considered, and insisted that if people began to reduce their contacts, the country could avoid going to Level 3 and Donegal and Dublin, which were already in Level 3, could avoid going to Level 4.

But Holohan had already told the health minister that morning that the situation was so grave that Level 3 would not be sufficient.

—

At the NPHET meeting, Holohan paid tribute to the 'excellent work' carried out by Glynn during his leave of absence before proceeding to, in effect, tear up the recommendation that NPHET had made under his deputy's chairmanship days earlier. Glynn was not bothered. In his view, Holohan was 'excellent' at making judgements on rapidly emerging evidence. 'If anyone ever asked me, would Tony back himself, I would say a hundred per cent,' Glynn later said.

The returning CMO was described by several of those at the meeting as strong from the outset on the need for a significant intervention, and that Level 3 wasn't enough. Mary Favier recalled that the one item on the agenda was to look at modelling and deterioration. 'The numbers weren't that different, but it's how you present them and put a tone against them. They were presented with much more urgency,' she said.

But the data was clearly worsening, rapidly and unexpectedly. In the three days since NPHET had met, there had been a 25 per cent increase in daily cases, a 27 per cent increase in the seven-day incidence rate, and hospitalisations had risen by a quarter over the previous week. '[When NPHET met on 1 October] we were on track for a further two thousand cases for that week. In other words, a stable, if very concerning, disease profile,' Glynn recalled. 'By that Sunday evening, we had three thousand cases in that seven days […] everything accelerated very quickly from Thursday to Sunday.'

Liam Woods, the director of the HSE's acute hospitals division, was always one of the most concerned at NPHET meetings, aware of the pressure a full-scale Covid wave would put on hospitals. Members recalled how on this occasion it was no different. The data showed that the average number of admissions to critical care had jumped from one per day on 29 September to two per day by 4 October.

While the official minutes do not record it, NPHET discussed the fact that 72 hours earlier it had recommended staying the course with Level 2 and some measures from Level 3. It was a radical change of tack. How would they justify this to the politicians? There was some discussion about moving through the levels incrementally, but the view – very firmly shared by Holohan and others in the room – was that that wouldn't be enough.

Consensus emerged around the need for 'proactive and robust measures'. 'We knew the disease was out of control. We knew the reproduction number was rising. We knew the level of intervention that was required to get it back down. We knew it was politically difficult to deliver,' Philip Nolan, NPHET's modelling chief, would later recall. But the recommendation that emerged was Level 5 for the next four weeks – and there was no dissent. 'Everybody realised we were in deep shit,' Nolan said.

The meeting concluded before 6 p.m. Holohan texted Donnelly to say that he would be available to brief him shortly. It would be the returning CMO's first briefing of the relatively new minister. The news would not be good. Around an hour later, a Zoom call was convened between Donnelly, O'Reardon, Holohan and Glynn, at which the Level 5 recommendation was relayed to Donnelly.

Donnelly informed the Taoiseach. 'I was annoyed,' Micheál Martin later said. He wondered how on earth the advice had changed in three days: 'The answer seems to me that a fresh pair of eyes came back – Tony came back – and looked at it differently.' But the Taoiseach thought NPHET was meant to be a team – 'it's not meant to be personality driven' – and later recalled, 'No one has satisfactorily explained to me how a body that's multidisciplinary arrives at a conclusion on a Thursday and then arrives at a very dramatically different escalation on the Sunday.'

He was not the only one struggling with the news. Leo Varadkar was at home; he was restricting his movements after being in close contact with a staff member who had tested positive. 'I was taken aback', he later recalled. He thought that, if the advice was going to change so dramatically in the space of three days, 'they would sit down with you and go through it'.

Finance minister Paschal Donohoe later recalled that he 'absolutely hit the roof' when he heard NPHET's proposal. He and public expenditure minister Michael McGrath were in the final stages of putting together their first budget, to be delivered nine days later. Now they were, in their view, being bounced into a lockdown – at a conservative cost to the State of €1bn for every month of harsh restrictions – with no prior notice. 'I think people were shocked and we weren't ready for it,' McGrath later said. 'That led to what happened in the following number of days.'

The reaction was more visceral elsewhere in Government Buildings. Martin Fraser got no heads-up and was annoyed about it. He would later be furious that the Level 5 recommendation ended up being leaked to the media. The structures he had set up in September alongside the *Living with Covid* plan included the Covid Oversight Group where the views of top NPHET officials were to be shared and discussed. He had expected that they would go up through the levels as set out in the plan. Now this structure appeared to have been rendered irrelevant by Holohan's desire to move fast. 'This is where we're at now. What the fuck are we going to do?' one colleague later recalled Fraser saying to them. The sense of shock that permeated the political system was palpable.

Could it have been avoided? Could the ground have been better prepared? Mary Favier later argued that it was the government's job to know – that the relationships should exist to enable 'clear and open communications' so there is 'no misunderstanding'. Holohan, she argued, had the skills and capability to communicate the importance of what was coming. 'It wouldn't be in his interest not to have done that,' she said. 'Someone should have told [the government]. Whose responsibility is it for that? That's the Minister for Health [...] the ultimate responsibility lies between Tony and Stephen Donnelly, and one of them cocked up.'

While this may imply that the fault lies with Donnelly, his position was that delaying nearly 24 hours before calling Holohan about the slide in the trajectory of the virus was not a big deal. In fact, it would annoy him that he had to answer questions in the Dáil about precisely what he knew, what he did and when. He viewed it as complete nonsense. 'We hadn't really worked together at this point,' Donnelly later said when asked if he could have handled it differently. 'It might have given us a few hours' more notice that a change in advice was being considered, which is better to know – though it wouldn't have changed anything in terms of the advice that came on Sunday.'

But others believed that time mattered. 'A day or two heads-up would have made all the difference between sounding composed and literally being completely on the back foot,' Paschal Donohoe would later admit. The Taoiseach was also clear that, if he had known on the Saturday the level of Holohan's concern, it would have made what followed easier.

But he does not blame Donnelly for that. 'NPHET, in retrospect, should have paused and slowed down,' Martin later said. 'I think it was the wrong way to go about it that weekend – and I said that to Tony. I think we should have been given a heads-up in relation to the enormous decision that was about to be made.'

Shock within the system soon spread to the general public. Initial reports were partial or partially accurate – that Level 3 was recommended or that undetermined 'tighter restrictions' were being called for nationwide. At 8.20 p.m. RTÉ's political correspondent Micheál Lehane broke the full story. 'NPHET recommend LEVEL 5 restrictions for entire country in letter to government. Party leaders set to seek meeting with the CMO tomorrow to discuss the recommendation,' he tweeted. Some in Cabinet were learning of the plan for the first time. 'A disgraceful leak,' one minister said via text. For months afterwards, senior figures in NPHET and government blamed each other for leaking news of the shock recommendation.

That Sunday night, as Lehane was imparting the 'strong political resistance' to the NPHET recommendation on RTÉ's *Nine O'Clock News*, Martin Fraser was emailing the Taoiseach with the HSE's daily operations update from acute hospitals. The PowerPoint, which had already been circulated to dozens of people in the health system, showed 215 confirmed or suspected Covid-19 cases in hospital with 36 confirmed or suspected cases in ICU. Not good, but not overwhelming. A counter-offensive against the recommendation was under way, and one of the anchors would be the situation in hospitals.

Data and conversations with hospital managers told Paul Reid one thing: hospitals were coping. He had relayed his views to the Taoiseach and he also spoke to the Tánaiste that weekend. He later said he had 'no sense' of a Level 5 being in the ether, or indeed being necessary. 'I wasn't there in terms of a Level 5 being required,' he said. The sudden recommendation shocked and annoyed him. No one had told the HSE chief executive that it was in the offing. 'I relayed my frustration: "I'm CEO of the HSE, is someone going to call me?" I was definitely annoyed […] jumping to that decision was wrong,' Reid would later say.

The HSE boss was also concerned about the societal impact of another lockdown and the future toll it could take on the health system. At 5.52 a.m. the following day, Reid woke up – he usually did at that hour – and tweeted, 'There's obvious concerns about the trends on #COVID19. But we also know the impacts of severe & regular restrictions in society on the public health, wellbeing, mental health and the economy. Level 5 recommendation to government has to be considered in this context too.' It was carefully phrased, but the subtext was obvious: Level 5 was a bridge too far.

The tweet set off alarm bells among some of Reid's HSE colleagues, who viewed it as an unhelpful intervention. NPHET members Colm Henry and Liam Woods told Reid that the data presented at the meeting had been compelling. Both were concerned that the projected increase in cases would leave hospitals at breaking point. 'I've seen those models and they're accurate in my view,' Woods told Reid, whose response was, 'How does that stand up from our hospitalisations? I can't rationalise it.'

Some HSE figures felt the tweet was wrong. In fact, such was the level of disquiet in the HSE over Reid's pre-dawn tweet that he was informally rebuked by members of the organisation's board over it. They believed it was a misjudged intervention or, as one board member described it, 'a fit of the mads'.

'He shouldn't have done it and it was a mistake. He seemed to be almost supporting a sort of party political position,' the board member said. The primary concern of many on the board, however, was that Reid's tweet could be used by the politicians to argue against the NPHET recommendation. They weren't wrong.

CHAPTER 20:

THE UGLIEST MEETING

5 October 2020
Cases: 38,032
Deaths: 1,810
Seven-day average of new cases: 453

From his home in Carpenterstown in west Dublin, Leo Varadkar, still restricting his movements, remotely joined a meeting in the Sycamore Room of Government Buildings. He wasn't happy.

'This is a bolt from the blue,' he told the three senior NPHET figures in the room. To Tony Holohan, Ronan Glynn and Philip Nolan, Varadkar's question was simple but devastating in equal measure: 'I want to know from each of you: do you accept government policy?'

It was a stinging criticism, and one that landed, particularly with Glynn. 'I hope I'm never asked that question again,' he said almost a year later. 'Where do you go from there?' Politicians asking civil servants if they, in effect, respect the power democratically vested in the political system is jarring. […] You begin to wonder if they have any understanding of what you're going through. They have a job to do, you have a job to do, and you're trying to do the best for the country in a situation unlike any that has gone before. You're not trying to further yourself for your own good. Yes, what you're saying is really difficult for them to hear. But what was the implication of a "no" there?'

The lines of communication and, more important, trust between the political system and its public health advisers had been damaged. The fallout from NPHET's sudden Level 5 recommendation echoed around the Sycamore Room. It would have implications for months to come.

—

The meeting had begun just after midday and was, one of its participants would later recall, 'the ugliest meeting I've ever been in – and I've been in some ugly meetings'. For over an hour, the NPHET representatives were subjected to 'an unbelievable level of bollocking […] kicked up and down the room' before being 'kicked out'.

Holohan sat at the top of the table. He drew most of the fire, with Glynn and Nolan sitting on chairs against the wall behind him. There was no welcome back for the chief medical officer after his leave of absence. The Taoiseach was annoyed and disappointed he had not been contacted by Holohan that weekend. 'I am the Taoiseach and you didn't even pick up the phone,' several participants recalled him saying. Martin is not sure that he did say that, but he did call Holohan the following day. 'I would have appreciated a heads-up,' he told the CMO.

In fact, some colleagues on NPHET had strongly urged Holohan to call the Taoiseach that weekend. But, defending his actions a year later, Holohan cited a clear line of reporting that he had adhered to. 'This was in effect my first real working engagement with the new minister, I wasn't going to go around back of the scrum, past a new minister with whom I hadn't established relations and say, "Well, to hell with you, I am talking to the Taoiseach."'

But that Monday afternoon, any such excuses found little favour with the angry politicians. At one stage in his response to the Taoiseach, Holohan was, in the view of Paschal Donohoe, equivocating. So the normally mild-mannered finance minister intervened: 'Sorry, Tony, that man is the Taoiseach of this country and you do not talk to him like that.' The level of Donohoe's anger struck many participants. Donohoe is hardly docile, but he is usually even-tempered. On that day he was furious.

Holohan tried to weather the onslaught. From his perspective it was more important to impress upon the politicians the need to get control of the virus. But the barrage kept coming, chiefly from Varadkar and Donohoe. The meeting, Micheál Martin later recalled, was 'hot and heavy'.

Varadkar criticised Nolan's models, pointing out that they had been wrong in April and May, when they had predicted 16,000 deaths, and argued that NPHET's assessment that hospitals faced being imminently overwhelmed was not shared by the HSE's chief executive. Reid's tweet, along with his private briefings to the Taoiseach and others in government that weekend, were now being used in exactly the way some in the HSE had feared.

A year later, Holohan was still scornful of Reid's intervention. 'It's a little bit like the tidal wave; if you judge whether the tidal wave is coming on the basis of how sunny it appears on the beach when you're waiting for it, you're going to misjudge it,' he said. 'On that day I don't think an assessment that everything was okay was a safe assessment.'

Glynn, meanwhile, believed that Reid's tweet focused on the situation in hospitals as it stood then. 'That wasn't the basis of our advice or the basis upon which decisions needed to be made,' he said of NPHET's recommendation. 'It wasn't about what was going to happen today or tomorrow, it was the trajectory we were on and how quickly the situation was likely to deteriorate in the days and weeks ahead.'

Back in the Sycamore Room that day, Varadkar asked for reassurance that four weeks of, what he would later publicly describe as, a 'circuit breaker' lockdown would be enough: what would happen if it didn't work? Would it be credible to keep the schools open during those four weeks? What should the government say to the 400,000 people who faced becoming unemployed once the lockdown was implemented? 'None of us were happy about just being in the position that we were being put in,' Varadkar would later admit.

Michael McGrath questioned why NPHET's advice on Sunday had changed so dramatically since the previous Thursday. In particular, McGrath felt that restrictions on household visits – as recommended days earlier by NPHET – should be given sufficient time to work. 'Going from Level 2 to Level 5 was a very big jump and people aren't expecting this,' he said.

For some time, McGrath, an austere but friendly and politically astute TD from Carrigaline in County Cork, had harboured concerns about NPHET's modelling. As far back as September, he had argued at meetings with colleagues for the need to have the modelling interrogated or, more specifically, peer-reviewed.

After all, the politicians were making decisions impacting hundreds of thousands of jobs, costing hundreds of millions of euros, and they were taking the modelling at face value. Some of them may have understood – or claimed to understand – the graphs and charts presented to them almost every week. But some felt they were being bamboozled with dozens of slides and complex graphs, often projected on to a wall or a screen that was difficult to see.

The NPHET response to the furious politicians, communicated almost exclusively by Holohan that day, was that the focus had to be on getting case numbers back under control and down to around one hundred per day. Otherwise, restrictions would be recommended for a longer period. But none of what Holohan responded with landed favourably with the politicians.

Despite the clear backlash, he was unwavering in his view. 'Can we not go to Level 3 or Level 4?' McGrath later recalled asking. He felt that there was 'not a great difference between Level 4 and Level 5 in many ways, but no, he [Tony Holohan] was adamant that was his view, that was NPHET's view and that was it.' Holohan was dug in. The politicians floated compromise positions: could Dublin or Donegal be put in Level 5? Would Level 4 do it? No. The advice was the advice.

Having borne the brunt of the government's anger on what was officially his first day back at work – Holohan was, in the words of one participant, 'savaged' – he and his two colleagues were asked to leave the room.

The relationship between the government and its public health advisers had reached its lowest point. Now critical decisions were being taken by the coalition, with the doctors outside the room, their advice disregarded. 'I think there was an agreement in the room that we wouldn't accept the advice, that it was that we were being forced into something,' Eamon Ryan later said.

The consensus among the politicians was that the country could not go from Level 2 to Level 5 in one fell swoop. Instead, the entire country would move to Level 3 for a period of three weeks. The decision was rubber-stamped by the Cabinet that evening. The government was now taking public health decisions without public health advice.

For NPHET, it had been a diplomatic disaster – and it was about to get a lot worse.

—

Addressing the nation that night, Taoiseach Micheál Martin attempted to explain why NPHET's advice was being rejected. Businesses and public health services were recovering; 'Severe restrictions now would have a very damaging impact, which those services and businesses may not be able to recover from,' he said from the rostrum at the front of Government Buildings.

As Martin spoke, Leo Varadkar was making his way out to RTÉ's television studios in Donnybrook for an interview with Claire Byrne. He had an altogether different mindset. 'I knew that rejecting their advice would be a problem for us politically, that the public would be divided. Some would agree with us and some wouldn't. And my objective in going there was to defend and explain the government decision,' he later recalled.

That may have been the objective, but his earlier fury at NPHET did not appear to have abated by the time he went on air; and that sober-minded explanation of his motivations, at a remove of just over a year, didn't come across that evening.

As Varadkar gave his interview, Stephen Donnelly was at a press conference in Government Buildings, insisting that relations with NPHET were 'absolutely fine'. But Pat Leahy, the political editor of the *Irish Times*, had to point out to the health minister that Varadkar was telling a different story to viewers of RTÉ One.

'I think what happened the last couple of days wasn't good for anyone, wasn't good for NPHET, isn't good for government, and really wasn't good for the Irish people, many of whom were worried sick today wondering whether they had a job tomorrow, wondering whether they were shuttering their business for the last time,' Varadkar told Byrne.

'So, we thought that this is not the right way to do things, land something like this on a Sunday night, without prior consultation, without being able to answer very basic questions.' The recommendation of a 'circuit breaker', he said, was not something that had not been 'thought through'.

But in his most cutting remark, Varadkar pointed to the membership of NPHET, 'all coming from medical or scientific or civil service backgrounds'. None of those people, he said, 'would have faced being on the pandemic unemployment payment yesterday', when they made the Level 5 recommendation, and 'none of them would have to tell somebody that they were losing their job'.

It was a stunning attack. The deputy head of government, the man who had been Taoiseach during the first wave and had, publicly at least, stuck to and implemented public health advice, was now systematically taking apart NPHET recommendations on live television. What's more, he was questioning whether they really understood what the public were contending with.

Sitting at home watching the programme, Ronan Glynn was very annoyed by this assertion in particular, given that his own family has a catering business, Glynn's Fruit and Veg, that stood to be impacted by any decision to lockdown. Some senior members of NPHET wondered if their positions were tenable, while seasoned officials wondered if Holohan would resign. (Holohan, typically intractable, never considered it.) One senior NPHET member suggested to a colleague that they would love to resign and, in the process of doing so, cite Varadkar as the key element undermining public health advice. A discussion between some senior NPHET members about publicly hitting back at Varadkar ensued over text and WhatsApp. 'We won't be able to stay silent on this,' one senior figure texted another. There were also some more concise and earthier dismissals of the Tánaiste. The idea of hitting back publicly withered on the vine.

At home in Terenure, Tony Holohan watched the interview with his wife and daughter. Holohan does not typically watch news or current affairs on TV, relying on the Department of Health's press office to keep him abreast of who is saying what. The TV goes on when there is sport or Netflix to watch. But he watched Varadkar's interview with an overriding concern that his wife, in the circumstances she was in with her cancer diagnosis, had to witness such an unprecedented attack by the deputy leader of the country on a group of civil servants led by her husband.

Before concluding his interview, Varadkar offered a chilly vote of confidence. 'I have confidence in NPHET to dispense public health advice. That's what they do. They don't advise the public; they advise the government and the government decided,' Varadkar told Claire Byrne, who could scarcely believe that the Tánaiste had gone as far as he had. 'It didn't help, if I can put it that way,' Holohan later said of Varadkar's interview.

Mary Favier believed that Varadkar's intervention ensured that the relationship between government and NPHET was 'never the same again', describing the intervention as the 'dividing line'. It was, she said, 'a very clear deterioration for everyone on NPHET, a wariness, a real sense you have to be careful here. [...] Members of NPHET were just furious he would use that language, that he would be so unprofessional, basically have a tantrum and try and take down the CMO in the middle of a pandemic [...] it damaged Leo Varadkar's reputation in the medical fraternities significantly.'

A year later, Varadkar expressed some regret over what he said that night. 'What I meant to say is that all of us around the table are essentially public servants. I used the wrong words,' he said. But in October 2020, with cases rising, the government was now in a new phase of its pandemic response. It was making decisions that were fundamentally at odds with the advice of its top medical advisers.

The doctors had left the room.

CHAPTER 21:

LOCKDOWN

11 October 2020
Cases: 42,528
Deaths: 1,826
Seven-day average of new cases: 643

Leo Varadkar feared the government had made the wrong decision to reject a second lockdown. Six days after excoriating NPHET on prime time television, the Tánaiste wrote in the *Sunday Independent* that a 'short, hard lockdown' or a 'circuit breaker', as he had taken to calling it, would be needed to reduce Covid-19 cases. Varadkar said that it 'breaks my heart' to think of a second lockdown, but increasingly that appeared to be the direction of travel.

The Tánaiste had spent the week being kicked around by the opposition in the Dáil, with Sinn Féin's Pearse Doherty telling him he 'took the legs from under our chief medical officer'. Varadkar maintained he never 'said a bad word' about Holohan on television that Monday, but he had already sought to make amends. The day after the Sycamore Room showdown he called Holohan. 'I didn't mean to say it that way,' he told the chief medical officer.

While some in the Department of Health wondered at that time whether the CMO was about to resign, Holohan never considered it, believing that to do so would have been a dereliction of his duty. 'He made contact with me, to be fair, and set up a conversation in which he first asked me about my wife, and then went on to talk about the interview,' Holohan later said of the phone call. 'We had a straight-up conversation and my objective, to be honest with you, was to facilitate the ongoing functioning of the relationship.'

Varadkar's dovish turn and contemplation of another lockdown was not a view shared by other ministers. A week after the row with NPHET, Paschal Donohoe and Michael McGrath delivered the tripartite coalition's first budget. Forced to make their speeches in the temporary Dáil in the Dublin Convention Centre – hired at the considerable cost of up to €25,000 per day to ensure that TDs could social distance – McGrath announced that the spending taps were remaining on.

There was a budget package of €8.5bn just to deal with Covid-19, alongside a recovery fund of €3.4bn. The deficit was forecast to balloon in 2021, but in truth neither minister had any clarity about what sort of financial situation they would be facing in the coming twelve months. They were spending huge amounts of money amid unprecedented uncertainty. Donohoe's mindset at the time was, he would later state, 'If I've an idea of where I am going to be next month … I would actually be over the moon about that.'

The drumbeat for lockdown, however, grew as case loads increased. On 14 October, two days after the budget, with the rate of disease worsening, the government decided to move the border counties of Cavan, Donegal and Monaghan into Level 4 restrictions, while the rest of the country was to remain in Level 3 but with a ban on indoor household visits. The Taoiseach was, colleagues recalled, becoming increasingly nervous. Throughout October he had aired his belief that hospitality and Covid did not mix. He was particularly explicit on this at a pre-budget meeting with the party leaders and McGrath and Donohoe on 12 October in Government Buildings. 'I don't think hospitality is compatible with Covid,' he told the meeting.

Five days later, on the afternoon of Saturday, 17 October, the Taoiseach chaired the meeting of the Cabinet subcommittee on Covid-19. It ran late into the evening and once again the location was the Sycamore

Room, a hybrid digital and in-person affair. In sharp contrast to the ructions twelve days earlier, the mood was sombre as ministers began to accept the inevitable.

On the table was another Level 5 recommendation, issued the day after the government banned household visits. The message was clear: 'You haven't gone far enough, you didn't move soon enough.' This time, the recommendation was for six weeks instead of four.

During the meeting Varadkar was conspicuously conciliatory, even complimenting the modelling work NPHET had done, work that he had previously savaged. His temporary conversion from hawk to dove on matters Covid was clear to others present, who believed the Tánaiste had formed the view he had overreached, been too harsh on NPHET, and created a personal political vulnerability for himself.

The NPHET team, led by Holohan, ran through a stark picture. The last time, they hadn't been able to even get through their presentation – the bollocking had got in the way. The short version of the slides was that things had been bad in early October, and they were worse now.

McGrath, who had wanted a peer review of Philip Nolan's work, asked detailed questions about how his models were structured. He teased out whether there was a variation of Level 5 where you allowed retail shops to open, noting that tens of thousands of retail workers were going to lose their jobs overnight. McGrath and Donohoe both believed that there was no real Covid-19 dividend from closing non-essential retail shops, believing that, with safety measures like mask-wearing and distancing, there was little evidence to show they were driving infections.

While the meeting was generally cordial, at one point a frustrated Donohoe took Paul Reid to task. The HSE boss had presented a paper on hospital capacity that, to the minister's mind, appeared at odds with what NPHET was saying about the hospital system's capacity to cope. 'I don't know what this is telling me,' he told Reid, holding up his paper. 'Can we join the dots here?' Reid thought it was unusual for Donohoe to intervene in such a manner, but the minister was reflecting frustration over mixed messages.

Once again the NPHET members in the room were concerned by what they were hearing from the HSE chief executive. Glynn was said by colleagues to have found it 'incredibly frustrating' that NPHET were asked questions where precise and accurate answers were expected, whereas the HSE appeared to get away with more vague answers. There were times when the HSE CEO had a different view of the world – different from even those senior HSE figures, such as Colm Henry and Liam Woods, who sat on NPHET.

The meeting adjourned without a formal decision to lock down – that would follow on Monday, when Cabinet formally approved the imposition of Level 5 restrictions from that Thursday, 22 October. Eighteen days earlier, on 4 October, when Level 5 was first recommended, the five-day average case count was 462. On 15 October, when NPHET again reiterated its Level 5 advice, the five-day average was 946 per day. By 22 October, it was 1,205 per day. 'I often think too much is made of it when you look at the totality of the pandemic,' Martin said over a year later in late November 2021. 'That's 300 to 1,200 cases; we're at a couple of thousand now and now we have vaccination, everything is relative to what came after that.'

The lockdown probably avoided a truly damaging wave in November, but cases never got down to the level envisaged. Almost a year later, Holohan suggested that the delay was part of the reason for this. 'We were 400 or 500 case numbers a day on the fourth of October when we said Level 5 for four weeks. Who knows where we would have gotten to with that, because we didn't follow that road,' he said.

Holohan argued that bringing in Level 5 later in the month, when cases were at 1,200 per day, meant they could never get to a low enough level by the start of December. 'We could have had a much better controlled situation early in December if we had moved in October as NPHET had recommended,' he said.

But Holohan's view sidesteps the fact that NPHET did clearly dangle the prospect of a significant and relatively smooth relaxation of restrictions at Christmas. Holohan's presentation to the Cabinet subcommittee that day clearly outlined how a six-week lockdown could get the virus under control.

The coalition leaders, ministers, advisers and civil servants were shown Philip Nolan's latest modelling which outlined that if the R number (the reproductive rate of the virus) was reduced to 0.5 for that long, 'we will be under two hundred cases per day' by the end of November. That in turn would open the door to relaxing restrictions such that the reproductive rate could rise to 1.4 without the disease spiralling out of control. Case numbers would rise – they always did when restrictions were loosened – but if that course could be maintained, the NPHET presentation stated, 'We will have only 200 cases per day by end-December.'

What's more, the presentation outlined the plan for the new year, where cases were projected to rise to 300 per day, but an unspecified 'intervention' (i.e. new restrictions) lasting two weeks from 2 January would bring cases down again to fewer than 100 per day.

This was the Christmas playbook, outlined in a presentation with Holohan's name on it in the middle of October. It wasn't a promise – clearly not – but the putative bargain that was offered is clear in the slides the politicians were shown. The blueprint for a meaningful Christmas – lock down, relax, lock down again – was put on the table that day.

While accepting the need to lock down, even that NPHET presentation seemed overly cautious to some in the room. Ministers did not, publicly at least, agree with the idea of getting the reproductive rate as low as 0.5 and cases hovering in the 100s.

Instead the lockdown was seen as a trade-off to the public: do this for six weeks and we can open up at Christmas. As he announced the Level 5 restrictions, the Taoiseach delivered a clear message that if people 'pulled together over the next six weeks we will have the opportunity to celebrate Christmas in a meaningful way'.

Asked at the press conference held afterwards what would happen after the six-week lockdown, the Taoiseach was clear: 'We want to go to Level 3, straight up. That's where the government wants to go on the first of December.'

—

As October turned to November, the country settled into a second, bleaker lockdown as colder, wetter weather and darker evenings ensured the novelty of the spring 2020 lockdown was long forgotten.

The focus of the political world shifted elsewhere, most notably to the significant fallout from revelations, published in *Village* magazine at the end of October, that Leo Varadkar had given a confidential government document outlining a GP pay deal agreed with the Irish Medical Organisation to his friend Maitiú Ó Tuathail, the head of a rival GP organisation.

The story had significant consequences for Varadkar, who survived a Dáil motion of no confidence in November but later found himself the subject of a criminal investigation that stretched into 2022. Micheál Martin backed his coalition partner but there was significant disquiet among coalition ministers over the affair.

Tensions were not just confined to the political arena. They were also evident at NPHET, where a long-running dispute about a key element of the State's management of the pandemic came to a head.

Along with Holohan and his top lieutenants, the HSE's chief clinical officer, Colm Henry, had become one of the most recognisable faces of the pandemic. A Cavan native and Gaelgoir, Henry has boundless energy and an expansive recall of film and literary references, often peppering his conversations with references to anyone from Gore Vidal to Oscar Wilde to Shakespeare. He totes a briefcase full of work materials, supplemented occasionally by back issues of the *New Yorker*. Henry lives in Cork, but while working in Dublin during the week he stays at the Stephen's Green Club, a private members' club on the north-west side of the city centre park.

Although not personally close, Holohan and Henry had known each other for three decades – the CMO was at UCD with Henry's sister. Their relationship had frayed over the pandemic and they had clashed over the Level 5 recommendation in October. Henry believed that Holohan had mishandled NPHET's communication to government and had told him as much in a testy phone call afterwards.

Weeks later, the issue was the Contact Management Programme (CMP). Since almost the beginning of the pandemic, test and trace had been industrialised by Niamh O'Beirne and her massed ranks of contact tracers in the CMP. Public health is an intricate discipline, taking in broader factors than the corporeal or clinical concerns doctors usually specialise in – epidemiology, screening programmes, and how disease and populations interact.

Holohan, who himself is a public health physician, had a long-standing view that contact tracing was something best done by public health departments around the country. But for the HSE, this was a view that might be correct in theory, but was divorced from the reality on the ground. Henry's team saw that the doctors in these divisions were exhausted and suffering from historic underinvestment.

There were also wider frustrations. Holohan felt that the key faces of the HSE's response to the pandemic did not include a single public health expert – Reid, Henry, O'Beirne and Chief Operations Officer Anne O'Connor were the main voices for the group. 'There's seventy or eighty public health doctors in the HSE and none of them are regularly pushed out to speak,' Holohan later said. 'That's the reality; we've been behind the scenes asking them to build capacity and intelligence in public health and there's been real resistance.' The HSE's public health function had 'effectively been demobilised' during the pandemic, Holohan said.

There was also a long-standing suspicion among senior NPHET members that Reid was leaning heavily on Henry and other HSE members of the group, who found themselves in the firing line whenever it produced a recommendation the HSE didn't like. As a member of NPHET and one of the top people in the HSE, Henry had one foot in the policy-making camp and the other in the operational side. He could also find himself navigating the choppy waters between Holohan and Reid, and the HSE and the department. All these tensions played out in the conflict over who should run contact tracing.

At one virtual NPHET meeting in late 2020, Henry outlined his work in a paper about the future of the CMP. Holohan, supported by Philip Nolan, pushed back against what he was saying. The whole affair was hampered by poor internet connections, but Henry felt that he wasn't being heard. He snapped, 'I am the chief clinical officer of the HSE, you must allow me to speak.' He was doing his best, and he expected support and collaboration, he said. Henry was furious and, as one source later recalled, would have walked out had the meeting been held in person (although he did stay on the call). It was, one NPHET member later said, 'the single biggest breakdown of a relationship' among the public health emergency team.

Word of the clash reached Paul Reid. 'I was mighty pissed off about it and wanted to take it off him [Henry] and wanted to deal with it,' the HSE chief executive later recalled. But Henry was wary of the row becoming a proxy for other turf wars, and wanted it to be sorted between himself and Holohan. 'He was adamant that he wanted to deal with this,' Reid said. 'He was adamant that he should not have been spoken to in the way he was spoken to at the meeting.'

From then on Henry became less active on NPHET calls. People on NPHET felt he also withdrew – or was withdrawn – from press conferences, but there was in truth no direct link. Other HSE people, ironically including public health doctors, were put forward instead. The Holohan–Henry row receded and the pair continued to speak, but the underlying tensions remained.

CHAPTER 22:

1 GOVERNMENT CENTRE

12 November 2020
Cases: 66,632
Deaths: 1,965
Seven-day average of new cases: 369

T he lockdown appeared to be working, but the public health team had already begun to manage expectations. Philip Nolan told the *Business Post* in early November of the need for tight restrictions right into Christmas. 'We are going to have to put pretty strict limits on the extent to which people can get together over Christmas,' he told the paper's reporter Rachel Lavin. 'That's a big thing to ask of people, but what it affords us is the possibility of a spring without escalating public health restrictions. That's the trade-off.'

The interview did not go down well in government. Days later Martin Fraser and Robert Watt both tackled Nolan at a meeting of the Covid Oversight Group. Watt reminded the public health officials of their obligations under the civil service code not to speak to the media. Fraser pointed out that only the chief medical officer was authorised to hold media briefings. It was not just Nolan who was the subject of disquiet in Government Buildings.

Mary Favier appeared on *Morning Ireland* on 16 November urging caution about reopening and also remarking, 'We'll need to have a cautious approach as to how alcohol is used over the next few weeks.' This sort of intervention 'pissed off' the government, one senior official later recalled. 'You can't have it both fucking ways, you can't be a trusted adviser when, before you give advice, you're going on *Morning Ireland*,' they said.

Eamon Ryan acknowledged that public pronouncements by NPHET – 'doing press conferences, writing letters, very much in the public space' – were a source of tension. 'There would be a sense in government that NPHET's public persona is pushing government in a certain direction or has huge influence on what you can or can't do.'

Many in government also suspected that the people making these media outings – especially Favier – were Holohan outriders sent on a mission to soften up the ministers and civil servants. However, this wasn't the case. Some were genuine solo runs, which Holohan and Deirdre Watters, the head of the Department of Health press office, subtly tried to control, raising them in meetings, offering guidance and assistance.

In some ways, Holohan was closer to the frustrations of the political side than they may have realised. 'If there were people pissed off in government, they were kind of entitled to be pissed off about it, I was pissed off about it myself,' he said about the solo runs and leaks from NPHET meetings. As time wore on, many media appearances and social media forays were carefully planned by the Department of Health press office.

In truth, frustrations about who said what on radio or in the newspapers were just symptoms of a wider problem. The trust between the government and NPHET was gone and everywhere there was suspicion. Nowhere was this more obvious than in misgivings over the numbers on which vital decisions were being based. As far as some in government were concerned, NPHET's mastery of data and modelling gave them the upper hand, setting the tempo for discussions. At the height of the mistrust between government and NPHET, some officials believed the public health team was withholding data from the political side, and they felt they were playing catch-up in key meetings.

There was a growing feeling that an imbalance between the role of NPHET and the role of government had to be addressed. As one public service veteran puts it, 'In our world, the person who writes the memo, who has the PowerPoint, who has the data – they're the most powerful person in the room.'

The coalition was not going to be bounced by virtue of not having analysis to back up its side. Ministers may not always have understood what they were being shown on the screen, but they understood power. Next time they would have their own bank of stats and graphs.

—

Since he first approached Nolan in March 2020, the power to frame the pandemic response with statistically backed arguments had rested with Holohan. Models and their outputs moved to the centre of the entire Covid-19 discussion over the course of the second lockdown.

There was a conscious effort on the government side to copper-fasten its arguments. One insider dubbed it the 'battle of the spreadsheets'. The Central Statistics Office (CSO), the Department of Finance and others were all asked to contribute, but so too were outside consultants. What emerged was an almost Orwellian plan, bizarrely dubbed 1 Government Centre (1GC).

The idea was hatched by the consultancy firm EY, whose managing partner Frank O'Keeffe excitedly emailed Martin Fraser, Liz Canavan and other officials in the Department of the Taoiseach in early October. O'Keeffe declared that he and his EY partners 'have spent the past 24 hours thinking through the art of the possible'. In emails over the weeks that followed, the chiefs of staff of the three government leaders were all looped into the discussions of the project, which mapped out a dizzying surveillance architecture plucked straight from a dystopian novel.

 Discussion documents circulated to government outlined a 'consol-idated view of performance and directing activities' that would 'direct the cross-government response' including 'compliance enforcement', 'tax and welfare interventions' and 'targeted Eircode interventions'. Some of the putative inputs were downright creepy: a section on surveillance suggested the 'use of computer vision on CCTV to assess location com-pliance to social distancing. Direct enforcement activities to address.'

The consultancy firm pitched a 'social distancing index' that provided a 'rolling 15-minute assessment' of people's adherence to the two-metre rule using 'mobile data from citizens who have registered for specific apps to count phones in 25m tiles [on a map] every 15 minutes'.

EY told the Department of the Taoiseach that users could 'anticipate potential concentrations that would need action to prevent pandemic spread'. It mapped out how there was a 'wealth of data available with varying ease to access and privacy concerns'. More than two dozen data sources were identified, including citizen location and movement, credit score and lending by customer type and region, use of mental health and counselling, public and private CCTV, Central Bank credit register debt levels, and government worker absenteeism.

A spreadsheet outlined the public health restrictions and what data types and sources could be used to monitor the public's adherence to the rules. Mobile data from Three Ireland would be among the most commonly used, along with contact tracing information from the HSE. Event plans and lists from Facebook, and eat-in versus takeaway spending data from AIB, the Central Bank and Visa would also be collected and analysed.

The most innocuous potential breaches could be monitored, including mining data from Libraries Ireland to inspect whether a restriction that libraries were to be available for online services only was being implemented, with the number of online users compared to pre-restriction numbers to be examined. Spending data from point of sale machines and cross-border spending patterns could be used to analyse whether people were staying within 5km of their home.

The government was told there should be a 'war room' set up to co-ordinate efforts, and there are indications that such a setting was established in Room 350 in Government Buildings, with subsequent briefing materials including photographs of it.

The EY team were also corresponding with a vast array of state and non-state actors over the project, the briefing materials show, including the CSO, the Department of Health, the HSE, the Revenue Commissioners, the Department of Social Protection, the Gardaí, the Central Bank, the National Transport Authority, AIB, Visa and 3Mobile.

Many of the measures seem to have been substantially a consultancy's fever dream. A government spokesperson said the social-distance index did not progress, but, they said, information from a variety of sources, including the 1GC programme, had been used as part of the process of introducing restrictions. The 1GC programme draws together 'existing data outputs' from publicly available sources, they said. Senior sources insisted none of the more intrusive methods were ever used: 'We never did anything Orwellian.' However, outputs from EY's analysis continued to form part of pandemic planning in the department in 2022.

But some of EY's data-crunching was later summarised in a presentation to the Cabinet subcommittee on Covid-19 on 26 November. It concluded that the introduction of the effective ban on household visits from mid-October drove a reduction in cases across most counties and that the reopening of construction and non-essential retail over the summer did not have a material impact on the 14-day incidence rate of the disease.

It confirmed what some in government had started to believe: that it was not Level 5 that had made a difference but the ban on household visits. All the lockdown had done was cause widespread economic damage and devastation at a combined cost to the exchequer of some €1.5bn and rising.

Michael McGrath believed it, so did his secretary general, Robert Watt, and so did Paschal Donohoe. All three and others were loath to implement severe restrictions that would cripple the economy and force the State to spend over €1bn per month keeping thousands of businesses and employees on life support. The view was not confined to those in the finance ministries. 'In my mind that CSO analysis, that EY analysis, was important,' Eamon Ryan later said – in particular what CSO research showed about the impact of lockdowns on mental health.

EY's work, however, did not impress Holohan or his officials. Nolan and the CSO's Padraig Dalton had been looped into the 1GC discussions and its wider work. In one meeting on 12 October, Nolan stressed the need to ensure that EY's work on the health aspect of the data gathering did not circumnavigate the existing line of command. It was now clear that NPHET was concerned about what impact this would have on the government accepting or not accepting their advice.

In person, they were blunt. Following a rushed presentation of the EY data at the Department of Health one morning, Holohan told Liz Canavan, 'This is a load of horseshite.' Philip Nolan would later recall that the analyses were 'incredibly naive' and that the senior NPHET members had told the Taoiseach's officials, 'That stuff is just toxic.' Ironically, in the final EY presentation, some points would chime with NPHET's outlook on risks around restaurants and holiday periods. In fact, EY's data-crunching had identified as far back as September that indoor hospitality was a problem with the spread of Covid-19 cases.

Holohan was alarmed. As far as he was concerned, this was a con- certed attempt to get more data inputs, but it was being done by people who did not understand the nature of an infectious disease. He would later state that EY 'are not epidemiologists, they are crunching data, their interpretations. We weren't impressed.' The chief medical officer recalled that he saw it as the government's clear intention to ensure 'they wouldn't be boxed into one particular view of things'.

Stephen Donnelly, meanwhile, thought the decision to bring EY on board was a very good move. The health minister valued the outside con- sultants' input; it was the kind of thing he liked to see, and he wanted to see more of it. Though not familiar with the 1GC initiative, as a general rule the former McKinsey consultant and self-described 'data guy' believed the more data the better. EY were Stephen Donnelly's type of people.

In autumn 2020, Donnelly was brought into Dr Steevens' Hospital, the HSE headquarters, for a meeting with public health doctors. The idea was to give him an in-depth briefing on what it is public health doctors do – the shoe-leather epidemiology that was a key part of controlling the pandemic. Two sources present said later that it was a really positive meeting, but towards the end, a public health doctor made a contribution. The doctor was vastly experienced, having worked on Ebola breakouts in Africa, and was now working on Covid outbreaks on halting sites in Ireland. He mentioned a piece of modelling technology, a fancy bit of kit that, theoretically, could help manage disease.

It was far removed from the reason Donnelly had been brought to the meeting, which was to give him an insight into the real, on-the-ground problems public health doctors were facing. 'And suddenly, Donnelly fucking seized on it,' one source recalled – models, technology, these were things we needed in Ireland, he said.

The doctor responded: look Minister, it's really interesting, but that's not where we're at. This is on the ground, grinding it out, there's no magic bullet here. 'And you could see Donnelly desperate for a magic bullet. But he missed all the humanity in the room,' said a source present. 'It was so divorced from what he just heard,' said another person present, which was 'a human angle, which was then to be neutralised by McKinsey'. A spokesperson for Donnelly later said the minister 'is aware that there are no silver bullets when it comes to the Covid-19 pandemic'.

Later, in mid-November, the minister called Philip Nolan and told him he had been impressed with his analyses but, as far as he was concerned, the data he was getting from NPHET was just linear data. It was just graphs; counting things up like case numbers and hospitalisations. It was all very useful, Donnelly believed, but he felt much more could be done.

Big data and artificial intelligence might yield deeper insights as to where the disease was spreading, Donnelly argued, and he was going to try to take it further. He had been talking to one of his counterparts in Australia who told him they had deployed artificial intelligence to their Covid-19 data to find patterns that human analysis would not. He felt this could all be used to target government policy responses. It was a view he repeatedly articulated in meetings with NPHET and Department of Health officials.

Donnelly convened a meeting on 20 November to discuss whether insights could be gained from big data, artificial intelligence and machine learning to suppress the virus as much as possible while minimising the societal and economic cost. But ultimately it was concluded that data-sets related to Ireland were messy, or 'antiquated' as Donnelly took to calling them.

The minister was disappointed but undeterred in his near-constant demand for data and information from his officials to inform his approach to the pandemic. He had spent one Sunday afternoon in the middle of October poring over graphs on hospital admissions, discharges and critical care patients, summarising what the data told him in an email to the Taoiseach and his chief of staff, Deirdre Gillane. 'Averages may be slightly off as reading figures from graphs,' he wrote.

Typically, a minister would delegate this sort of work to officials, but Donnelly's predilection for data-crunching was emblematic of a different way of doing business. Sometimes it led to ideas that were original and worthwhile, but it could also, some people felt, lead him down blind alleyways. They feared it distracted him from appreciating how issues played politically.

While not related to Covid-19, an example of this came in late 2020 at a meeting with finance minister Paschal Donohoe about the spiralling costs and delayed timelines at the National Children's Hospital, which had become a budgetary nightmare and a noose around the government's neck.

Donnelly saw the issue as one of time and money. 'How you match up money and time is how you get a solution on this,' he told a meeting of senior ministers and officials on the children's hospital issue. But the health minister had missed one other important element: for a politician, he seemed not to register how voters would feel about the fiasco. 'Politics,' Donohoe, the veteran minister, reminded his colleague, 'the politics of this are disastrous for the government.' Donnelly was many things, but as his time in office went on, many in government harboured doubts about his instincts, his natural feel for politics.

CHAPTER 23:

LEVEL FUN

25 November 2020
Cases: 71,187
Deaths: 2,033
Seven-day average of new cases: 304

The NPHET meeting went on for over eight hours. It was so long one member went to the dentist, while continuing to listen to proceedings on their earphones.

At the start of the month, some officials in the Department of Health had been talking about 'Level Fun', an amalgam of the various levels with some restrictions still in place over Christmas but enough freedom for people to enjoy themselves. But the sharp decline in daily case rates at the start of November stalled as the month wore on.

On 19 November, Holohan had told a press conference that people had 'slipped' in adhering to the lockdown. At the NPHET meeting held earlier that day, Cillian De Gascun posed the question of whether Level 5 should be extended into December. Some members agreed, asking whether a proposed move to Level 3 should take place later in December.

Something had to be identified for Christmas, something that would work, both politically and in relation to the disease. As a crunch point approached, the newspapers were awash with speculation about reopening. By the time of its eight-hour meeting on 25 November there was a strong view among NPHET members against reopening hospitality. But some at the meeting noted the perception of a social contract with the public, who believed six weeks of Level 5 would result in a 'more open, normal Christmas'. The HSE raised concerns that some of the options being discussed would fall short of the public's expectations.

NPHET ultimately concluded that hospitality should remain closed for another two months, recommending an 'enhanced Level 3', allowing visits to private homes from one other household – a maximum of six people – from 2 December, with this increasing to six visitors from up to three other households for a two-week period over Christmas.

'If some element of hospitality is retained,' Tony Holohan wrote in his letter to Stephen Donnelly that day, 'the NPHET is of the view that the recommended easing of measures with regard to household mixing over the two-week festive period as set out above could not also be retained.'

The following day, 26 November, politicians, civil servants and their senior public health advisers gathered across two rooms in Government Buildings, joined by a video link, to decide on how – not if – they could reopen the country over the festive period. Paschal Donohoe was in no doubt about what was needed as Christmas approached, laying down a marker early. 'This is costing too much,' the finance minister told the meeting of the Cabinet subcommittee on Covid-19.

Donohoe was concerned that if the country did not move out of lockdown over December it faced being under harsh restrictions right into 2021. That was untenable. He later described 'a real sense that if we didn't try to make a real move out of lockdown at that point and moderate the public health measures in some way [...] we were going to be in a state of semi-permanent Level 5 throughout the entire Christmas period and into the new year'.

The meeting heard from Paul Reid, EY and the CSO. NPHET was privately scathing about both the EY and CSO presentations. Philip Nolan, whose models were suddenly not the gospel they had been hitherto, pointed out in his presentation that the effect of restrictions on household visits, introduced on 15 October, was 'not knowable'. It was a deliberate attempt to push back at EY's analysis and the view among the politicians that this measure had been responsible for driving down infection.

The public health advice was now different from the blueprint that had been sketched out in NPHET's presentation on 17 October. A relaxation of lockdown was advised, but trammelled along particular lines. Given the high rates of disease, opening up too quickly would combine with Christmas to cause a 'third wave of disease [that] will ensue much more quickly and with greater mortality than the second,' the presentation stated.

Nolan told the meeting that if the reproductive rate – the R number – exceeded 1.2, and if there was a significant increase in infections at Christmas, then case numbers would exceed 400 a day by early to mid-January. This figure of 400 was important. NPHET told the government that a short, sharp intervention when the disease was at this level could bring the virus back under control. That was the central scenario that was highlighted in the text of Holohan's letter to Donnelly and that formed the core of Nolan's presentation. There were overly optimistic assumptions underpinning this, however, including modelling that cases would fall to a lower starting point – 100 cases per day by the beginning of December.

Much depended on the pace and angle at which this 400 a day threshold was crossed, which would be determined by the R number – the speed at which infections were growing. The higher the R number, the higher the cases, and the earlier that number was reached, the sooner public interventions would be needed. If the R rate was between 1.4 and 1.6, 'rapid exponential growth' beyond 400 cases a day could be expected early in the new year. The government was told that even under the most benign assumptions, there was too much virus in the community to allow the reopening of hospitality as well as household visits.

Across the coalition, the consistent defence of the decisions taken in the run-up to Christmas has been that NPHET did not predict the surge that came. It is true that neither the published graphs nor Holohan's letter sketched out anything approaching the scale of infection that followed Christmas. However, the presentation to the subcommittee, released to the authors under Freedom of Information, includes a previously unpublished slide showing a striking vertical red line where cases would exceed 1,500 by late January if the reproductive rate of the virus reached 1.6 as a result of increased socialisation. That wasn't a peak. The red line escalated skywards, straight up past 1,500 and literally off the charts. The red line was not emphasised to the subcommittee, and the numbers underpinning it were an underestimate, but the pattern of what was to follow in January was there. There was a low chance, NPHET predicted, but the slide does show that cases could skyrocket beyond control.

In reaching their decisions on what to reopen, the politicians seized on an element of Holohan's letter they believed offered them the ability to open hospitality while delaying allowing household visits. Page 6 noted data from SAGE, the UK equivalent of NPHET, which suggested that closing hospitality might reduce R by between 0.1 and 0.2 and that preventing mixing between households might have an equivalent effect. In response to a question from Leo Varadkar, Nolan told the Tánaiste that the effect on R of opening hospitality would be the same as allowing household mixing – increasing it by 0.2.

'We said in theory, these things [hospitality and household mixing] are equivalent,' Nolan would later recall. 'But that whole point was that doing them together would have a cumulative effect.' He conceded that the letter may not have been clear enough, but said it was clear in their presentation. 'No doubt about it. At no point did we say you can do one or the other, you can mix and match.'

NPHET officials believed they had offered a straight binary. The politicians believed they had choices, they could fine tune the approach within those choices and they could effectively balance things out. 'It was there in writing on page six of their letter that the impact of the two would be about the same. We chose one, they chose the other one,' Michael McGrath later said. Simon Coveney aligned with this view, as did others in the room. Paschal Donohoe felt that NPHET had left a degree of ambiguity.

Stephen Donnelly believed there was a choice and that keeping household visits restricted for longer left space to be more liberal on hospitality. What the government was doing was in keeping with the spirit of the NPHET advice, he believes. He would later state publicly that the coalition had followed public health advice all along and that there was no way of knowing if keeping hospitality closed would have led to less spreading of the disease – a view he holds today.

The argument that government went against public health advice 'simply doesn't stack up', the health minister said in autumn 2021. 'There were a lot of measures in place, with the government decision lining up closely to the NPHET advice. The advice included an option to go further in terms of hospitality. We chose households on the basis that this is where the large majority of transmission was happening,' he argued. 'So we went further than the advice on households and a little less on hospitality. Nobody can say what would have happened if we'd done it the other way around. Maybe there would have been less transmission, maybe there would have been a lot more transmission.'

The view of ministers was shared by the party leaders. 'There was a balancing out,' the Taoiseach later said. 'We felt we were more conservative on households, NPHET less conversative on households.'

Eamon Ryan later characterised the mood that day. 'If you're looking at the language from NPHET in the room, it wasn't, "you're taking risks here, you're going further". The CMO was saying, "we're not in bad shape, the modelling is reasonably optimistic". It wasn't all warnings,' he said, describing the difference between government and NPHET as 'marginal'.

However, not everyone who sat on the political side of the room that day believed the government had sufficient cover for the actions taken. 'The NPHET warnings were quite stark,' Ed Brophy – Paschal Donohoe's adviser who subsequently left politics in 2021 – said later. 'It was binary: we could either allow for more hospitality or allow more mixing at home, but not both. I was [in] no doubt whatsoever that their position was that things could get pretty bad if we did both.'

Nolan ultimately felt that NPHET had failed to convince the government. He continues to feel guilty and 'pissed off', but that is tempered by how he feels about the other presentations – the EY and CSO data. 'We were pissed off about other presentations that were made; they seemed to me to have misrepresented the seriousness of the situation and confused the picture. Fundamentally, I still can't get it out my head that if we had presented our arguments and data differently, if we said it differently, they might have got the right message – probably not, but that's how I felt.'

The government decided that the country would reopen in three stages over December under the guise of Level 3. On 1 December, non-essential retail, hairdressers and gyms would reopen, followed by hospitality three days later. From 18 December, households could mix with up to two other households and people would be allowed to travel outside their county.

The coalition hoped the right balance had been struck – a big emphasis on family time, some element of socialising, or as one senior source put it at the time, 'At least don't go tearing the absolute arse out of it. Plainly and truthfully, that's what the government are saying.'

NPHET, however, was 'stunned' by the decision. 'Oh my God, they're going all the way – opening everything,' was Ronan Glynn's reaction, according to Nolan. For his part, Glynn believes that NPHET was 'very clear about hospitality not opening' and that what the government decided was a significant departure from that advice.

Holohan said it 'isn't the case' that his letter offered a choice. 'Our advice was that we thought that in the circumstance of Christmas, it might be possible for people to have a safe amount of socialisation, but that couldn't happen if pubs and restaurants were open,' he said later. 'We recommended firmly and fully that pubs and hospitality should not reopen.'

But sitting in the Taoiseach's office exactly a year after that meeting Micheál Martin was adamant that the NPHET advice was not against reopening hospitality. 'I don't think it was crystal clear,' he said. His defence was strident, focused on the period when hospitality was open and household visits permitted simultaneously, but not on how the two may have interacted with each other over the course of December.

'Are we now seriously saying that from the eighteenth to the twenty-third [of December] was the key moment?' he said. 'That doesn't stack up, it doesn't. We went to Level 3, NPHET said go to Level 3. I think we need to stand back from it all and say, are we seriously suggesting that a subset of Level 3 is responsible for the enormous case numbers that subsequently happened?'

Varadkar holds a similar view, railing against the 'simplistic' narrative that if only the government had followed NPHET advice there would have been no third wave of Covid-19. 'I think that's untrue because NPHET recommended going from Level 5 to Level 3, and recommended that we allow household gatherings two weeks before we did,' he said.

Varadkar is 'absolutely sure' the third wave would have happened even if NPHET's advice had been followed to the letter with home visits allowed from the start of December. It would, he argued, have driven socialisation in two million homes rather than across 11,000 bars and restaurants. 'The error was to accept the advice to go from Level 5 to Level 3 when we should have followed our own plan and gone to Level 4 first,' he said a year later. 'I think that the gap between what they recommended and what we did has been overstated.'

The following day, after Cabinet approved the measures, Micheál Martin told the nation it had a responsibility to 'manage risk'. He noted there had been much speculation as to what a 'meaningful Christmas will look like' but argued that his plan struck 'a safe balance between maintaining the pressure on the disease and creating space for families, friends and loved ones to be together this Christmas'.

At a later press conference, Varadkar confessed to having had 'cabin fever' over the course of the previous six weeks and outlined plans to go to the gym, get a haircut and go to a restaurant that weekend with friends he had not seen for months. The Taoiseach struck a more reserved tone, saying he might head out for a meal, but he was most looking forward to 'lazy days at home at Christmas'.

Asked to reflect on those contrasting messages nearly a year later, Holohan said, 'I thought that was a very responsible message from the Taoiseach.' As the country prepared for Christmas the chief medical officer recalled being 'genuinely worried and concerned' at what lay ahead. 'I didn't know where we were going to end up, to be frank.'

The answer would soon become devastatingly clear.

CHAPTER 24:

SERIOUS TROUBLE

18 December 2020
Cases: 78,254
Deaths: 2,149
Seven-day average of new cases: 392

P hilip Nolan remembers the text Tony Holohan sent him a week before Christmas Day 2020, after he had sent him a screenshot of the 'epi curve' showing the daily case counts. The last few days, he told Holohan, looked 'scary'. The reply from the chief medical officer was brief and to the point: 'Very much so. We're in serious trouble.'

The first signs of difficulty had come a week before that. All the NPHET modelling at the end of November had presumed cases would fall below 200 per day, and the hope was for even fewer, between 50 and 100. But as non-essential retailers, hairdressers and gyms opened on 1 December, 269 new cases were reported.

In early December, cases generally stayed in the 200s, only once dipping below 200. 'You kind of think you have time to respond,' Cillian De Gascun said later. 'But that's not how the virus operates, so when we opened up at two hundred and fifty to three hundred cases per day – around twenty-five times what we saw in summer – we didn't see a further decline as we had seen when restrictions were eased in the summer […] we didn't even get to Christmas.'

On 10 and 11 December, the daily case count tipped above 300. NPHET had expected case numbers to rise as the country reopened and be at around 350 per day going into Christmas week. Even though daily case numbers drifted up past 300 earlier than expected, public health officials still believed their main job was to prepare the government for a mini-lockdown in January, as had been outlined in their presentation in October, and alluded to again in November.

But on the day Nolan and Holohan exchanged texts, 18 December, there were 582 cases. This was far beyond what had been hoped for a week from Christmas. It was also the same day that households could begin to mix again, after two weeks when indoor hospitality had been open for groups of up to six, from six different households.

The government resolved that it would not be spooked by the case numbers. The coalition briefed that there would of course be concern at the rising case numbers but that Ireland was still performing well compared to other European countries. At the last Fianna Fáil parliamentary party meeting before Christmas, the day before home visits restarted, Micheál Martin told his TDs and senators that there was a need to 'keep an eye' on infections. During December, Martin told his restive party that the government envisaged never having to close retail again, a view shared by ministers across the coalition.

But the days leading up to Christmas were punctuated by several alarming letters from Holohan urging a change in course. The day before restrictions on household visits were relaxed, he wrote to Donnelly to say the increase in cases was 'clearly related' to the earlier relaxation of restrictions on retail and hospitality. 'This deteriorating situation is all the more precarious as we commence into a further period of relaxation of measures from the 18th December,' he wrote.

The chief medical officer advised that Christmas should, in effect, be ended on 28 December rather than 6 January (which had been the plan), with indoor dining closed and visits to homes from one other household only. NPHET was now seriously worried. An outright cancellation of Christmas was discussed, De Gascun later said. He also wondered retrospectively whether alarm bells had been rung loudly enough with the politicians. 'You do look back and wonder should we have been more forceful in our advice in the run-up to Christmas,' he later said. 'It was a complete disaster.'

As Christmas Day approached, the government briefings to political correspondents signalled that new restrictions were likely before the end of the year. Effectively, ministers were planning to meet Holohan halfway by closing hospitality from 30 December but allowing inter-county travel to continue. But in a matter of days, that plan fell apart as Ireland was plunged into its most damaging surge of infection – and was facing a new threat.

On 14 December, the Department of Health had been notified of a concerning Covid variant by an EU early-warning system that noted its 'numerous spike mutations' and rapid spread. The same day, the UK put large parts of the south-east of England into a pre-emptive lockdown based on preliminary indications of what the new variant could do. Four days later, as Holohan and Nolan exchanged worried texts, and household visits resumed, the UK's New and Emerging Respiratory Virus Threats Advisory Group (NERVTAG) published a paper suggesting that a Covid-19 variant it had identified in Kent, in the south-east of England, had a 'substantial increase in transmissibility compared to other variants'.

The emergence of variant B117 drove a shift to panic stations in Ireland and, after nearly a year of pandemic fatigue, the traditional Christmas break suddenly became a period of frantic change and mounting dread.

SUNDAY, 20 DECEMBER 2020

Across Europe, countries began to sever their connections to the UK. For Ireland, this was particularly complicated. People had been travelling between Ireland and the UK in their thousands. In addition to people having been away from their families for a year, it was Christmas.

From 14 to 20 December, some 17,917 people had arrived at Dublin Airport from the UK. Eamon Ryan, the transport minister, had been speaking with his British counterpart Grant Shapps, who warned him that the variant was going to change everything. Stephen Donnelly got the same message from Matt Hancock, the British health secretary. On

20 December, Ireland put in place a 48-hour travel ban from the UK and later extended it to the end of the year, but many Irish residents were now marooned in Britain.

The government took the view that they could not be left there and decided to charter jets from Ryanair and Aer Lingus to get them out. It was a 'calculated risk', Simon Coveney later said. 'We were effectively banning travel between Britain and Ireland, the first time ever in our history that had happened. We had to try to deal with a specific group of people who had to come home for all sorts of reasons.' A travel agency was in effect set up in the Department of Foreign Affairs over Christmas and between then and 6 January, some 1,349 people were flown into the State on these airlifts.

But for those who couldn't get airlifted, the State's open border with Northern Ireland allowed thousands of people into the south via Belfast. Not for the first time, Coveney raised concerns with the Northern Ireland Executive about what he would later describe as 'effectively an open back-door that we couldn't police'. But the response from First Minister Arlene Foster was not what he had hoped. 'It was made clear to me that they were not going to stop flights,' he recalled. 'They weren't going to shut down connectivity between Northern Ireland [and Great Britain].'

On the same day the travel ban was announced, Holohan convened a small group of NPHET members for an emergency meeting. Fear hung in the air at the Sunday meeting. It was partially a response to the worsening situation, but it was also tactical. 'We needed to say to the minister, conscious of what happened in October, the shit is about to hit the fan,' a senior NPHET source said later. The intention was that the political system would be primed for a Level 5 recommendation.

The letter arising out of the meeting was sent the following day, but Holohan sent a message to Donnelly that Sunday, specifically about the Kent variant. He told the minister of 'interesting, and concerning' features in the new strain. In his letter, which was never published, he wrote, 'It is possible that this new variant could cause more severe disease or influence the immune response, but there is no evidence for either of these outcomes at this time.'

The B117 variant – the Kent variant, later known as the Alpha variant – was a wicked thing. It had mutated much more quickly than expected. Holohan wrote that it had 29 mutations from the original Wuhan strain, whereas the 'wildtype' coronavirus strain that causes Covid-19 accumulates between one and two mutations a month. On whether there was definitely extra transmissibility associated with the variant, the letter was hedged. While the initial analysis suggested it could be 70 per cent more transmissible, Holohan also wrote, 'This new variant has emerged at a time of the year when there has traditionally been increased family and social mixing.' He cited WHO opinions that there was 'insufficient evidence' to determine if the strain had an impact on disease severity or transmission.

Nonetheless, with 'significant inbound travel' anticipated from Britain in the days ahead, Holohan advised that sequencing should be ramped up to hunt for the variant. He further advised that people arriving from Britain should have to self-isolate rather than just restrict their movements for 14 days. This advice would be backdated to people who had arrived from the UK since 8 December. The advice was implemented as policy; there is no way of knowing how closely it was heeded by the public, or heard.

MONDAY, 21 DECEMBER 2020

There was no shortage of dissonance washing around Government Buildings the following day. With rapidly rising cases and the emerging variant, ministers fretted that the population at large had not woken up to the threat. And yet one government source briefed, 'Christmas will happen, it will take an asteroid to prevent Christmas from happening and allowing people to come together in some sort of a way.'

That same day, however, a Cabinet source confided that some politicians were already changing their own plans to see family over Christmas. 'The bit that's gnawing away is the numbers and the intergenerational mix[ing],' they said.

At a Cabinet subcommittee on Covid-19 meeting, ministers decided to close hospitality on Christmas Eve and to end inter-county travel on

26 December, except for those travelling home. However, the decision, while de facto taken and widely briefed to the press, still had to be signed off by Cabinet the next day.

Holohan was at the subcommittee, and wrote to Donnelly that day with the intention of getting his analysis of the situation into Donnelly's hands before that Cabinet meeting. 'The epidemiological profile of the disease is deteriorating rapidly and there are now clear signs of exponential growth similar to or greater than that seen at the peak of the second wave,' he said.

There was, he wrote, an 'imminent risk' of increasing deaths; multiple clusters were breaking out everywhere, with secondary and tertiary spread. Holohan flagged the ongoing risk around hospitality and other indoor gatherings, 'which facilitate inter-household mixing and which may act as loci for "super-spreading" events'.

Officially, the chief medical officer had no mandate from NPHET – which would not meet until the day after the Cabinet, 23 December. But his letter clearly indicated that a recommendation for a new lockdown was coming. 'My considered view is that measures as set out in Level 5 of the Government's plans are necessary,' he wrote.

For the third time since October, a gap began to emerge between the CMO's advice and the government's approach.

TUESDAY, 22 DECEMBER 2020

While Cabinet signed off on what was described as Level 5 restrictions to be introduced from 24 December, there were a number of exceptions, most notably that one household would be able to visit another until 31 December. Level 5 envisaged no household mixing. NPHET's advice would ultimately be to end that on 26 December.

And Covid was combining with other threats. The economic impact of closure would be dire and there was also the prospect of a no-deal Brexit, still live in the days leading up to Christmas. The Cabinet memo warned ministers:

There is a significant risk of many businesses not being in a position to continue in existence into the new year in this scenario, with consequent impact on employment across a range of the worst-affected sectors. Obviously there is a potential reinforcement of these economic impacts in the event of a failure to conclude a free trade agreement between the EU and the UK.

The hospital system was coping, the memo outlined, but the disease was spreading among the over-65s. A significant impact on healthcare had been avoided during the second wave as the lockdown cut off transmission of Covid-19 before it had spread substantially into older groups. There could be no guarantee of the same happening again, the memo warned.

While it had been a trend throughout the pandemic for the public to exercise caution in reaction to rising case numbers, Christmas appeared to have clouded people's judgement. Even as 'sharp increases in cases became apparent towards the end of last week, early evidence is that people's mobility did not decrease', the memo stated. Traffic volumes for private cars were up 16 per cent. Despite high levels of compliance, the Cabinet was told, the Gardaí had found a number of pubs over the previous weekend that were non-compliant with regulations. Thanksgiving in the US and Canada had sparked a wave of infection that was now materialising in North America. A similar effect could now follow Christmas in Ireland, ministers were told.

WEDNESDAY, 23 DECEMBER 2020

The huge spread in the disease was also being felt in the contact tracing system. 'We saw 1,407 lab reported positives by 10 p.m. on 23 December and 1,777 by 24 December,' Niamh O'Beirne, the HSE's lead on testing and tracing, would later recall. 'At that point we saw it was a definitive problem.'

On Christmas Eve, she held emergency calls with her management team. These usually took place three times a week, but they were now happening daily.

Holohan felt the decisions didn't go far enough, and following a NPHET meeting on 23 December he wrote to Donnelly telling him as much. 'The fact that the level of infection is growing faster in December than it was in October is underscored by the fact that current estimates of reproduction number (1.5–1.8) and growth rate (6–9 per cent) are higher than they have been at any point in the pandemic since March,' he wrote.

He also flashed a warning about the health system, which was 'in an extremely precarious and fragile position, is at heightened risk of becoming overwhelmed and is facing into difficult decisions in relation to the ongoing provision of care'. All available actions had to be taken, he wrote. What's more, he said that NPHET did not believe the decisions Cabinet had taken the previous day – with various carve-outs from Level 5 – were enough.

The deterioration would threaten health, education and childcare services in the new year, he told Donnelly. 'The NPHET is of the view that all indicators for the application of Level 5 measures have been met and that there is now too great a risk in waiting to assess the impact of measures announced yesterday, and advises the full suite of Level 5 measures are introduced with effect from midnight on the night of 26th December,' the letter stated.

The NPHET meeting that day had discussed going even further than what was recommended in Holohan's letter to Donnelly. 'We discussed that idea of "Do you just cancel Christmas?"' De Gascun later said. The messaging from NPHET afterwards was pretty blunt: revise Christmas plans, people were told. Yet officially its public health advice still allowed for the mixing of three households over the following three days.

But the government's advice went further than that, allowing two households to mix after Christmas, until 1 January – a decision taken against a backdrop where there were active concerns over compliance and the degree to which public behaviour was shifting in response to the rapidly worsening situation.

MONDAY, 28 DECEMBER 2020

The number of confirmed close contacts per case – the best way to deter-mine how much social mixing was going on – remained, according to HSE data, very high over the following days, peaking at an average of almost five close contacts per case on 28 December. Some individuals were reporting 10 to 15 close contacts.

After reading Holohan's 23 December letter, Donnelly was as worried as he had been at any point during the pandemic. The new variant, plus another troubling mutation from South Africa, the rise in cases, the spread in older people – all pointed to disaster. Increasingly, his personal view was that the only way to address the rise was through March 2020-style measures, over and above the five-level framework: a total lockdown. He had met the nursing homes sector two days earlier and delivered a chilling message: pull down the shutters, cancel visits, keep them alive and we will get to you pretty soon with vaccines.

But the Cabinet did not meet before Christmas to discuss Holohan's 23 December letter, and extra restrictions were not considered when it met on 28 December – the day close contacts peaked. On the same day as that second festive Cabinet meeting, Holohan wrote again: 'I am of the view that the current set of measures, which are less than the full suite recommended by the NPHET last Wednesday, will not be suffi-cient to bring the current trajectory under control.' Yet the following day, the *Irish Times* ran a story citing a government source who said that while further action could not be ruled out, 'We're at Level 5 with a few tweaks.'

The Cabinet met again on 30 December and accepted Holohan's rec-ommendations in full. A total lockdown was to be imposed with schools and construction given a reprieve. The delay between the advice being issued, considered and implemented still rankles with Holohan. 'We issued that letter related to the twenty-sixth of December, and we issued a subsequent letter […] they didn't all get considered until the thirtieth,' he said. 'Our view […] of what was needed is set out on the dates on which it was set out; it didn't happen. Those are matters of fact. And clearly I didn't believe that was sufficient, because that was our advice.'

There was, Holohan later said, a 'substantial amount of disease transmission' over the Christmas period, and that had consequences in the weeks and months that followed. 'We experienced a level of transmission and mortality as a result of that, as well as the pressure on the hospital system as a direct result of the scale of transmission that occurred over the course of Christmas,' he said.

The Taoiseach, however, is firmly of the view that raking over the issue of when households were allowed to stop mixing is in the realm of what he pithily calls 'post-match analysis'. 'It's really splitting hairs,' he later said. There are limits to what governments can do, especially at Christmas, his argument runs. 'There is a natural thing over Christmas that no government is going to stop. It wouldn't have made a difference.'

WEDNESDAY, 30 DECEMBER 2020

The effect of lockdown, once introduced on the day before New Year's Eve, was clear in the close contact data. A presentation by NPHET's modelling group on 7 January showed that it had begun to fall rapidly around 30 December, down from the high of 4.7 two days earlier to just 3 close contacts per confirmed case of Covid-19 on 5 January.

But the third wave of Covid-19 had already begun to crash into the healthcare system. A joint note for NPHET from the Department of Health and the HSE warned that hospitals were under 'significant pressure', and even though there were over 900 free beds in the system, that 'should not be regarded as a sign that the system is under control'. In fact, 'the situation across all settings is now deteriorating', the note warned.

There were 51 outbreaks in public hospitals and 46 in nursing homes. The percentage of tests coming back positive from the serial testing programme in nursing homes was surging to double its standard rate. There had been 10,481 cases reported in the two weeks up to 27 December and mixing over Christmas would, the note said, 'result in an even greater number of cases being reported in the coming days', potentially leading to 'an overwhelmed system in which quality care is compromised and outcomes are poorer'.

It was a dire warning and Holohan's assessment was as bleak. In a letter to Donnelly he characterised the situation as 'the most concerning observed since the onset of the pandemic in Ireland' and that it 'repre-sent[ed] an immediate and grave threat to all key public health priorities [...] and the continued delivery of education and childcare services'.

Not even the modelling being given to Donnelly captured what was happening. The vertical axis on Philip Nolan's slides maxed out at 4,000 cases per day, and hospital numbers at 1,400 per day, but the analysis now showed that in the three worst-case scenarios, the line was going almost directly vertical, again literally off the charts, just like the slide shown to ministers on 26 November.

'It was chilling that for each model run we had to expand the y-axis [the vertical axis] on the outputs to accommodate unimaginable num-bers of cases,' Nolan later recalled.

On 30 December, Micheál Martin addressed the nation to explain why it was returning to lockdown. He pointed the finger squarely at the threat from the variant, mentioning it for the first time in the second sentence of his speech, and several times afterwards.

'It is already very clear that we are dealing with a strain of the disease that spreads much, much more quickly,' he said. 'Indeed, it is spreading at a rate that has surpassed the most pessimistic models available to us.' The threat of the Irish health system being overwhelmed and the risk of increased sickness and death among the most vulnerable was, he said, 'obvious'.

It was 33 days since he had stood at the same podium at the front of Government Buildings announcing the start of a meaningful Christmas.

On 8 January, 8,248 new cases of Covid-19 were reported in Ireland and ten days after that, 2,020 people were in hospital. It was beyond the worst nightmare scenario.

CHAPTER 25:

THE SURGE

1 January 2021
Cases: 93,532
Deaths: 2,248
Seven-day average of new cases: 1,348

What's happening has a medical name, but most people would just see another human being in extreme distress. Grabbing the arm of the chair they sit in, or the edge of the hospital bed, their rate of breathing sharply elevated, eyes wide. Less than twenty minutes earlier, the patient may have been relaxed, breathing with supplemental oxygen or high-flow oxygen therapy, through a mask.

But now, the fibres of their neck and arm muscles are tensed as they use all their power to suck down oxygen, battling the effects of the coronavirus which is wreaking havoc in their lungs. The technical description of this is 'utilising the accessory muscles of respiration'. In common terms, the patient is crashing, losing the ability to breathe for themselves.

An intensive care doctor will come to their aid. The critical care team is scrambled and the patient is brought into the intensive care unit on their narrow hospital bed and transferred into the wider intensive care bed. The violence of this movement can accelerate the distress, causing the patient's condition to deteriorate further, putting more pressure on the team caring for them.

The patient is sedated. Now that there's no gag reflex, a consultant, going in through the mouth, uses a device called a laryngoscope, which has a small camera mounted on the tip, to look into the trachea. The white vocal cords, strung tightly when a person is conscious and talking, are relaxed, fallen open. Using the scope to watch their progress, the breathing tube is inserted, through the vocal cords, down and into the middle of the chest. The ventilator is switched on and begins to breathe for the person, now intubated, incapacitated and in intensive care.

By 23 January 2021, there were 139 Covid-positive people in Irish intensive care units who had undergone this procedure. Including non-intubated Covid patients in intensive care, the number peaked the following day at 221. At the start of Covid, Ireland had 255 beds. By January, this had risen to a baseline capacity of 280, but it was unprecedented to have so many filled with people all suffering from the same disease. In the second week of January alone, 138 Covid-positive people were admitted to ICU, and stays for Covid-19 patients in intensive care could last for weeks.

It was 'off the scale', Michael Power, an ICU consultant in Beaumont Hospital and the HSE's clinical lead for critical care, said later. The HSE had a total surge capacity of around 350 beds, which was described as a 'manageable' scenario, but was managed only by a daily redeployment of dozens of nurses from their base hospitals to ICUs around the country.

Slides from the HSE's internal ICU audits show a thick red line strung across the graph at 350 beds. Above that is 'beyond surge capacity' and an 'unmanageable clinical scenario', Power said. Beyond that? 'We get Bergamo.' The State's ICU occupancy peaked in late January at 330 beds, between Covid and non-Covid patients.

What happened in the hospital system was similar to a car hitting a kerb, a senior HSE doctor later explained. It's not so much the hitting of the obstacle; it's the speed and the severity you encounter it at.

Ireland had hit the kerb fast, and in January and February 2021 saw a weeks-long effort to recover from and manage that impact, as hospitals came terrifyingly close to collapse. An HSE internal census later found that, although the 350 limit was never breached, at a national level many hospitals experienced overwhelming surges of patients critically ill with

Covid-19; and there were not enough specialised nursing staff available to provide the critical care they needed.

'Surges of critically ill patients occurred locally following geographic clusters of Covid patients,' the census found. 'In these hospitals appropriate critical care nursing staff ratios were unavailable, the care of critically ill patients was not assured and the clinical situation in these hospitals quickly became overwhelming.'

—

Collapse, or the prospect of collapse, within a hospital or a healthcare system doesn't happen with one single incident. It's individual parts of complex systems being pushed to breaking point. At the sharp end is dealing with human remains.

Many of the logistical problems that arose during the first wave had been solved. Gravediggers were no longer afraid of digging graves, for example. But the temporary mortuary at Kilmainham Hospital in Dublin had been deconstructed, and the seven refrigerated facilities ordered in March were distributed around the country. With an average of 34 deaths per day in January, the limit of capacity to hold bodies loomed into view, particularly in the capital, according to Ciarán Browne, the general manager of the HSE's acute hospitals division.

'There was a couple of times our Dublin hospitals came close to having more remains than spaces in their mortuaries,' he recalled. Browne had organised temporary morgue facilities in March and April 2020. Now, ten months later, Tallaght and Naas were touch-and-go heading into some weekends, when fewer people working and funerals not taking place on a Sunday exacerbated the issue – but people were still dying at the same rate.

Reflecting on the crisis much later, Browne felt a Bergamo-style situation was more likely in early 2021 than spring 2020. The number of cases was skyrocketing and the vaccine programme was only starting. 'Some days there were fifty to a hundred Covid-related deaths on top of the number of people who might have died that day,' he said. The HSE

planned to move bodies from hospitals elsewhere or to ask local authorities to erect temporary facilities in car parks.

The lack of dignity for human remains weighed heavy on the minds
of officials and medics, as did the prospect of families seeking to collect
their loved one's body only to be told they had been moved elsewhere.
'There were a couple of Fridays when hospitals contacted us to say they
didn't know if they could cope over the weekend if more deaths happened
in the hospital,' Browne said of that period. 'We had plans, but these were
plans we didn't want to put into operation – to move remains from one
hospital to another or to start using hospital wards to store remains. We
were honestly afraid some of those days.'

The flow of patients through hospitals and into ICUs was also managed. The HSE knew that 1,000 new cases would transfer into 50 hospital
admissions with a lag of between two and three weeks, so it was clear
shortly after Christmas that an enormous wave was looming over the
hospital system. 'We were looking at a pipeline that was horrendous,'
Paul Reid would later say.

But the situation had changed, in some ways for the better, with
more known about the disease. As Covid admissions surged, people who
would previously have been admitted to intensive care were managed
with high-flow oxygen therapies – through bi-level positive airway pressure (BIPAP) and continuous positive airway pressure (CPAP) machines
– where oxygen was forced into their systems to help them breathe. At any
given time outside the pandemic, Ireland might have around a hundred
people receiving these therapies. In January and February, the number
peaked at over four hundred.

Patients were also being managed at home, using devices to measure
pulse oximetry while they were monitored by clinical staff remotely. It
was a crisis of unprecedented proportions. 'The third surge was much
worse,' Colm Henry later recalled. 'It was different in every way. A nasty,
absolutely uncontrolled surge.'

There was constant focus on keeping individual ICUs from falling over.
Every morning 52 phone calls were placed, two to each intensive care unit.
The first assessed bed capacity, monitored by an HSE bed information

system (BIS) programme. The second was to senior clinical nurse managers, to assess their rosters and their level of need; who had capacity and who needed resources, which nurses could be shuffled where. Every day for 35 consecutive days, this information was crunched by a group of doctors and managers comprising the critical care major surge working group.

This was where serious threats were detected, such as what emerged in Mayo University Hospital, Castlebar, which was dealing with the after-effects of heavy socialisation at Christmas in Belmullet, which drove a huge cluster in the vicinity. The working group spotted that the hospital had five beds, but ten patients.

As a last resort, the Mobile Intensive Care Ambulance Service (MICAS) was deployed, effectively evacuating patients from hospitals that were about to be overwhelmed and distributing them around the country to hospitals where they could be accommodated. There were 68 MICAS movements in January alone, equivalent to around a quarter of the previous year's total, and triple the expected month-on-month level of activity. 'If MICAS had been unavailable these hospitals would have been overwhelmed,' the HSE's internal census report stated.

Ireland's health system pulled itself back from the brink, not because the wave was not enough to overwhelm it – it was – but rather because hastily rigged breakwaters managed to save it.

—

At a meeting of NPHET on 30 December 2020, Kevin Kelleher, one of the HSE's most senior public health specialists, bluntly declared, 'Public health cannot cope.' The people responsible for tracking and managing the disease outbreak had been overwhelmed. There had been years of chronic underinvestment in public health – most notably, its specialists were not on consultant grade contracts, an issue that was not resolved until late the following year.

The former director general of the HSE, Tony O'Brien, claimed this underinvestment was a result of successive governments ignoring the problem. 'You can never fix something through an annual financial process or service planning round if you haven't previously fixed it in terms of government policy around healthcare,' he said.

While adequate funding would not have prevented the pandemic, it did mean that when Covid-19 hit, public health did not have any capacity to deal with it. Scotland had four to five times more staff in public health than Ireland, Kelleher said. 'This was the most catastrophic tsunami,' he said. 'Our defences were a two- to three-inch wall. Whereas you would have expected it to be two to three feet.'

As late as October 2020, Colm Henry, the HSE's chief clinical officer, wrote in a confidential memo that resources in its public health function – medical, nursing, research and surveillance, management and administration – were 'insufficient at all levels to respond to the challenges posed by Covid-19 over the next six to eighteen months'.

At the start of the pandemic the HSE pulled contact tracing into the national contact management programme run by Niamh O'Beirne. While regional public health doctors understood that the sheer scale of the crisis meant this had to happen, there were concerns about how it was done.

Mary T. O'Mahony, the public health doctor in HSE South who traced 780 cases from the first case of community transmission in the country, said it meant that her team was no longer getting information that enabled them to identify sources where transmissions and possible transmissions were happening. Public health in the region had been fully tracing each case, which, she believes, helped control the spread in Cork and Kerry.

But, she said, a request to continue this intense form of contact tracing was refused, as it became more centralised. The centralisation was needed and valuable as cases grew rapidly, but nonetheless, O'Mahony said, the system wasn't integrated well into pre-existing public health structures. In a presentation made in May 2020, she argued that the centralised format led to incomplete data, poor recognition of complex cases and settings and an apparent lack of understanding of urgency of cases.

Sometimes cases were not contacted, she said, because after three calls went unanswered, the file was simply closed. In one instance, she flagged some 1,681 positive cases found on the system that had been marked as 'resolved cases – unable to inform patient'. She later said she flagged this up the line through the contact tracing system and the public health infrastructure.

Trickier calls, including those to non-Irish nationals without English as a first language, might not, she observed, get the same attention from centralised contact tracers working their way through a list, who could select the cases they were to work on from the pool. 'HSE South staff noted that cases with foreign-sounding names were less likely to be selected out in this way.' She said this issue was 'regularly discussed' among public health doctors in the region.

The third wave of Covid-19 exploited long-standing weaknesses across the health system, such as the computer system used for tracking and counting disease – the Computerised Infectious Disease Reporting system or CIDR (pronounced 'cider'). Kelleher compared it to an Amstrad computer, a range of personal computers made by a company of the same name that ceased producing them in the late 1990s. 'It's run on an almost obsolete system,' he said.

CIDR has no capacity to link disease cases to wider information about the nature of an outbreak, such as whether it was in a restaurant or pub. Much of that information is still captured on paper. Cases of infectious disease are uploaded from a testing lab and then created manually in public health departments. The data is used to draw up monthly or weekly reports on the prevalence of different diseases.

For Covid-19, a specific platform was set up to process the volume of cases involved. But that left a difficulty: when contact tracers called a person with Covid-19 and created more data from a questionnaire, they had to figure out how to get that information into CIDR. Initially this was done manually, but then the volume of information became too big. A technical solution was developed, where 'bots' would trawl the huge data lake, transferring the data across to CIDR. But it was far from perfect. The bots would throw aside cases with anything irregular, leaving it to the humans to sort out.

When cases surged after Christmas, the bots began discarding cases at a huge rate, swamping the humans monitoring the system. At its peak, there were 42 bots churning through the data, throwing new cases at CIDR. Over Christmas, some public health staff who tried to log in to upload cases were met with blue screens. The system was not working and within days it collapsed entirely.

While the issue did not stop positive cases being contacted or contact traced, it did mean that in early January, the true Covid-19 situation was worse than official figures stated. It also meant that the reported daily case numbers, which punctuated the pandemic for ordinary people, bore less relation to the reality of the disease on the ground. News of the CIDR collapse deepened the public's sense that the system had lost control.

While the backlog was eventually eliminated on 7 January, the incident served as a reminder of what Ronan Glynn later described as the 'absence of integration' of the data systems being operated across the Irish healthcare system. 'It must be a clear learning from this pandemic that there must be a concerted and sustained focus on improving and integrating health information systems and health data, and we must build up our workforce capacities around public health surveillance and modelling,' the deputy chief medical officer said.

—

With residents and staff in nursing homes on the cusp of being vaccinated, Covid-19 once again rampaged through the system.

In the aftermath of the first wave in spring 2020, HIQA resumed its in-person inspections of care facilities, concentrating on 44 nursing homes that had significant outbreaks.

The results showed that even after the first wave, when it was clear what Covid-19 could do, there were significant issues relating to non-compliance with regulatory standards. None of the homes was found to be fully compliant, and just five were mostly compliant. Eleven were not compliant with at least one-third of the regulations inspected.

Some 58 per cent were not compliant on governance and management; half were compliant on infection prevention and control, with inspectors finding that one nursing home had left bedroom doors open for residents who had tested positive for Covid-19. The premises of 32 per cent of homes inspected were deemed not up to scratch, while 21 per cent were non-compliant on staffing.

HIQA has been unable to publish many of the regulatory reports into these centres as some homes are challenging the findings, either by judicial review or in some other way. As January went on, the reports being sent from HIQA to the HSE were depressingly similar to those from April and May 2020.

On 19 January, Chief Inspector at HIQA, Mary Dunnion, told the HSE that HIQA had been notified of 19 unexpected deaths across 17 designated centres. Staffing deficits were rampant, with operators advised to seek public health advice on possible derogations from regulations and post-infection guidelines to allow staff to return to work.

Reports from the centres of greatest concern on that day described 'a chaotic situation on the ground [...] Exacerbated by unclear/confused governance arrangements'. HIQA was forced to remind one provider of its duty to ensure the care of residents, and its responsibility to provide a person in charge at the centre. Inspectors reported 'a lack of clinical oversight'.

In another centre, HIQA pointed out that the person in charge was not a nurse, and there was a nurse in the centre only for a number of hours each morning, Monday to Friday. The HSE was providing support but 'the concern here is that care staff would not have the clinical knowledge to recognise and respond to a resident who might deteriorate', the regulator said. In another, staffing arrangements didn't allow for separate teams over the weekend to run the different parts of the home where people with and without Covid would live – an important infection control measure.

Over a 100-day period, 1,000 vulnerable citizens died – for the second time in a year.

CHAPTER 26:

THE TUNNEL

3 January 2021
Cases: 101,887
Deaths: 2,259
Seven-day average of new cases: 2,251

Pale and exhausted, Ronan Glynn appeared on Sunday's edition of RTÉ's *Six One News* imploring people to stay home. The news was unrelentingly grim, and hospitalisations and ICU admissions had doubled in less than a week. 'There are many people listening to this programme who are infected and who unfortunately will end up in hospital in the coming days,' he told presenter Ray Kennedy.

Glynn would later recall how he had scared half the country, even his own family. 'It was obvious to us that we were in massive trouble now,' he said. 'It was clear that there was significant mortality coming.'

Earlier that day, Holohan had convened an emergency virtual meeting of senior officials on NPHET and from the HSE to, one participant later recalled, prime the health service to 'kick ass and be ready for a surge' as well as gather information for the government. Models drawn up by Philip Nolan were by that point suggesting that there could be between 1,300 and 2,000 people in hospital by the last week in January. Covid-19 was everywhere.

The country had been shut down for three days, but even under Level 5 restrictions, the plan was, in theory, for some sectors to reopen. On New Year's Day, there was already a sense that that would slip away. Construction was one sector that fell by the wayside soon enough, being largely closed on 7 January.

Schools were due to reopen within days. There was not a single person involved in the Covid-19 response who was not deeply unsettled by the damage done to children by closing schools in spring 2020. The even deeper scarring to children with additional or special needs, and those from disadvantaged areas, motivated a strong desire among some to keep schools open at all costs.

Politically, it had been a landmark achievement for the nascent coalition to get schools open again in September 2020 with the aid of hundreds of millions of euro to make them safer environments. Through the autumn and early winter, HSE public health teams, led by Kevin Kelleher and HSE public health specialist Abigail Collins, worked with schools to develop protocols that kept them open even during the Level 5 lockdown in October and November.

Schools were a heady cocktail of forces, often bucking against each other: political, industrial relations and disease management. Public health specialists faced down incredulous teachers and argued that the classroom was a safe environment. Above all was a core political priority: the maintenance of full-time education for children throughout the most acute phases of the pandemic. Micheál Martin, a secondary school teacher by profession, a former education minister, and a parent, placed almost unrivalled emphasis on the continuation of schooling.

As case numbers had begun to climb in December, there were indications that the structures put in place to keep schools open were creaking. Claremorris Boys National School shut its doors on 11 December after a number of students tested positive. The department squared off against the school – as it did throughout the pandemic whenever there was an unapproved closure of a school – and ordered it to reopen.

But the bigger challenge as schools broke for Christmas and cases soared to unprecedented levels would be to get them open again in

January. Just before the new year, some on NPHET argued that a delay in reopening of one to two weeks should be considered. But while the public health team agreed there was a serious threat to schools, the position was that they should reopen as planned from 6 January.

In late December in the Department of Education, Minister Norma Foley, her advisers and senior officials had some confidence that they could get schools reopened as planned. But there was already bad mood music coming from the teachers' unions, and the situation was deteriorating rapidly. By 30 December, as he announced the enactment of the full Level 5 lockdown, the Taoiseach said that schools would reopen on 11 January – five days later than planned.

The hope was that an extra weekend might allow time for cases to come down. However, even though it wasn't expressed at the Cabinet meeting earlier that day, inwardly politicians knew that the plan was crumbling. 'It's always the last thing that you relinquish: sending children to school,' Public Expenditure minister Michael McGrath, a father of seven, later said. 'But I think even at that point, we knew that they weren't going back.'

By the time of Holohan's emergency virtual meeting on 3 January, the writing was on the wall. The need to keep schools closed indefinitely, and other painful messages, were conveyed to the government at a meeting of the Cabinet subcommittee on Covid-19 two days later. In sharp contrast to October and November, there was no recrimination or anger at the meeting.

Reopening schools would be a more tortuous and painful process than the government might have imagined. The teaching unions torpedoed a plan to bring Leaving Cert students and children with special needs back into the classroom on a part-time basis from 11 January. This ratcheted up the pressure on Foley and her department. In addition to the pressing real-time education needs of students with additional and often complex needs, there was, for the second year running, the overwhelming institutional weight of the Leaving Cert. Every week students spent out of school made it less likely that a conventional exam could be run.

There were endless meetings with the unions. 'It felt that we were always getting it to a point where we were almost getting it over the line, and then it would roll back,' a source involved recalled later. A deal was then struck in principle for pupils with special needs to return to the classroom. But the teachers themselves were restive and unconvinced that it would be safe to go back.

A webinar with Glynn was organised for teachers on 18 January. It was an unmitigated disaster. The organisers quickly shut off comments on the platform on which they were running the webinar, which had an astonishing 16,500 participants. But it was also going out live on YouTube and some of those in attendance unloaded mercilessly on the public health doctors. The comments were angry. The doctors were told they were peddling a 'pack of lies'; they were 'patronising'; many participants called for a strike. 'THEY HAVE PROVEN THEY DON'T CARE'; 'We'll obviously have to strike. You lot don't care if we live or die'; 'DRAIN THE SWAMP'. It was ugly and, in some instances, unfair.

Some on the government side felt the comments stream had been taken over by a militant and more vocal group of teachers whose views did not reflect those of the majority view (though politicians and their advisers often reassure themselves with versions of this story). In reality, it didn't matter. Even if the negative comments were not truly representative, they were a barometer of wider unease. Some in the department felt that the volume and depth of feeling showed that the unions would not be able to bring their members with them. The plan to get special schools back up and running collapsed the next day. Foley and the unions publicly exchanged barbs, and the minister went on radio and accused INTO – The Irish National Teachers' Organisation – rep John Boyle of being 'disingenuous'.

The pressure then came on from advocacy groups. AsIAm, the autism advocacy group headed by Adam Harris, brother of Minister for Higher Education Simon Harris, was an articulate and visible presence along-side Inclusion Ireland and Down Syndrome Ireland. Parents of severely disabled or autistic children did first-person pieces with newspapers and radio stations, while vaccines began to be rolled out and the number of new infections collapsed.

Towards the end of January, the government felt that public opinion was shifting, and this put wind in the sails of a plan to get pupils back in the classroom. A deal to bring special schools back was struck on 1 February, but it would be the guts of a month before the Taoiseach confirmed a phased timeline for the resumption of in-school education for other students. By 12 April all students were back in class; some had been out of the classroom for more than three and a half months.

The HSE's clinical lead for infection control, Martin Cormican, who was brought onto NPHET early in 2021, is firmly of the view that, in both 2020 and 2021, schools remained closed for too long. While the risk of a novel pathogen that was not understood meant closing them in March 2020 was, in many ways, a rational move, keeping them closed after Easter of that year, he believes, could have been avoided.

Similarly, in early 2021, when the argument for keeping schools closed was about keeping mobility in wider society at as low a level as possible, he believes there was a miscalculation. 'There's a risk of infection spreading in any situation where you bring people together. The question is what is the risk and what is the benefit. The consequences for children's welfare long term, and the consequences in particular for children in areas of deprivation of long-term closure and their long-term ability to develop was profound, and I think that needed more weight than it was given.'

Cormican believes that schools could have opened at a 'manageable level of risk much earlier' and that the consequences of closing them, and the profound impact this had on children of all ages, 'outweighed the benefits that we got from it in terms of stopping the risk of infection'.

His view is not unique. Seven days into the new year, Kevin Kelleher – who knew he would be retiring before the end of 2021 – told a meeting involving Foley and her officials, 'One of the greatest regrets I have in my very long career is that we allowed schools to be closed, and we now know this had a massive impact on our children – and that is totally wrong.'

—

In early January, Tony Holohan told a NPHET meeting that the Covid-19 situation was 'the worst the country has faced since the beginning of the pandemic' and asked members of the group to reflect on that.

On the political side, the coalition was rocked to its core, hoping against hope that the hospital system would not collapse and leave it contemplating the sorts of scenarios it had feared in spring 2020. These were, Michael McGrath would later reflect, 'the darkest days that we've had in government so far', when ministers looked at hospitals almost hourly and with 'a real sense of dread about how bad this would get'.

Paschal Donohoe would recall sitting at his desk one day in January pulling out his Cabinet papers. 'What did I miss? What could I have done differently?' he asked himself, later admitting that the decisions had weighed heavily. From the government's point of view, the disaster at Christmas was also a clear political vulnerability.

There were two lines of defence. First, NPHET had not warned the government that this could happen. The second was the impact of the B117, or Kent/Alpha, variant. In October 2021, these were still the two pillars of Simon Coveney's argument: 'Nobody could have predicted and our models didn't predict either that in January the pace of spread would accelerate the way it did under a new variant.'

In December and January, both in public comments and background briefings, there was a clear emphasis on the variant. A senior source in the Taoiseach's office briefed one of the authors of this book that Alpha was linked directly to a 75 per cent increase in cases and a surge in hospitalisations. Into January, it was consistently cited, with government ministers arguing that it had been imported weeks previously, which suggested that it had been playing a meaningful role in transmission for some time.

By late summer 2021, McGrath said that what happened was 'a combination of pent-up demand, exuberance, Christmas time, hospitality, household mixing and [the] Kent [variant].' Leo Varadkar said the third wave was 'initially driven by socialisation, and then was compounded by Alpha'.

There is a thread, too, in the government's position that its own advisers weren't alive to the threat quickly enough, or that the virus mutation got the jump on the State. Donnelly later said the Christmas fiasco was caused by socialisation plus the new variant, which 'subsequent analysis revealed was in Ireland earlier than was previously understood'. On 14 December 2020, Matt Hancock had moved large parts of the south-east of England to the highest level of restrictions due to the emergence of the variant, which was likely to be behind 'very sharp exponential rises in the virus'.

On 15 December, De Gascun had told RTÉ that 'when a novel variant like this emerges, it's always important that we assess it and keep an eye on it, but at this stage there's nothing to be overly concerned about'. Varadkar was critical of this position in an interview in late 2021. 'The view of Cillian certainly, maybe not NPHET, was that these were of academic interest and that we shouldn't invest too many resources in even looking for them, or gene sequencing,' he said.

De Gascun had sparked controversy on New Year's Day when he tweeted that results at that stage suggested that Alpha was 'not responsible' for the surge. Professor Mary Horgan, the president of the Royal College of Physicians in Ireland and a recent government appointee to NPHET, took on her new colleague on the public health team. In a reply to the tweet, she said that the 'sample size [is] too small to make this conclusion'.

The tweet irked De Gascun, who later contributed to a paper which argued that, while the surge 'appeared to coincide with the arrival' of Alpha, there was a 'disconnect' between the peak in case numbers and the peak prevalence of Alpha eight weeks later. De Gascun's view, and that of other senior NPHET members, was clear: Alpha had an impact. It made the wave bigger and harder to tackle. But the level of socialising by people in the run-up to Christmas mattered much more.

A virus depends on its host for survival and relies on that host's behaviour to transmit it to someone else. So Alpha was always going to become dominant. It was growing in Ireland from November 2020, accounting for around 7.5 per cent of cases in the week beginning 14 December. By the week beginning 4 January 2021, this figure was about 46 per cent.

'The fact that Alpha was more transmissible certainly resulted in more cases in January, and an epidemic that was more challenging to control with existing public health measures,' De Gascun said. 'But it didn't drive anything: it did what viruses do, and rode the wave of increased human interaction and socialisation in the pre-Christmas period.'

Perhaps the strongest view held on the role of Alpha is the Taoiseach's. 'Compounded it?' he said in late November 2021. 'Alpha drove it wild.' Citing Horgan by name, Martin said the variant was in Ireland 'in early December and it was a factor'. He also said he rang Tony Holohan before Christmas about the variant 'and I was told it wasn't an immediate concern'.

He also referred to the concerns shared by Angela Merkel at the time. In the days after Christmas, the Taoiseach took a phone call from the then German chancellor. She was uneasy about the Irish case trajectory. 'I see the Irish graphs,' she told the Taoiseach. 'Up.' She said this to him again 'at the bloody EU council meeting,' Martin said later.

The Taoiseach argued that this view was echoed by doctors in hospitals, who told him that the minute the Alpha variant of the virus got on to a ward it infected everyone on it, which would not previously have been the case. 'There was a difference of views. Public health would not accept, by the way, the clinicians' view here,' Martin said. 'Stephen [Donnelly] would have discussed this with Ronan and Tony and was told the clinicians are getting this wrong.'

As to the view that Alpha wasn't the driving force behind the wave, Martin is clear: 'I don't buy that, I don't accept that, the evidence demonstrates that, the exponential growth in cases, the fact that in hospitals it spread like wildfire, unlike the previous variant.'

To this day, Glynn, Holohan and Nolan believe the more fundamental factor was how socialising played out up to 30 December. 'I can't prove it was hospitality but what I know for a fact is that hundreds of thousands of people came together in indoor settings in the middle of December,' Glynn later said. It grew 'not because that virus was more transmissible, it was happening because more people were coming together', the deputy chief medical officer said.

If Alpha had never arrived, Holohan believes, there would still have been mass mortality and incredible pressure on hospitals, due to 'massive socialisation'. 'We absolutely would have,' he said. 'It's a factual statement, saying, "Here is the level of disease, this is the level of socialisation: A multiplied by B gives you C." That's what we were looking at. It wasn't difficult to work out [...] Alpha played a role, obviously, after Christmas, in January. But what happened at Christmas and through Christmas [was] caused by socialisation.'

Philip Nolan shares this view. Alpha, he said, 'made it bigger, made it last longer and made it harder to suppress'. But more than anything, the devastating third wave was, in his view, caused by 'the very intense social mixing' from early December. 'There can't be any doubt, in retrospect, that the decision for a near complete societal reopening at the beginning of December was the primary trigger of the January surge.'

The grim aftermath of the meaningful Christmas shifted the power dynamics of the pandemic again. The politicians and their public health advisers were once more in lockstep. 'The room for latitude with NPHET at that point was very small, if not gone,' Paschal Donohoe would later say.

And it was the finance minister who would sum up the mood of uncertainty and trepidation at the Cabinet subcommittee meeting on 5 January. As the reams of gloomy data and projections were presented to politicians, Donohoe asked Holohan and his team, 'How long is the tunnel?'

The truth was, they didn't know.

CHAPTER 27:

SHOT IN THE ARM

21 January 2021
Cases: 181,922
Deaths: 2,818
Seven-day average of new cases: 2,695

'**W**e are planning our programme based on a supply of vacc- ines that would mean every citizen can be vaccinated by September,' Stephen Donnelly told the Dáil on the third Thursday in January. Less than 100,000 shots of the Covid-19 vaccine had been administered across the State. Three weeks into the new year, 532 people were already dead as a result of the virus, and hundreds more deaths were inevitable.

The health minister's statement to the Dáil was littered with caveats and qualifications, with words like 'indicative', 'assumptions', and 'tentative' thrown in for cover. But in the dark days of Ireland's devastating third wave it was a beacon of hope. The September date was all that made the headlines that day.

It was, however, simultaneously a hostage to fortune – a promise the government would be held to and for which it would be castigated if it failed to meet it. Even if some circumstances were beyond the control of ministers, the weary public, entering their second year of Covid-19, would not forgive the coalition if it mishandled the way out of the pandemic nightmare.

—

'Hopefully he knows something we don't,' the anonymous Department of Health source told the *Irish Examiner*. 'Maybe he'll hook us up?' It was 15 September 2020 and sources in Miesian Plaza were pushing back strongly against the Tánaiste, Leo Varadkar, who the previous day had told journalists that a Covid-19 vaccine would be available and could be administered in the first half of 2021. The story quoted a senior department source saying, 'we're highly unlikely to have an approved vaccine in January', further noting that they were only getting around to setting up a committee to decide on how one might be rolled out.

The story worried Varadkar, who thought the remarks were dismissive – but also just plain inaccurate. He had been told by Paul Reid (no relation to the HSE's Paul Reid), the CEO of Pfizer's Irish operation, earlier that month that a vaccine would be ready by the end of the year. 'It wasn't a figary, it was something that the company manufacturing the vaccines was telling me,' he would later say. 'I was a little bit insulted, and I was a bit worried that if this was the view in the Department of Health, that they weren't adequately prepared for the fact the vaccines might be available in December.'

Pfizer had been adamant it would have a shot ready in December and would soon have 100 million doses manufactured. Privately, Varadkar thought that even his publicly indicated timeline for the new year was being cautious – and he was right. The first Pfizer shots were administered in Ireland just before the new year, and by the end of the first half of 2021, around half of the adults in the country would be completely vaccinated.

It was perhaps no surprise that in September 2020 the Department of Health believed vaccines were some time away. It had only just set up its vaccine strategy group, which met for the first time at the end of August. It was chaired by the tireless Fergal Goodman, the same assistant secretary who had been given new responsibilities during the shake-up of the department earlier that year, and who would shortly have to contend with the thorny issue of mandatory hotel quarantine.

Early meetings of Goodman's group identified many of the issues that would leap to the centre of the political agenda in early 2021. How would the State facilitate vaccines for the entire country? How would it handle the likelihood that initial supplies would be small? Who would administer the vaccines? Would it be through GPs, special clinics, pharmacies? Would there be special storage requirements for the different vaccines? If so, would there be sufficient cold storage for some vaccines? Would some shots be suitable for some cohorts of the population but not others? Would vaccine passports be needed? What about an IT platform to track the rollout?

The minutes of the group indicate that it was grappling with the key issues but doing so with a typically cautious civil service incrementalism. Groups, subgroups and working groups were being convened, one-page strategies drawn up, along with key issues for circulation, draft action plans for review and comment. A second group had been established within the HSE and began to meet in October. The minutes of the final meeting of Goodman's group made vague reference to a shake-up, that its structure 'may need to be reappraised to maximise [...] output and to avoid duplication of effort'.

Five days after that meeting, news broke that trials showed Pfizer's vaccine was incredibly effective against Covid-19. Suddenly, what had been abstract and hopeful became real and vital. In the Department of the Taoiseach, Martin Fraser called up Professor Brian MacCraith, the former president of DCU.

Since leaving his academic role, MacCraith had embedded himself in the semi-formal shortlist of the great and the good the State called on when it wanted to outsource the deep thinking – and maybe some of the hard choices – about policy (or, indeed, to kick a thorny issue into touch). He had led a review of public health training in 2017, carried out a rapid view of the scandal-hit CervicalCheck programme in 2019 and he was chairing the government's commission on the future of media. Now Fraser wanted him to head up a vaccine taskforce.

MacCraith got the impression that there was a concern in Government Buildings, and more specifically in the Taoiseach's office, that 'things weren't moving rapidly enough, or there wasn't sufficient focus'. He was not wrong; Fraser had formed the view that the State was not ready to vaccinate nearly the entire population and needed to significantly upgrade its capacity to run a programme that could draw not just on the HSE but on expertise from people in logistics to those working for the large multinationals based in Ireland. The UK, which would initially tear ahead in its vaccine programme, had been working on these issues for months, under its vaccine tsar, venture capitalist Kate Bingham. MacCraith was told to pull together, in a matter of weeks, a plan for how a vaccination programme would work in practice. When he went to work, he later recalled, he found 'there wasn't a high level of preparedness'.

MacCraith and the newly established vaccine taskforce were given a floor of an office building owned by the Office of Government Procurement in Dublin's docklands. Before long, the taskforce had moved into the glistening Liffey-side headquarters of consultancy firm PwC, which was providing consultancy services. Across 2020 to March 2021, the HSE alone would pay PwC €5.1m for Covid consultancy

It wasn't plain sailing; one early meeting was described by a person present as a 'shitshow'. Multiple people with similar functions crowded around a long meeting table in PwC or took part in massive Zoom calls. On one early call with vaccine manufacturers, a source recalls how MacCraith inadvertently asked them to divulge information that would be tantamount to discussing trade secrets on a call with competitors.

At an emergency meeting in the Department of Health on 3 January, MacCraith told NPHET that by the end of the month, 40,000 shots would be given per week, but a source at the meeting wasn't convinced they were ready to go. It sounded like they were unprepared and having difficulties with IT and workforce, the source later recalled. Another person on a call with MacCraith and his team in January said it was 'comical' with 'lots of people trying to have a hand in the vaccine programme, [and who] were pushing out actual experts'.

That was a view shared by some in the HSE, MacCraith later surmised, which had experience in vaccination programmes such as the annual winter flu vaccine and the schools immunisation programme.

'There may have been some resentment that those who routinely would have run vaccinations suddenly had this superstructure coming in,' MacCraith later said. 'You could sense a bit of that and that had to be worked through.' However, he was acting with the stamp of approval from Fraser, the Taoiseach and the HSE's Paul Reid.

Public service turf wars were only one of State's concerns as it prepared to roll out life-saving vaccines. An Garda Síochána were worried that anti-vaccination groups would intercept shipments of the jabs as they came in, or try to prevent them from being distributed around the country from the HSE's cold storage facility in Citywest. The vaccines, because of how they were stored and the complexity of shifting them around the country, would present a perfect opportunity for an asymmetric attack that would be easy to mount, extremely visible, and could have a significant impact.

'One of the concerns we had early on in the programme is that if there [is] resistance to vaccines and there is an anti-vax campaign, it does not take anything sophisticated to interrupt that distribution chain,' a senior HSE official later said. 'Simply blocking a road for a period of hours is something that compromises the distribution chain and the cold chain.'

—

Gardaí believed that anti-vaccination groups, taking their cue from anti-nuclear campaigns of the 1970s and 1980s, might chain themselves to machinery or fences, lie down on the road and not let trucks roll out. The force's digital intelligence unit – which had its roots in monitoring the online chatter of water charges protests years earlier and had grown to monitor terrorist groups and other subversive activity online – was called upon.

The anti-vaccine groups in Ireland were not well organised, but Gardaí did put certain individuals under surveillance, with undercover policing of digital groups to the fore. Such protests never materialised, but roving patrols were put in place around mass vaccination centres when they opened later in the spring, amid concerns they would be targeted by protests.

The problems that would bedevil the first phase of the vaccine roll-out began to materialise as early as mid-December, before any shots were even administered. The first intervention from the National Immunisation Advisory Committee, whose job it was to provide clinical advice on the vaccine rollout, came on 17 December 2020 when its chair, Karina Butler, wrote a panicked email to Tony Holohan and Ronan Glynn shortly before 5 p.m.

NIAC, she explained, now only wanted the shots to be given on sites that had medical facilities, in case someone had a bad reaction. Anaphylaxis was a particular concern. In a follow-up email Butler said there were concerns about 'trying to do it in too many centres at once'. Her concerns were reasonable, on a clinical level as well as on a human level – the last thing anyone needed was a serious and high-profile adverse reaction claiming someone's life in a remote nursing home. But it presented a serious logistical and operational challenge for the HSE, which had been finalising plans to administer jabs in nursing home settings.

'What the fuck?' Paul Reid responded when news reached HSE headquarters in Dr Steevens' Hospital. It was a big problem. Nursing homes are not clinical settings; they are places where people live. Most have a GP who provides in-house services, but their capacity to deal with a really serious incident would be extremely limited. There were a few nursing homes co-located on or near acute hospitals or big healthcare centres but not many. Amid rising Covid-19 numbers, the pressure was immense.

Ultimately, the fears about people going into anaphylaxis after being vaccinated subsided, and the programme was pushed into nursing homes around the country in early January. But there were still teething problems. The vaccine rollout started before an IT platform to record progress was ready, meaning that in nursing homes people were writing down information on scraps of paper.

Confidence was gradually growing, however, to such an extent that a policy of holding 50 per cent of the vaccines in reserve was relaxed, and, at the insistence of Stephen Donnelly, the programme was accelerated courtesy of early deliveries from Pfizer. A Cabinet memo on 12 January outlined that residents and staff in nursing homes would all have their first shot in the next fortnight.

In sharp contrast to the convulsions over supplies that would follow, the memo also outlined how Ireland could have a 'substantial excess' for resale, donation, distribution or use in boosters. That eventually came to pass, but the route taken was much more bumpy than was anticipated.

The following week, ministers were told that around 770,000 doses would be given in March. But that target would be missed by some margin. The first indications of issues with supply began to emerge, ironically from Pfizer, which would ultimately prove rock solid in terms of reliability. An issue at a Pfizer plant in Belgium forced it to slash deliveries, and panicked meetings were held in Miesian Plaza amid fears that up to half of the consignments Ireland was due would not turn up. This issue flared up and disappeared again, but much bigger problems lay ahead.

—

The term 'game-changer' still draws an 'Oh, Jesus' from MacCraith. In early 2020, it was the phrase du jour, particularly when it came to AstraZeneca's two-dose Covid-19 vaccine developed in conjunction with Oxford University. The jab was easier to store and administer than Pfizer and Moderna shots, which were based on a novel mRNA technology that required ultra-low-temperature storage. The plan was to roll out the AstraZeneca vaccine to the State's GP network, massively increasing the speed of the programme.

The UK had already given AstraZeneca the green light and was racing ahead of its former colleagues in the EU in vaccinating its population. Pressure was growing in Dublin, and such was the enthusiasm for the AstraZeneca jab that Stephen Donnelly publicly proclaimed in mid-January that he was seeking early delivery of Ireland's allocation. He wanted it in the country before it was approved, and distributed to doctors' surgeries up and down the State so that it would be ready to plunge into arms once greenlit by the European Medicines Agency (EMA).

But MacCraith knew it wasn't a runner. 'I had to bite my tongue a lot,' he later said. Sure enough, it was a firm 'No' when he looked into it. 'I suppose anything that raised expectations unrealistically, just overall probably, was unfortunate.' Three days after Donnelly had raised the possibility of early deliveries, the European Commission publicly said it wasn't possible and the minister had to concede that it had been an 'ambitious ask'.

Ultimately, the problem with AstraZeneca was not in securing early deliveries – it was in securing deliveries at all. The company welshed on schedules that proved wildly unreliable, and it would contact the HSE or the taskforce, sometimes with only a day's notice, to slash delivery numbers. This had a knock-on effect all the way down the chain as appointments were rescheduled, creating major logistical and operational difficulties.

Before the end of January, a bitter row broke out with the European Commission after the drugmaker told Brussels there would be serious shortfalls due to manufacturing issues. This prompted a brief but damaging diplomatic crisis when the EU triggered an emergency provision of the post-Brexit Northern Ireland protocol, Article 16. In effect, this would have meant controls on vaccine exports from the EU in order to avoid Northern Ireland becoming a back door for vaccines to be shipped to mainland Britain. It was a major error and reversed within hours, but it was interpreted by the British government and Northern unionists as a hostile act. In Dublin there was disbelief that it was allowed to happen.

The State could cause plenty of trouble for itself, too. After AstraZeneca's shot was approved by the EMA on 29 January, NIAC ran the rule over it to determine how it could be included in Ireland's programme. Late on the evening of 1 February, RTÉ's health correspondent Fergal Bowers tweeted that NIAC had recommended to Holohan that AstraZeneca would be used as 'an option' for people aged 65 and over.

However, that was only half the story. NIAC's recommendations were much more restrictive. The group had met twice over the weekend, and nerves were growing frayed in the HSE at the lack of a firm indication. Across Europe the atmosphere was not good. There were genuine concerns about the low number of 65+-year-olds included in the AstraZeneca trial. In a bizarre intervention, French president Emmanuel Macron said the jab was 'quasi-ineffective' for older people. France, Belgium, Italy and Germany all ruled it out for older people.

The delivery of advice from NIAC is a convoluted process. NIAC acts on a request from the chief medical officer, and after it sends its advice to Tony Holohan, he formulates his own advice for the minister. Sometimes this differs from what NIAC has told him. The minister then sometimes (but not always) goes to Cabinet to seek approval for the decision. Holohan then has to tell the HSE what the policy is, with health officials then having to figure out how the policy will be operationalised. In this case, to put it in layman's terms, they have to work out how and when jabs will be put into arms.

On 3 February, two days after Bowers's story, the HSE's chief clinical officer, Colm Henry, confirmed the AstraZeneca vaccine could be used for older people, but the strong preference was to give them an mRNA vaccine; either Pfizer or a jab produced by Moderna. In a narrow sense, it was an option, but in reality, this all but ruled out AstraZeneca for the over-65s.

The HSE and taskforce were now scrambling, and the pressure was coming on from the Taoiseach's office, who told them a new plan was needed by Thursday. The prospect of leaving older people without vaccine cover was a political non-starter. 'That grouping of seventies and above in the country, obviously, is a very important voting group,' MacCraith later noted.

The plan was approved late on Friday night and GPs were told they would be giving Pfizer, not AstraZeneca, to over-65s. Due to the complex storage arrangements, they would have to come together in 'buddy' surgeries or in the first mass vaccination centres.

It was the sort of volatility that would characterise much of the vaccine programme in the spring and early summer of 2021. The problems Ireland faced were not unique in the EU; but the US and the UK, which were more visible, were streaking ahead. At the end of February, Martin Fraser texted the Taoiseach two graphs showing that, while Ireland lagged way behind the US and the UK, it was above the EU average in terms of vaccines administered per 100 people. 'The only fair way to compare our performance is in the EU context and while we're not the very best we are doing very well,' he wrote.

Fraser was trying to land a point at a time of acute political pressure for the Taoiseach and his government. Indeed, many senior figures involved in the rollout were confident even at that time that the floodgates would eventually open; that there would be weeks in the summer where hundreds of thousands of people would be jabbed. But amid harsh restrictions, uncertain supply lines and the mounting post-Christmas death toll, this seemed very far away – and barely credible.

CHAPTER 28:

SNAKE OIL

20 February 2021
Cases: 214,378
Deaths: 4,135
Seven-day average of new cases: 797

Mark Ferguson knew how to make an entrance. In the depths of lockdown, sartorial standards had slipped on NPHET's Zoom meetings, like everywhere else. But at his first meeting since being appointed, Ferguson almost seemed to be sending a message with his garb: a hoodie and a crumpled baseball cap. If that didn't do the trick, his Zoom background would: a fiery CGI alligator, drawn in flames, on a black background, filled the screen behind him.

The backdrop was a nod to Ferguson's unique research pedigree. Long before he was head of Science Foundation Ireland and chief scientific adviser to the Irish government, he researched cleft lips and palates in humans, which, in a peculiar turn, led to experimenting with alligators and crocodiles, since their palates are remarkably similar to humans. Ferguson has been known to remark that working with alligators and crocodiles prepared him well for a career in the Irish public service.

A glittering research career led to the Northern Ireland-born Ferguson being made a Commander of the British Empire in 1999 for services to health and life sciences. He was made director general of Science Foundation Ireland, the State's body for co-ordinating and funding scientific research, in 2012, and appointed chief scientific adviser later that year. Ferguson had been in situ for almost a decade and yet he was a peripheral figure to much of the Covid-19 response, unlike his UK counterpart, Professor Patrick Vallance, who became a visible and integral part of the British effort.

That changed in January 2021 when Stephen Donnelly rang Ferguson and told him he was 'looking to refresh NPHET'. As Ferguson later recalled, 'He wanted more of an external perspective.'

The health minister had been examining a NPHET restructuring as far back as September and October 2020, but it had been overtaken by events as the virus ran out of control. He believed it had plenty of medics – in fact he thought it had too many members overall – but was light on science. Donnelly also wanted to add himself. He had asked Holohan as much. 'When I came in, I put that to the department – because I am a hands-on sort of a guy,' Donnelly recalled. 'I like to be involved in the detail.' Multiple people pushed back against the suggestion. At the core of the concerns was that, as Holohan had told Harris in March 2020, ministers change the dynamic of a meeting. However, if he could not be on NPHET, Donnelly believed he could add more members who were not necessarily Holohan appointees. It was a view shared by the coalition leaders. 'I particularly wanted Mark [Ferguson] on, I think Micheál was kind of keen on Mary Horgan as well,' Leo Varadkar would later recall, saying the pair were added 'for their qualities, particularly their support for antigen testing'.

Horgan, the president of the Royal College of Physicians of Ireland, is an infectious diseases expert and, while her credentials were unquestioned, her appointment raised eyebrows among some senior NPHET members. First, there was a curious choreography around the decision to add her, which Donnelly told Holohan had been discussed at Cabinet level. But an appointment to an advisory panel within a government department is something that doesn't even need ministerial-level approval, much less a Cabinet discussion.

The same NPHET members believed her specialism – infectious diseases – was well covered and, as time went on, they harboured suspicions that Horgan was briefing the Taoiseach bilaterally. They noted similarities between views she would express privately and what Micheál Martin would say in public. There was nothing improper here; Martin made a point of using his long car journeys to and from Cork at the start and end of his week to check in with all manner of people involved in the public health response. Nonetheless, Horgan and Ferguson were, in effect, political appointees to a medical advisory group. Their CVs were hardly out of place, but some on NPHET couldn't shake the feeling that they were fifth columnists. The appointments had been made at a time when the pendulum of pandemic policy had swung firmly towards the public health advisers; there was little appetite or scope for departure from NPHET advice, but the long-standing ambition to reshape the advisory body, perhaps from within, remained.

The traumatic aftermath of Christmas meant the whip hand was with NPHET. The politicians knew it, senior NPHET people knew it, and it was clear to the outside world as well. In February 2021, Trinity College Dublin's Covid-19 Law and Human Rights Observatory wrote that 'NPHET's advice has at times appeared to carry determinative or close to determinative weight'. There is a risk, the group said, 'that expert advice, limited to public health, captures the whole decision-making process, such that the advice becomes the decision'.

Yet despite this, the appointment of Ferguson in particular heralded the start of a major scrap between the political system – more specifically, Stephen Donnelly – and NPHET throughout the course of 2021. It would prompt bitter battles behind the scenes, damage key relationships and raise questions over who called the shots.

—

Aside from the striking backdrop, Ferguson's first contribution did not impress some NPHET stalwarts. He gave what one participant later claimed was a short and fairly elementary lecture about viral evolution, genomics and transmission, which one NPHET official acidly dismissed as having 'clearly just been picked from the *Atlantic* magazine'.

NPHET was packed with infectious disease experts, virologists and civil servants who had been given an 18-month crash course in pandemics and the coronavirus. Now here was Ferguson telling them about how viruses mutate, the importance of ventilation and, most important, about rapid antigen testing. It was something, he said, that worked just like a pregnancy test. It was a remark that raised hackles among some veterans on the group, who felt they didn't need any easily grasped analogies to help shape their thinking on antigen tests.

Rapid testing was already a divisive topic. Its proponents fell somewhere on a spectrum between a belief that it could enable a fundamental shift in how the pandemic was managed, to a feeling that, at the very least, it should be considered as a useful tool in the State's armoury. At its most utopian, antigen evangelists imagined a near-normal version of life alongside the virus, with nearly all activities facilitated by a universal system of rapid, cheap antigen testing. Donnelly wasn't quite that zealous, but he did have a deep conviction that the technology could have a meaningful role. He told an Oireachtas committee in November 2020 that it could be a 'game-changer'.

NPHET had long resisted the widespread adoption of antigen testing, arguing that there was no evidence base to warrant its wider use in society. Chief among Tony Holohan's concerns was that symptomatic people who got a negative result from the test would falsely believe it was a green light to go about their lives and partake in risky social activities. Or, as Philip Nolan once bluntly observed in a Twitter post that earned a potent backlash: it was 'snake oil'. Nolan would later express regret over the post, which would be serially thrown back at him, weaponised as evidence of NPHET's dismissive and inherently hostile approach to things it didn't like.

The appointment of Ferguson in early 2021 was Donnelly's way of laying down a marker and finding a way to make NPHET play ball. Privately, he likened the powers that rest in his office to a 'ministerial bulldozer', which he could get into and drive around when he wanted something done.

He made his feelings clear in a letter to Holohan on 22 January. 'As you are aware, I have been pressing for the need to expedite antigen testing for some time,' he told Holohan. Beyond putting Ferguson on NPHET, he was also granting him his own vehicle to drive through change. 'I am disappointed at the lack of progress made to date and have decided to set up a small group to examine and advise on this issue as quickly as possible.'

Interventions in healthcare are overseen by a framework known as 'clinical governance', which is designed to ensure oversight, quality and accountability within healthcare. It's a key pillar of many modern medical systems. Faced with resistance from within the healthcare establishment, Donnelly's move was to reverse-engineer this and set up his own expert group on rapid testing. 'One of the challenges in rolling out something like this is that as well as the normal operational considerations, there needs to be clinical governance, which is difficult to get when the clinical view was different to mine in terms of where and how antigen testing should be deployed,' Donnelly said later. Rather than be beholden to the advice coming from the CMO's office, Donnelly's clear view was that it was his prerogative to outflank that advice if he saw fit. 'I think it's important that ministers can go against advice,' he said. He believed the advice coming from Holohan and Glynn was given in good faith, and knew it was also broadly supported by the HSE. 'I just had a different view.'

He picked the other members of this bespoke group, which Ferguson would chair: Horgan; TCD professor of experimental immunology Kingston Mills; and infectious diseases consultant Professor Paddy Mallon. 'All have accepted and are on board. They will be reporting directly to minister (quickly),' Susan Mitchell, Donnelly's policy adviser, wrote on 20 January in an email sent just after 7 a.m., copying in the new Department of Health secretary general, Robert Watt.

Watt had arrived at the department just 18 days earlier to relieve Colm O'Reardon, who had been six months in the post – longer than he or anyone around him expected. Though appointed on an acting basis, it soon became clear that Watt was also in the running for the role on a permanent basis, and was seen as the clear favourite. The €292,000 salary (€81,000 more than a standard secretary general wage) would sweeten the pill of arguably the most challenging job in the civil service. It would also cause Watt and the government months of difficulties as they defended what, on the face of it, appeared to be – as Sinn Féin put it – a 'stroke of the highest order' – something all parties involved in the appointment firmly deny.

Discussions around Watt's appointment had, in fact, begun shortly after the previous October's budget. Watt had to move anyway from DPER due to limits on the length of time secretaries general can remain in post. There was a view, shared by the Taoiseach, Paschal Donohoe, Michael McGrath, Fraser and others, that there was a lack of structure and process in Health. Memos were being drawn up for Cabinet without advance discussion with other departments and the interface between public health advice and government decision-making had been badly damaged over the course of October and November. A couple of days after Christmas, Fraser called Watt and told him the Taoiseach wanted him to go down to Baggot Street. There would be an open competition, but Watt was sent in with a mission from the Taoiseach: sort out the department. 'We needed to do something at that stage in the Department of Health, it had to be done,' Martin later said. 'What we're saying [at the time] is we need to solidify health, we need to get some certainty around it.' He said there was a 'vacuum' at the official level in Health – not just Covid, but the children's hospital.

Watt arrived into the department the day after New Year's Day to put his arms around the situation, meeting Tony Holohan, establishing the ground rules for how they would work together. The primary goal was to avoid the sort of communications breakdown that had happened the previous October. No more surprises. Shortly after he received Mitchell's email on 20 January, Watt forwarded it to the CMO: 'We might have a word later.'

Watt did not think the expert group was a good idea, he didn't understand why it was being formed and did not necessarily agree with the minister's and Mitchell's direction of travel. Later that night, Watt told

Mitchell that he, Holohan and Donnelly had spoken. While 'everybody is happy' that the group could proceed, there would be a need for 'further expertise' on the group, he wrote, and its work would be considered by NPHET. The subtext was clear: if rapid testing was to be considered, the healthcare establishment would be involved. Holohan would have a presence. Mitchell pushed back; it was to be a 'small group that moves quickly'. Donnelly initially suggested that Glynn could be appointed to the group to 'ensure efficient cross-fertilisation' – although he never was.

A brief tug-of-war followed; Holohan suggested the issue be looked at by a NPHET subgroup – keeping the topic firmly under his eye. Ultimately, the independent group went ahead, albeit with two additions. The first was Darina O'Flanagan, a former director of the HPSC, whom Holohan had called out of retirement when the pandemic hit. O'Flanagan was on a par with Glynn, Nolan and De Gascun as key confidantes of Holohan. 'She's not afraid of anybody or anything. She's not afraid of me,' Holohan later said. 'She tells me if she doesn't agree with me […] and that's what I want her to do.' The second addition was Dr Lorraine Doherty, a senior HSE doctor who had worked on the health service's use of rapid testing.

Before long, Holohan would be gone, taking his second period of compassionate leave as his wife entered hospice care. But in his absence, the conflict over rapid testing continued.

—

As the rapid testing group set about its work, Donnelly and his allies went on a major offensive in support of antigen testing. On 27 February, he replied to a Twitter user: 'I appointed the government's chief scientific adviser, Professor Mark Ferguson, to lead an urgent review of rapid testing. He's reporting back very soon – my view is that there's an opportunity to deploy these tests.'

In early March, a series of briefings conveyed the position that antigen would be among 'key elements' of the government's reopening plan to be presented in the middle of the month. When the *Irish Times* health editor Paul Cullen reported on 1 March that the use of rapid tests was to be given the green light for use in monitoring outbreaks in schools, it prompted a furious reaction from the HSE, whose job it would be to implement any such changes.

Colm Henry, the HSE's chief clinical officer, emailed Glynn, copying in his boss Paul Reid, and Watt. 'This highlights the concerns we have over governance of antigen testing policy,' he fumed. 'Parallel decision-making on antigen testing policy can lead to confusion in public health response. Any decisions made in this area should be fully integrated into existing processes in both DOH and HSE.'

Watt sought to pour oil on troubled waters, reassuring him that this was 'media speculation' based on a report that had not been finished. 'No policy position has been decided – and we will decide any advice to the minister in tandem with yourselves,' he told Henry. Notwithstanding the 'nothing to see here' explanation proffered to the HSE, Watt was concerned. That afternoon he sought out the draft report from Glynn and that night emailed him raising issues about its content, saying that he had spoken to Donnelly about it, 'express[ing] the view that significant work [is] required'. Donnelly, Watt told Glynn, was 'supportive of the view that the report needs more work'.

Four days later, Ferguson told his group that he had just submitted to Donnelly his final report – or what he thought was the final version. Just minutes later both O'Flanagan and Doherty told him to take their names off it. Doherty's PA had already emailed that morning on behalf of both: 'We feel it does not adequately meet the terms of reference as set up by the Minister for Health for this working group nor the requirements of pandemic control in Ireland.'

But Ferguson appeared not to have seen the first email at 4.25 p.m., when he emailed the group with a copy of the 'final report and my cover letter which I submitted to the minister today'. Twenty minutes later, Doherty wrote again: 'In case the report has already gone to the minister, my name should be removed' and she emailed again seven minutes after that: 'I hope you received my letter this morning? My name should be taken off the final report as I cannot support it.' Four minutes after that, she wrote again: 'Darina and I wrote to you this morning indicating we could not sign off this report. We asked for our names to be removed from the report.'

It was another hour before this landed with Ferguson, and it knocked him sideways. He had just sent a report broadly endorsing the use of antigen tests to a minister who had made it a political priority. Now, it seemed, the rug was being pulled from under him. 'I have spent all of yesterday and today finalising and submitting our report. I was therefore shocked to find the attached letter amongst my emails when I returned to my routine work,' he wrote back. The previous morning, he had asked that issues should be flagged by midday. 'It is unfortunate that no one had the courtesy to inform me about the contents of the attached letter earlier, or by telephone, before I submitted our report to the minister,' he added.

Ferguson had to go cap-in-hand to Donnelly and tell him that the report in fact no longer enjoyed the support of the entire group. What was more important was that the two dissenters were from the bodies responsible for developing and implementing policy. What good is a report if the actual people who are responsible for nuts-and-bolts implementation have disavowed it? If the Ferguson group was a political attempt to circumnavigate the healthcare establishment, this was the returned volley of fire. 'I am not sure where we go from here,' Ferguson wrote to the group. 'I am very disappointed by this turn of events.'

Donnelly gave the group another fortnight to submit a unanimous report. On the day it was due to reconvene, 16 March, O'Flanagan emailed to say she was discussing changes with Doherty, who was unable to attend and was going on leave, and they were 'endeavouring to get recommendations which are realistic and can actually be implemented and not merely aspirational'.

Ferguson later told Donnelly that O'Flanagan 'felt the report was unbalanced and too strongly in favour of introducing rapid testing'. In the end, neither O'Flanagan's nor Doherty's names were on the final report. Submitting it to Donnelly, Ferguson outlined in exhaustive detail what had happened, how support had been withdrawn 'to my great surprise, and at the last minute', and his later efforts to persuade O'Flanagan and Doherty to sign off on the document. Nonetheless, he told Donnelly that the recommendation was that alongside other measures 'widespread rapid testing is introduced in Ireland as another layer in our response to Covid-19 and to maximise our chances of a successful sustainable reopening'.

Senior NPHET and HSE officials thought the report was dreadful, scoffing at the inclusion of an endorsement from a Nobel Prize-winning economist (Paul Romer, a professor at New York University, who argued for regular serial mass testing and reviewed the report in advance of its submission) in a paper on health technology as an example of 'eminence-based medicine' or 'policy-based evidence making'. A senior HSE source later described the report and antigen testing in general as 'really a proxy for a struggle for power between a minister who was struggling to get purchase […] versus someone who understood how to exercise the maximum power from the weakest position'.

That someone was Tony Holohan. Although he was on leave, his office, at that point headed by Glynn, filleted the report in early April. 'The role of these tests is also overstated in parts of the report where it is purported that widespread testing can prevent further lockdowns or significant levels of restrictions and provides no substantive real-world evidence in this regard,' Glynn wrote. While the report was launched with an accompanying press conference, rapid testing, beyond some pilot programmes and a couple of scaled-up examples, had a limited role for many months.

The entire healthcare establishment had effectively dismissed the report and the HSE showed little interest in using antigen tests. In May, the Cabinet was told that the HSE had used fewer than 300 rapid tests in acute hospitals. By contrast, the Department of Agriculture had used nearly 11,000 across food and meat processing facilities. Donnelly's first effort to make antigen testing work had largely fallen flat. But behind the scenes, the conflict rolled on.

—

Into the late spring and early summer of 2021, Donnelly remained insistent, badgering Watt for an update. He wanted to bring a memo to Cabinet in late April, and again in mid-May. In June, he emailed Holohan (now back at work following the death of his wife) amid growing concern over the Delta variant and its importation to Ireland. 'I'm also of the view that rapid testing should be available and offered at ports of entry for travellers returning from GB,' the minister wrote.

A week later, Watt asked Glynn and Holohan for another update. He was feeling the pressure from his minister. In the same month, Donnelly told Watt he wanted to set up a group on implementing wider anti-gen testing that would be chaired by HIQA. Watt emailed Glynn and Holohan: 'I suggested HIQA would not work but the Minister is clear that a group is to be established which drives policy and promotes use in: critical workplaces, schools, colleges, live events, etc.'

Holohan replied that NPHET was reviewing its approach to the matter 'given the persistence of this issue in public debate' but said he hadn't seen anything new 'that gives me any assurance regarding antigen testing in the settings mentioned in your email'. In a cutting broadside, the CMO concluded his email by saying he was happy to address the issue alongside two of his senior officials, who would be there to see 'any discussion which might lead to operationalising an instruction from the minister, especially if it is at variance with the public health advice provided by me'. The implication was clear: if Donnelly was going to reject his advice on antigen tests, and figure out a way to move them to the centre of Ireland's Covid policy, Holohan wanted witnesses.

Holohan found Donnelly's persistence strange, but it was unrelenting. Donnelly would often talk about conversations he had had with Susan Hopkins, the Kildare-born deputy director of Public Health England, on the UK's rollout of hundreds of millions of rapid tests free on the NHS, a project the CMO considered a waste of money.

In early July, Holohan upped the ante with an official letter to Donnelly, taking on his intention to establish a group for deploying rapid antigen tests among asymptomatic people, which the *Irish Independent* had a few days earlier characterised as the minister preparing to 'sideline' NPHET.

It wasn't safe, Holohan told his minister. 'The hypothesis that antigen testing could be a precursor or enabler for the safe recommencement of certain activities which would otherwise not be deemed to be safe [...] poses several risks both to the individuals engaging in those activities and to those around them, as well as to the wider public health response.'

Holohan said that pursuing this policy could endanger the whole project of keeping Covid-19 under control and variants of concern at bay: 'Crucially, such work should not compromise the finite expertise and resources that are currently fully engaged in the other critical arms of the public health response as this would present significant risks to our country's capacity to continue to effectively respond to the pandemic, particularly given the immediate threat of the Delta variant.'

—

The email betrayed Holohan's deeper concerns about how Donnelly handled his advice more generally and how he represented it to the Taoiseach and his colleagues around the Cabinet table. He, Glynn and Nolan sat in meetings of the Cabinet subcommittee and observed how Donnelly spoke only after the three coalition leaders and other ministers had had their say.

On one occasion in April 2021, NPHET were beamed into the Sycamore Room via video conference from the Department of Health advising a further delay in relaxing public health restrictions. An hour and a half passed before Donnelly spoke – and when he did it was with a non sequitur outlining his worries about whether the government would be able to get third-level education back in September. 'Why are you worried about that?' the Taoiseach snapped, pointing out that there was a minister (Simon Harris) responsible for that sector.

Some Cabinet ministers had formed a similar view, privately, that Micheál Martin could be dismissive towards Donnelly, but to those watching this on a video screen in the Department of Health, it was a revealing moment as to where their minister stood.

Martin later rejected out of hand suggestions that he was curt with his health minister. He said he 'cuts to the chase' in meetings and that there was one meeting where he did address Donnelly with 'Look, Stephen, we'll go straight to the team.' As for a lack of questions from his health minister, the Taoiseach argued that Donnelly speaks frequently to Holohan. Donnelly said the same: before these meetings, he receives extensive briefings from the CMO and others, where he raises questions and discusses issues at length.

But ultimately, senior NPHET officials, including Holohan, did not feel their advice was being supported or represented well by the health minister – certainly not in the way it had by Simon Harris at the start of the pandemic. Their concerns stretched all the way back to October 2020, when Donnelly, in their view, bungled the urgent communication of the seriousness with which Holohan viewed the Covid-19 situation at that time. Then Donnelly ultimately sided with Cabinet colleagues in rejecting the Level 5 advice.

His relentless pursuit of the wider use of antigen testing was, to senior NPHET figures, more evidence that the minister could not be relied on to represent their views. They found the antigen row unhelpful in that it created a sense of division about how the State should respond to the pandemic.

It was not that NPHET thought their word should be taken as gospel – Donnelly was free to disagree with them and express his own views – but they believed that once it was arrived at, it was his job to represent the NPHET advice faithfully to the government, which could then decide whether or not to follow it. They also had doubts about whether Donnelly was able to clear the way politically for the types of policies NPHET wanted to progress. Donnelly has consistently downplayed any tensions with NPHET, saying that he felt he always had an 'excellent working relationship' with his top advisers, praising them as 'dedicated doctors and public servants' that the State was lucky to have. 'Of course we don't always agree – I'd be worried if we did,' he explained.

The truth, however, was that the minister swam against the tide in a way that left the public health officials uncomfortable. In the course of late 2020 and through to 2021, Holohan came to the conclusion, which he shared with others on NPHET, that his advice was not safe in the hands of the health minister.

CHAPTER 29:

QUARANTINED

26 March 2021
Cases: 233,327
Deaths: 4,651
Seven-day average of new cases: 574

I n the early hours of the last Friday in March, around twenty bleary-eyed passengers stepped off a bus that had travelled under army escort from Dublin Airport to the Crowne Plaza Hotel in Santry, north Dublin. They were the first arrivals into Ireland's new mandatory hotel quarantine system, implemented in the face of massive institutional and political resistance.

Ireland was in the midst of its longest lockdown, and the extra infectiousness of the Alpha variant meant cases were proving harder and harder to push down to the level they had been at the previous summer. In March, many feared, in fact, that slippage in compliance and weariness could drive another surge. Even after weeks of relentless restrictions, there were concerns that Ireland could tip back towards disaster. On 19 March, Martin Fraser had texted Micheál Martin:

> Taoiseach, we had a good look at the data and had discussions with various key people today. It's clear that we can have growing confidence in the successful impact of the vaccination

programme by June/July but there are very big risks in April/ May. The disease is definitely plateauing at a higher level than in previous waves. So you're right not to speculate or to raise hopes of significant reopening. Today's test results are 766 cases 5.5% positivity which is the worst Friday for a while and just bears out what we're seeing.

It was typical of Fraser – a concise but comprehensive update on where the State stood in its battle with a devastating third wave – and it injected a note of caution. Fraser was preaching to the converted; throughout the spring Micheál Martin was adamant that nothing should be done to threaten the steady progress Ireland was making in driving down case numbers. Any reopening of society would be cautious.

He was on the same page as NPHET, which would provide the Cabinet subcommittee on Covid-19 with grim projections if ministers pushed to reopen society in any substantial way in April. Many restrictions would have to remain in place until early summer as the vaccination programme shuffled along. Just over 865,000 doses were given out by the end of the first quarter, just half of what had been projected, as supply stuttered.

The journey to that chilly March morning in Santry had begun almost a year earlier when NPHET first examined how to prevent the virus from reseeding in the late spring of 2020. Tony Holohan believed that the State was in a unique position to introduce restrictions on overseas arrivals that would curb the risk of importing the disease. On 8 May 2020, he wrote to Simon Harris to outline NPHET's view that a 'mandatory regime of self-isolation for 14 days at a designated facility' should be considered.

Such systems were in place in Asia, New Zealand and Australia, but it was an idea without precedent in western Europe. Holohan knew his proposal would not be welcomed in government, as did Harris, who had been aligned with his CMO on the public health advice from the start of the pandemic. Sure enough, it encountered immediate resistance.

In one meeting, Martin Fraser told Harris, Holohan and Jim Breslin, the secretary general of the Department of Health, that NPHET's idea had come with no specific proposals, while pointing out the State's obligations under EU law and the Good Friday Agreement. Voices were raised; Harris came away from the meeting feeling Fraser had been condescending and patronising – and that his stance was also likely informed by the fact that Harris and the government would shortly be out of office. It was very late in the day to be rushing in with a policy that could upset delicate legal, constitutional and industrial policy balances. But Fraser was also trying to tease out how the policy would get done.

Harris later brought a proposal on hotel quarantine to Cabinet, but it was qualified by what amounted to a lengthy shellacking of the proposal by the Department of the Taoiseach, also included in the memo for government. 'Specific proposals on how this would be done have not been presented,' it stated. 'A number of complex issues arise, such as what facilities would be made available, how would they be operated, how could sufficient capacity be assured, what costs would arise and how would they be met, would it be open to circumvention by travel via Northern Ireland, and how would compliance be assured/enforced.'

As well as warning ministers that categories of exemptions would have to be agreed, the memo outlined concerns that the facilities would be compared with State-provided accommodation for, among others, homeless people and asylum seekers. 'There could be legal challenges on the basis that a more restrictive regime was being applied to inbound travellers with no symptoms or history of the disease, than to citizens who test positive or have been in close contact with persons with the disease,' it said, adding that the regime would be contrary to recently issued European Commission guidance.

The then justice minister Charlie Flanagan was also unimpressed and railed against the idea in a series of meetings in late spring and early summer. He told Varadkar directly that he thought it would be unworkable and bristled at those who pointed out that it was working in Australia. 'The Australians don't have a great track record in terms of human rights anyway,' Flanagan told colleagues, pointing out how they put asylum seekers on ships and islands. It would, he said, make direct provision 'look like a tea party'. Others were concerned; Paschal

Donohoe worried that the government would be taking on another gigantic public health project that it would be unable to deliver. Harris had no support from his fellow ministers or from the government system and the memo reflected as much. It was as good as a 'no' from the senior ranks of the civil service, and more specifically from Fraser.

Ultimately the Cabinet referred the proposal to a group of officials, headed by the Department of the Taoiseach's second secretary general, John Callinan, for further examination. Harris understood that work on the proposal was still ongoing when he left the Department of Health in June 2020. 'When it was introduced, I think the complexities of it became clear,' he later said. One senior NPHET official later quipped that that summer the hotel quarantine proposal was sent to 'Fraser's Rest: The Nursing Home for Ideas That Don't Go Anywhere'.

That summer, with case numbers falling to single digits, there appeared little appetite to quarantine passengers arriving from overseas. The outgoing Cabinet did sign off on plans to make it mandatory to complete the passenger locator form (PLF), with those failing to do so facing a fine of €2,500 or a prison term of six months. That was a debacle of its own, with responsibility bounced around between different government departments. Travel policy in general was ever-changing, the oversight was opaque, and enforcement was patchy.

Internal emails from the Department of Justice's border management unit reveal a convoluted process for managing PLFs. Staff were to place the forms received from arriving passengers in envelopes for a specific flight. The information written on them was then manually inputted into various password-protected spreadsheets for individual flights and then master spreadsheets for the day's arrivals. These were used for follow-up calls to check that passengers were complying with isolation or quarantine requirements. It was messy and compliance was uneven.

Hundreds of calls were made with the answer rate by those who had filled out the PLFs ranging from 58 per cent to 85 per cent in late April and early May. The emails record staff frustration over airlines not handing out forms. 'Unless this becomes a requirement of boarding the non-compliance issue will continue,' one official emailed in early May.

Eventually, the Department of Health outsourced the follow-up calls for PLFs to the digital services business Capita, which, as of January 2022, was paid over €2.6m for operating call centre services.

An Garda Síochána were ultimately asked to carry out spot checks on people who were supposed to be quarantining at home. But at Garda HQ in the Phoenix Park, they railed against the 'crap data' they were sent, with some passengers putting in fake names and addresses. In one instance a passenger gave their name as 'Mickey Mouse', a source later recalled.

A pilot scheme to carry out checks was rolled out in six of the 28 Garda divisions and never went any further. It later emerged that spot checks were carried out on fewer than 10 per cent of the tens of thousands of people suspected by the Department of Health of failing to comply with home quarantine.

—

A few weeks into his term as health minister, Stephen Donnelly signalled his own concerns about Ireland's weak border control. In August he floated a proposal to introduce a red list banning all non-essential travel from countries with high rates of Covid-19, including the USA and Brazil. The idea never got off the ground.

Then, in early November, Donnelly and Holohan clashed in a series of emails over the issue of mandatory quarantine. This was prompted by an emerging issue in Denmark where a new strain of coronavirus was found to have been transmitted from mink to humans, resulting in the Danish government announcing a cull of more than 17 million mink. The UK put strict restrictions on arrivals from Denmark, and Donnelly's Stormont counterpart Robin Swann urged him to introduce the same measures in Ireland. Concerned by what Swann was telling him, Donnelly emailed Holohan and his officials asking that they engage directly with their counterparts on the matter, describing the UK position as 'decidedly more robust'.

Holohan felt that the North was trying to dictate to the government in Dublin and that the UK response was an overreaction. Holohan's relationship with his Northern counterpart Michael McBride was also occasionally more strained than was publicly known at the time. In January, McBride wrote to Holohan seeking an arrangement to share passenger locator form data, insisting that there was no 'firm legal barrier' to collecting addresses of passengers arriving in the South bound for the North. Holohan responded that in fact there was and that he did not understand the detail of what McBride was proposing. 'These are genuine concerns of a legal nature and not merely related to best practice in data protection,' he wrote.

The mink issue caused a snippy exchange between Donnelly and Holohan. The CMO wrote back to the minister concluding his email with a stark warning on the 'relative weakness' of Ireland's border security, saying that it did not give him 'assurance', which therefore meant he could not assure Donnelly that appropriate public health controls were in place to prevent importation of the virus. 'This is particularly concerning now that such a potentially serious development as mutation has arisen,' he concluded.

Donnelly replied tersely, 'It would have been useful if you had aired your concerns, or indeed any concerns whatsoever in regard to border controls, when asked for your view at the Cabinet subcommittee some weeks ago where the border control protocols were being discussed and agreed.'

What ultimately forced the government's hand on quarantine, however, was not the public health advice – it was the public. On 18 January 2021, an Ireland Thinks poll found an astonishing 90 per cent support for the idea. The views of the Independent Scientific Advisory Group (ISAG), which advocated for a zero-Covid approach in which the disease would be entirely eradicated by strict border controls, were getting purchase with the opposition, further shaping the debate.

Paschal Donohoe would later reflect that the hotel quarantine debate morphed into 'one of the most dangerous challenges we faced during the disease at a political level, which was the false lure of zero-Covid'. Total elimination was something the government never felt was possible. NPHET wasn't agitating for mandatory quarantine, but its position had not changed.

Tánaiste Leo Varadkar told the Dáil three days after the poll that mandatory quarantine would not be proportionate or workable. But the government could not hold back the tide of public opinion as frustration and fatigue grew under lockdowns with no clear end point. Announcing six more weeks of Level 5 restrictions on 26 January, Taoiseach Micheál Martin also confirmed a policy shift on hotel quarantine which would now be applied to arrivals from high-risk countries where there were variants of concern.

Later that evening, Varadkar stood at a podium endorsing the proposal he had dismissed five days earlier. Against the desires and instincts of large swathes of the political and State apparatus, the weakness of the government in the wake of the Christmas disaster meant that hotel quarantine was now a reality.

—

While Donnelly was fully supportive of the policy, he did not believe it should be operationalised by his department. He was concerned about capacity in the department and HSE as it was, and now they were to be responsible for an entirely new policy and system. His counterparts in New Zealand and Australia advised him to seek help from elsewhere, specifically from those in uniform. He appealed to ministerial colleagues across Transport and Justice to shoulder the burden. 'Some departments really rowed in, like Defence,' he said later. 'Certainly there was an opportunity for certain departments to do more.' This was in keeping with a wider trend in the pandemic for Donnelly, who saw his department's work multiply time and again on Covid policy, while others escaped. 'I would have raised things at Cabinet; for example there would have been conversations where I said I strongly recommend against the Department of Health taking on X or Y,' Donnelly later said.

But at the Cabinet meeting to sign off on the plan, the Taoiseach squarely located responsibility within Donnelly's department, and more narrowly in his office, describing the Wicklow TD as 'the lead minister for quarantine'. This was primarily because the law underpinning almost all pandemic policy gave the health minister – and only them – powers to make regulations. You couldn't just ask another department or the Dublin Airport Authority to run the quarantine system. Donnelly's attempts to argue that others should be encouraged to step up to the plate fell on deaf ears, and so hotel quarantine landed in the Department of Health and on to the shoulders of Fergal Goodman, the soft-spoken and effective assistant secretary who was already at the coalface of the nascent Covid vaccination programme.

Goodman had to design a bespoke system to confine hundreds, if not thousands, of people to hotel facilities, with no clear blueprint. He had to devise how it would actually work, not just on paper. He knew that what happened to each individual in the hotel quarantine system was going to be tracked back to his desk. If something went wrong, he would have to account for it, probably before some Oireachtas committee or, worse, a public inquiry.

As the legislation underpinning the new system wove its way through the Dáil and Seanad, Goodman's team, who included officials drafted in from other departments, spent much of February and March working out how it would operate. Hotel operator Tifco secured the contract for the system, with the department providing health support in each of the hotels.

Towards the end of February, Ronan Glynn set up a Travel Expert Advisory Group to begin deciding the countries from which arrivals would be designated for mandatory quarantine. Glynn wanted a specific process that would have a clear scientific rationale for why a country would go on the list. This system trundled along, relatively controversy-free, until the morning of Monday, 30 March when the *Irish Independent* reported a leaked list of 43 countries, including the USA, France, Germany and Italy, that were to be added to the quarantine list.

It sparked an immediate backlash from Simon Coveney, whom Donnelly was legally obliged to consult, but his department hadn't heard from their counterparts in Health. 'I wasn't the only person reading the list. They were also reading it in Paris, and Berlin, and Washington and all these other places,' the foreign affairs minister later recalled. Donnelly rang Coveney that evening to apologise. 'We spoke that night and he said, "Jesus, Simon, of course you should have got that letter, and for what it's worth, I didn't leak anything,"' Coveney later recalled.

In the days that followed there was a caustic briefing war between the departments with one senior Health source telling the *Irish Independent*: 'Minister Coveney seems to think there is a milder variant of Covid within the EU which is clearly not the case.' Even though both ministers insisted they did not fall out over the issue, there was no disguising Coveney's unhappiness about it all months later.

'We were sort of bounced into this and then, the impression was being given that Coveney was trying to block this because he didn't believe in mandatory hotel quarantine, and actually that wasn't the case,' Coveney said later. All the trouble it caused for the government could have been avoided 'if Health had simply followed procedures they were required to follow in law, to consult with me as foreign minister', the Fine Gael minister maintained.

In the weeks that followed, it was also hard to miss comments from the chief executive of Greencore, one of Ireland's gilded corporate elites, who tweeted that it was 'hard to overstate the incompetence and lack of foresight' in the government's plan. It was equally hard to miss that he was Coveney's brother, Patrick.

The government had to endure a spectacular pile-on from some of Ireland's most important diplomatic and trading partners as the embassies of Italy, France and others called Ireland out. The European Commission announced that it was examining the policy 'as there are some concerns in relation to the general principles of EU law'. Meanwhile, some business figures worked the back channels between politics, commerce and the embassies, stirring up trouble.

Eventually, as spring turned to summer and the Covid-19 situation improved across Europe and the Western world, the list of countries on the quarantine list grew smaller and smaller. Carve-outs for vaccinated people meant fewer of them had to go into the hotels, until the system was formally disbanded in September, with ten thousand people having passed through the process.

An Garda Síochána, which had steadfastly refused to operate a permanent presence at quarantine hotels, despite repeated overtures from Health, reported in the same month that it was still investigating 143 confirmed breaches of the regulations underpinning the regime, including absconders and other offenders.

Donnelly judged the policy – one he succeeded in landing and executing in the face of strident opposition – a 'big success'. 'It was definitely worth it, and in fact I wanted to bring it in sooner – I had been advocating for border controls for quite some time,' he said, arguing that as passenger numbers from high-risk countries collapsed, the policy likely bought extra time before the even more infectious Delta variant came to dominance in Ireland.

Having originally estimated the cost at €7m, figures published by Donnelly on the Dáil record in January 2022 put the overall amount paid to Tifco for operating the hotel quarantine system at more than three times that amount – €22.5m.

The episode still rankles in Fine Gael. 'It died with a whimper,' was Varadkar's judgement in early November 2021. 'I think we had to do it politically, but [it achieved] not very much, I don't think.'

CHAPTER 30:

HAPPY TONY

14 April 2021
Cases: 242,105
Deaths: 4,812
Seven-day average of new cases: 397

The mood was grim around the Cabinet table on the Tuesday after Easter as ministers grappled with the latest change in clinical advice which meant that the AstraZeneca vaccine could no longer be used on under-60s because of concerns about blood clotting. Delays and similar clotting fears with another vaccine, a one-shot jab produced by Johnson & Johnson that was once itself heralded as a game-changer, only compounded matters. The period was characterised by torturous over-and-back dialogue with NIAC, endless reorganisation of the vaccine rollout, and simmering public and political dissatisfaction. The programme could not move fast enough, and despite best efforts, it couldn't find top gear. It appeared destined to stutter on into the summer with fewer jabs in arms, ultimately meaning little prospect of reopening society in any substantial way. There was no clear way out of the longest lockdown yet.

Suddenly the Taoiseach was asked to step out of the Cabinet room to take an urgent phone call.

On the line was Ursula von der Leyen, the European Commission president, confirming that Ireland was in line for an immediate shipment of 540,000 doses of Pfizer's vaccine – enough to pick up the slack from AstraZeneca and Johnson & Johnson's underperformance. The company had confirmed an extra 50 million doses to the EU in the second quarter.

Martin returned to the room with the good news, only for Varadkar to interject that it was already in the public domain. Old rivalries remained, it seemed, as the coalition's big beasts jostled to take hold of the glad tidings. But it was an injection of optimism that was needed after several turbulent months with the vaccine programme.

—

On 25 March 2021, the *Irish Daily Mail*'s Craig Hughes had revealed that the Beacon Hospital had given Covid-19 vaccines to 20 teachers at a private school in Wicklow – a school that the hospital chief executive's children attended. It was a dynamite story that plunged public confidence in the vaccine programme to an all-time low. 'It bruised the programme,' Brian MacCraith would later recall. It damaged credibility at a time when the government could ill afford the public to lose confidence in the vaccination programme.

There had been huge pressure on the coalition to provide certainty to different groups on when they could expect to be given their shot, but there just wasn't any certainty to give. As health minister, Stephen Donnelly had become the face of a vaccine rollout programme freighted with the hopes of the entire population – and people began to feel their hopes were being dashed.

Donnelly made several speeches in the Dáil across the first quarter of 2021 outlining when vaccines would arrive and when people would get their shots. They were heavily qualified, but they were also taken as promises by a weary public. 'I must have caveated what I said five times, in an effort to try and give everyone a bit of a line of sight on where we were going. I tried to be really clear in terms of these being provisional dates,' he said, 'but that got missed by some'. It didn't help that his contributions could be pockmarked with avoidable errors and inaccuracies.

He said that every citizen would be given a shot by the end of September, later correcting himself that it would be every resident. He told the Dáil at the end of January that 48,000 doses of vaccines were due that week, but it was less than half that.

Throughout the spring, Labour leader Alan Kelly called him out, as did many other opposition TDs; they repeatedly asked for information on the vaccine rollout, which Donnelly would promise but often fail to deliver.

In one particularly vicious exchange in April, Kelly roared at Donnelly across an empty Convention Centre. 'What the hell is going on here? [...] This isn't about having confidence in you. This is about incompetence.' Donnelly stared impassively into the distance. 'So that's what your resting bitch face looks like,' someone later remarked to the minister.

Donnelly was lashed by the media, with the *Irish Examiner* accusing him of dealing in 'false promises, unattainable targets [...] and blatantly unachievable suggestions'. Privately, the criticisms were landing hard with the minister. He was working 100-hour-plus weeks, and felt he was getting punched in the face time and again. 'It was a high-pressure time,' Donnelly said later. 'Getting the vaccine programme right was so important, so much depended on it that you wouldn't be human if you didn't feel that responsibility. It certainly doesn't make the job easier.' There was no release, he said, no trip to the pub at the weekend with friends to blow off steam, and much more important, he would go weeks without seeing his children awake. Sixteen-hour days – or longer – were common, six or seven days a week, and the pressure was unrelenting. 'I remember running in the dark in the snow one Monday morning in January and the first four items on *Morning Ireland* were on healthcare and Covid, and I just thought, "Dear God, this is intense."'

In mid-January he snapped at the Leas Ceann Comhairle Catherine Connolly, the gentle and universally admired Galway TD, in the Dáil, angrily muttering 'un-fucking-believable' after she told him he had run out of speaking time. He had been trying to respond to Fianna Fáil backbench rebel Marc MacSharry. He had to apologise to Connolly the following week.

His family saw the criticism and the abuse and in some instances were directly impacted by it. In February, the Office of Public Works erected a six-foot security fence outside the family home following a number of incidents where items were thrown at the windows or left on the doorstep. Cabinet colleagues grew increasingly concerned for Donnelly and the toll it was taking on him. 'I think Stephen probably would have thought at the time he was carrying all the burden,' Eamon Ryan later said.

Tánaiste Leo Varadkar did not think the criticism of Donnelly was fair or warranted and had to calm his own troops when Michael Ring told one Fine Gael parliamentary party meeting that the embattled health minister had 'foot-in-mouth' disease. The Taoiseach was less concerned, noting as a former occupant of the office that 'all ministers for health get flak'. Donnelly was of the view that more 'incoming' fire could be expected for the health minister during a pandemic, but that didn't make it easier.

Ministers and others in government saw the pressure he was under. Under enormous strain and working extremely long hours, sometime around St Patrick's Day, Donnelly became ill while working in the department. He was tended to by Rachel Kenna, the chief nursing officer, who is a registered practising nurse working in Miesian Plaza. Kenna advised him to go to hospital. The minister attended a Dublin hospital and underwent tests before being sent home. Donnelly, through a spokesman, declined to comment. His performance was a constant point of potential vulnerability for the coalition, and the health minister also felt he had to watch his back. When, in the early days of the vaccine programme, the *Irish Times* revealed that family members of doctors in the Coombe Hospital had received jabs, Simon Harris told journalists it was 'concerning' that there was seemingly no protocol in place to deal with leftover shots. The following day Donnelly rebuked Harris, without naming him, by pointedly telling Cabinet there was a strategy for spare doses, and that if his colleagues had any concerns about it, or questions, they should come to him.

It was correctly interpreted by those around the table as a thinly veiled warning to Harris, the former health minister, to stay in his lane.

It was also the culmination of months of frustration with his predecessor, and constituency rival in Wicklow, for wading into Covid-19 policy during media appearances.

Donnelly eventually formed the view that Harris would brief against him, undermine him and criticise him behind his back. He had considered saying it to his Cabinet colleague, but did not, although he did raise it with other Fine Gael ministers, who did nothing to disabuse him of his notion, more often responding with wry smiles.

There were also indications that Donnelly was preoccupied with Harris, who had endured a torrid time at points while in Health, but had left on a political high note. In January, an analysis was drawn up comparing mentions of the minister by the Department of Health's Twitter account to mentions of Tony Holohan. It also compared it to mentions of Harris by his department's official account. When the analysis was released later to Simon Carswell in the *Irish Times*, Donnelly sidestepped it, saying on radio that he had not seen the story, and distanced himself from the document, saying that it had been drawn up by a member of his team.

Paraic Gallagher, Donnelly's new press adviser, said that he had conducted the research, yet records show that Robert Watt had sent the analysis to the department's communications chief Deirdre Watters with a note that 'the Minister' had completed it. What's more, the handwriting on the document was strikingly similar to Donnelly's, which he had displayed in Twitter videos when he was in opposition, sketching out ideas and criticisms of the government on a whiteboard, sleeves rolled up.

—

An insatiable thirst for information about the vaccine rollout frustrated the HSE no end. Paul Reid and other senior executives tried to control this as much as they could. 'The more we are setting targets, the more we are setting ourselves up [to fail] because we haven't got the forecast delivery to meet them. We want to build confidence in the programme,' Reid told one meeting of the vaccine taskforce early on.

But the message never seemed to land. The political system was, one HSE insider later said, 'just fucking addicted to it, and Donnelly in particular was addicted to the fucking numbers'. Increasingly the HSE exercised caution in the information it provided to the minister for fear he would tweet it five minutes later. Reid would advise Donnelly: leave the operational stuff to us, because we can take the flak on it.

Donnelly was, his spokesperson later said, 'directly involved in all operational aspects of the vaccine programme', but throughout 2021 he continued to engage in what some in the HSE considered unnecessary and unhelpful meddling. In July, the HSE drew up plans to expedite the rollout of AstraZeneca to under-35s and to roll out the one-shot Johnson & Johnson vaccine to the same cohort through pharmacies. This was to be announced at the HSE's usual Thursday afternoon media briefing, but earlier that day Donnelly asked the health service to slow down because he had to brief the Taoiseach.

At a meeting that ran late into the evening, they debated endlessly whether the age group should be split further. HSE sources later recalled that word came back that Donnelly wanted to announce it in the Dáil the following day, Friday. But instead, the next morning the minister went on RTÉ's *Morning Ireland* and revealed the plan. It was unchanged from what the HSE had originally proposed to him. The only difference was that he was announcing it, not the HSE. The minister's spokesperson later said he was a 'strong believer in transparency and has consistently pushed for ambitious targets and the sharing of as much information as possible', having committed to doing so with Dáil colleagues.

It simply was not Donnelly's nature to sit back; he wanted to get involved in the nitty gritty. In fact, he began sitting in on vaccine task-force meetings. Unlike Tony Holohan, who jealously guarded his NPHET meetings, MacCraith saw no big issue with this, despite being 'quite aware it was unusual'. Donnelly was generally an unobtrusive presence, primarily listening and only rarely hitting the button on Zoom to raise his hand for a contribution. There is a difference between the taskforce and NPHET – the former doesn't advise the minister, the latter does. Nonetheless, some members quietly wondered – is he not busy enough with other stuff?

There were occasions, however, when Donnelly could not be found, such as the night of Saturday 13 March, when NIAC made a sudden recommendation to suspend the rollout of the AstraZeneca vaccine following reports of blood-clotting incidents in Norway. With thousands of vaccination appointments set for the following day, the advice landed with Ronan Glynn, who was still the acting chief medical officer, late that evening. 'That was a very lonely night,' he would later recall.

Sitting on his couch at home, with his laptop in front of him, Glynn picked up his phone and phoned Donnelly at about 11.30 p.m., but the minister could not be reached. He then sent a text to Donnelly with the details before midnight. But it seemed no one was able to get the minister on the phone that night, and it would be the following morning before he was looped into what was a seismic intervention in the most important vaccination programme the State had ever run. Instead, the phone traffic that night was between Glynn, Watt, Martin Fraser, the Taoiseach and Reid – who conveyed his 'shock' over the move and spoke to officials several times into the early hours of Sunday morning.

Over the course of those hours it was made clear to Glynn that there was 'very significant concern within the political system and the HSE at the potential consequences of this decision and it was clear that the department – and NIAC – were going to have to lead on the communication and own the rationale behind the decision'.

In other words, it was going to be the department that took ownership of the bombshell. To that end, a press release from Glynn was issued at 9.03 a.m. the following day, Sunday. MacCraith, the chair of the taskforce, was also out of the loop – the first he heard of it was on the radio bulletins that morning.

—

Much of March and April 2021 was characterised by these rapid reversals. None was as dramatic as the pausing of AstraZeneca that Saturday night, but delivery issues continued to disappoint and frustrate, to the extent that the Taoiseach sought a call with its chief executive, Pascal Soriot, in mid-March.

One participant on the call later remembered how pointless it seemed: the respective sides lining up on Zoom to exchange their mutual sense of disappointment about how things were proceeding. Soriot's side could offer no reassurances that things would get better. The Taoiseach could offer no incentive or threat to ensure they would do so. Rather than a high-powered face-off, it was flat and ultimately ineffective.

In April, NIAC ruled that AstraZeneca should not be given to under-60s, a full reversal of its stance from February, and another regulatory bombshell dropped with little warning. The opaque and convoluted process around NIAC advice was leading many in government to tear their hair out as they sought clarity over who could get what vaccine, and when. There were remarks about the structure of the body – its members were absolute experts in their field, but doing voluntary work on NIAC in addition to their day jobs.

The Taoiseach, while appreciative of NIAC's work, found the process 'challenging' and concluded that NIAC's structure was not fit for purpose. 'I just feel the system has to improve,' Micheál Martin later said. He would have given booster shots to healthcare workers earlier in the autumn of 2021 – a view shared by Varadkar – and thinks European authorities should have the ultimate say in public health issues. The EMA approves vaccines, 'why does every individual member state feel the necessity to interrogate it?'

MacCraith and others believe that NIAC's rigour engendered confidence that people could trust the vaccine programme. 'Their abundance-of-caution approach might have frustrated, but ultimately it was good for the programme,' he said. Glynn was strongly of the view that NIAC's approach was the right one. 'If you have a system and you don't back it, then you need to change it,' he later said.

But it was easy to lose sight of this when Karina Butler's group spent days ruminating over a change in the programme or, conversely, when its decisions landed with little notice, forcing wholescale restructuring of the process and turning the air blue in Government Buildings. Senior members of government and the HSE would often not get a sense of what was coming until it had been recommended. 'It would be better if a method could be found to couple clinical recommendations with the operational considerations,' MacCraith later argued. 'Because, operating in the isolation of just the clinical recommendations and not considering what that means from the operationalisation perspective, there was some frustration around that.'

NIAC's most significant decision, however, came in late March, when it advised the government to ditch plans to vaccinate people on the basis of their occupation. While no one could quibble with the initial list of those who got their shots – nursing home staff and residents, healthcare workers, and the old and medically vulnerable – the decisions would become more contentious as NIAC worked down the categories.

For weeks, the Department of Health had grappled with the cohort classified as 'key workers'. In February, it wrote to other government departments seeking a list of workers in the sectors they oversaw who might be considered 'key'. Departments risked facing the wrath of interest groups they left off their lists; on the other hand, they could include everyone and then blame Health when the mandarins on Baggot Street inevitably had to sort it out.

Sure enough, when the responses flooded in, it turned out, as one senior figure involved in the programme later joked, that 'there were 7.5 million people who were deserving'. It turns out everybody is special, they said. But on a serious level, this wouldn't work.

The solution, with NIAC's blessing, was to throw out the remaining phases of the plan and change to an age-based approach. The decision would be controversial, officials knew, and it was teased out away from the prying eyes and leaking lips of politicians. At the last Cabinet meeting in March, Donnelly arrived with the memo seeking approval for the change under his arm.

He encountered significant pushback from at least three ministers: Roderic O'Gorman, who oversaw childcare; justice minister Helen McEntee, who the Gardaí had been lobbying for early access to the vaccine; and education minister Norma Foley, who thought the proposal would spark a major backlash from teachers who had been promised they would be among the first one-third of the population to get a jab.

Ministers privately griped that there had been no clear idea of the proposal until it was signed off by the party leaders the previous evening, and even then, it wasn't certain it would come to Cabinet that week.

Foley was correct. The teaching unions absolutely hated the idea. She and her staff scrambled to get someone to explain it to them, finally getting Glynn on to a video call with the heads of the unions. At the time, Kieran Christie, the general secretary of the Association of Secondary Teachers, Ireland (ASTI), was on the road to Sligo, where he lives. He turned the car back to Dublin and dialled into the meeting from the union's offices – delivering a flat 'no' to the proposal. But the unions ultimately relented. The clinical advice set out by Karina Butler was compelling: the older you were, the more likely you were to die from Covid-19. The revised order was adopted, and it cleared the way for a streamlined rollout.

That did not prevent some out-of-sequence vaccinations going ahead, however. Emails show that, after lobbying from Garda Commissioner Drew Harris, Stephen Donnelly approved the vaccination of 634 frontline garda personnel at Citywest on 10 April 2021.

Eleven days later, on 21 April, Minister for Justice Helen McEntee wrote to Donnelly urging him to consider prioritising the vaccination of 300 prison officers who escorted prisoners to medical facilities, including some who had Covid-19. On 26 April, Donnelly effectively turned down the request before reversing his decision four days later. By the start of June, Donnelly, citing evidence from the WHO, would approve the vaccination of all prisoners and prison officers under 40. In the outside world, some people under 40 had to wait until July for vaccines.

April proved to be a turning point for Ireland's experience of the pandemic. It was the week after the EU-orchestrated Pfizer bailout of the vaccine programme that Tony Holohan returned to work (following the death of his wife in February). It could not have been more different from his last comeback. A week after his return, he signed off on a set of recommendations that took the political system by surprise – in a good way, this time.

As NPHET met, political operatives briefed journalists, 'Word is of a happy Tony.' Outdoor dining was to be reopened earlier than expected, numbers at weddings increased, and inter-county travel restrictions relaxed through April and June. Ireland's long march out of lockdown was finally picking up pace.

In the end, the much-vaunted target set by Micheál Martin in the dark days of February, that 82 per cent of adults would be offered a first dose by the end of June, was missed. But it garnered little attention as the country reopened.

CHAPTER 31:

DELTA

29 May 2021
Cases: 261,306
Deaths: 4,941
Seven-day average of new cases: 456

What Tony Holohan saw when he drove into town at around 8.15 p.m. on the last Saturday in May so appalled him, he felt compelled to tweet. The post strayed from his usual sober public health messaging:

> Absolutely shocked at scenes in South Great George's St, Exchequer St, South William St area. Enormous crowds – like a major open air party. This is what we do not need when we have made so much progress.

Ireland was enjoying its second summer of living with Covid-19 as much as it could. With pubs and restaurants closed until 7 June, takeaway pints were the beverage of choice for thousands who thronged the narrow streets of Dublin city centre. A few days later, Holohan said it was 'like Jones' Road on a day of the All-Ireland'.

It was an ill-judged foray. The tweet did not go down well online, or in Government Buildings, but it caused absolute ructions in Garda headquarters. Gardaí had for weeks found themselves stuck in the middle trying to help support the reopening of society while trying to maintain public order. Holohan's focus on South William Street caused particular angst in the Phoenix Park.

'Tony might have phrased the tweet a bit better,' a source later said, explaining that the tweet and its notoriety almost acted as a draw for people, with many convening on one street in the city centre. 'Basically South William Street became scumbag central, for want of a better phrase, so that's where we had to focus the policing effort.'

In the days that followed, gardaí blocked access to the street, which is lined with trendy bars and restaurants. The public order unit was called in and there was a social media backlash about heavy-handed policing. The lockdown was really beginning to fray – but it was also coming to an end.

—

Ironically, the day before Holohan's tweet, the Taoiseach had announced plans to accelerate the plan with the reopening of cinemas and theatres and some outdoor events added to the list of restrictions to be lifted from 7 June.

In mid-May, the HSE had suffered a major ransomware cyberattack, which caused nearly all of its IT system to shut down. While the initial disruption to some hospital services was overcome, its internal systems and some in the Department of Health would be crippled for months. It was enormously difficult for senior health bosses at a time when public frustration was building after a full five months of effective lockdown.

However, disruption to the Covid-19 response, including the vaccination programme, was for the large part avoided, and regulatory and supply issues were largely ironed out. As spring turned to summer, the evenings became brighter, and the HSE turned the afterburners on the vaccine programme. It took from January until the start of June to vaccinate 25 per cent of adults, Brian MacCraith later pointed out; and then just a month to double that tally. At its peak, in the week beginning 5 July,

392,196 doses were given – around 10 per cent of the eligible population in a single week.

Vaccines changed everybody's lives. But a race was emerging between the vaccines and another threat: a new variant, later named Delta, first detected in India in early October 2020, where it eventually ripped its way through the second most populous country on the planet in April and May 2021. The deadly Delta wave saw India's health service virtually collapse. Hundreds of thousands died. The enormous human tragedy played out on the nightly television news bulletins and prompted questions for decision-makers in Dublin.

The liberating power of vaccination and the threat of a highly infectious mutation came into conflict over plans to reopen indoor dining.

NPHET's initial recommendation was that indoor events, including hospitality, could restart from 5 July. The government happily went along with the measure, but the Taoiseach would later reveal that Martin Fraser and other civil servants, including Liz Canavan, were sceptical, believing it was reopening two to three weeks earlier than the general population expected. 'We had doubts about that – that the fifth of July was too early – and I asked those questions and I was told they [NPHET] were happy and comfortable with the idea of pubs opening on the fifth of July. I felt that might have been a bit early and, what happens then on the fifth of July? It gets deferred,' Micheál Martin said.

The first cases of Delta were detected in Ireland on 19 April. A combination of travel restrictions, including mandatory hotel quarantine, and the continued curbs on socialising limited its spread. But it was inevitable that, just like Alpha, it would get the upper hand, not least due to the continued open border with the UK via Northern Ireland. Despite this inevitability, the old tensions between NPHET and the government would be given another outing.

Tánaiste Leo Varadkar subsequently came to the conclusion that the response to the threat Delta posed was too slow before it hit Europe. While Varadkar said he did not want to pin the blame on anybody, he nonetheless cited the guidance of the public health team at the time. 'The initial advice from Tony, and I think from Cillian [De Gascun], was that Delta probably wasn't something to be that concerned about,' he later said. 'The initial view from NPHET was that Delta wasn't going to change the epidemiological character of the pandemic dramatically.'

In contrast, Micheál Martin later insisted that there was a general view that Delta would not be controllable and argued that NPHET was 'much slower on Alpha' than on Delta.

On the NPHET side, some blame was levelled at government. At the end of April, the public health advice was that hotels, and their restaurants, should reopen after the June bank holiday weekend. 'What NPHET generally tends to do is recommend the easing of restrictions on the Monday after a weekend, or on the Tuesday after a bank holiday,' Cillian De Gascun later explained.

But the government reopened hotels before the bank holiday weekend. Subsequent data showed that shortly afterwards, Alpha's dominance was replaced by Delta. The data suggests the extra socialisation from that weekend likely played a role. 'From my point of view, they're the kind of things that are quite frustrating,' De Gascun would later say. 'NPHET tries to structure the easing of restrictions taking into account societal behaviour, and based on what presents the least risk, and then government says, "Ah sure, it's a bank holiday."'

—

The blame game, such as it was, was markedly less intense than the bitter fallout from Christmas and Alpha. This was partly because the eventual dominance of Delta was seen as inevitable and its impact was mitigated by vaccination. But it was also down to organisational changes put in place at the turn of the year.

Despite occasional minor differences in emphasis or timing, in 2021 there was significantly more alignment between the constituent parts of what Micheál Martin had taken to calling 'the edifice' – the combination of government, HSE, NPHET and NIAC. Again Martin Fraser was in the middle of the new process, alongside Robert Watt, now installed as the Department of Health's secretary general.

Watt's reputation preceded him, and the NPHET team appreciated his skillset. 'Robert is an operator, an accomplished operator,' said a senior NPHET member. 'He goes to bat for his department.' On divisive issues like antigen testing, Watt was often found more in the camp of the department and its senior officials, including those on NPHET, at one point telling a meeting of the Covid Oversight Group, 'Look, we aren't going to antigen test our way out of this.'

His assertive style and forthright manner came with him to his new post. In one meeting in early July, over a deal to buy surplus vaccines from Romania, Watt was irked that it had been announced before it was finalised. It was the Taoiseach who had broken the news, but it was Donnelly who felt the heat. 'We'll find you good things to say, Minister, don't worry about that. Just let people do their jobs,' Watt told the meeting.

Some felt this was the secretary general managing his minister, but Watt, contemporaries observed, had never been shy about asserting himself, even in front of taoisigh, never mind ministers. Nonetheless, Watt's arrival marked a shift in the department. Some in Miesian Plaza had a nickname for him: 'Minister Watt'.

There were subtle but important shifts within NPHET itself after Holohan returned to work in mid-April. Rather than playing out across sprawling and unwieldy Zoom meetings, activity became more concentrated on the chief medical officer and his small group of key lieutenants.

Philip Nolan, the modeller, and Ronan Glynn, Holohan's erstwhile deputy, were supported by Darina O'Flanagan and De Gascun. Also in the orbit was John Cuddihy, the head of the HPSC, along with senior civil servants in the department, including Fergal Goodman and Deirdre Watters. The chief medical officer, allies said during the summer, needed a 'tight expert group to allow him formulate advice to government'.

The team was smaller and separate from the HSE and its members were, for the most part, happy to maintain their own separate identity. It also detached Holohan's inner circle from government appointees like Mark Ferguson and Mary Horgan, who didn't have the trust of some of his team.

The shift wasn't lost on members of NPHET. By summer 2021, Mary Favier, the former president of the Royal College of GPs, took the view that all the substantive decisions made by the group had been decided before a full meeting had been convened. 'It's become a fig leaf, it's now a decision-making cover. It worked much better in the earlier days,' she said. Not that she saw this as especially problematic in itself. 'It's only a problem if it's not acknowledged or described for what it is,' she added.

It meant that even as Delta gained dominance over the summer, there were fewer NPHET meetings. The disease was also, relatively speaking, controlled, and as the country opened up, people took well-earned breaks. There were two NPHET meetings in June and two in July, and just one towards the end of August, after a break of nearly a month.

—

As the year wore on, the pillars of the new system worked more as had been intended in 2020 when Fraser had set up the Covid Oversight Group. The COG, as it became known, met with NPHET and controversial proposals were shared and discussed, before a full NPHET meeting decided on new policies to be suggested to the Cabinet subcommittee on Covid-19, which were then in turn passed to the Cabinet, which usually (but not always) rubber-stamped them.

Watt's presence in the Department of Health brought a sense of order and structure that the Taoiseach had been seeking for some time. He was permanently appointed to the role in mid-April following an open competition that few, if any, believed would have thrown up an alternative candidate. Watt agreed to forgo the controversial €81,000 salary increase until the economic situation improved. 'I had no issue with him becoming SecGen,' Micheál Martin later said. 'We needed to do something at that stage in the Department of Health, it had to be done.'

Watt would hold Monday afternoon meetings of senior department officials, including Holohan and Donnelly, to focus on the issues at hand. It worked well. There were no meandering conversations. All this was underpinned by a constant back and forth between the principals.

Relationships of trust had built up since Christmas.

'We had a common problem,' Philip Nolan later said. 'And relationships of trust built up right across the political and administrative system, where anybody felt they could pick up the phone to anybody else and go, "Don't surprise me now."' As society gradually reopened, the channels were permanently open between Holohan, Watt, Fraser and, ultimately, the Taoiseach.

Conversely, the Department of Health's relationship with the HSE swung back and forth. Watt publicly love-bombed Reid, at one point calling the HSE boss 'one of the most impressive public servants this country has ever produced', with a 'phenomenal' record of delivery.

Behind the scenes, though, frustrations continued, especially with Reid's media strategy, from his broadcast appearances down to his tweets. This stretched back to 2020, but during 2021, Department of Health officials would grow exceedingly annoyed with Reid's media prominence, cursing him for commenting on a wide range of healthcare matters they thought were outside his lane. Holohan and Glynn were among those who privately groused about it.

At one point, around October 2021, Stephen Donnelly called Reid into the Department of Health and raised this with him, telling the HSE boss that others had asked him to bring it up, and that he should step back. The HSE board had given their executives a mandate to appear frequently on media about the pandemic, and Donnelly's intervention left the Finglas man unmoved. Nothing changed. Privately, sources said Reid dismissed it as not an issue to be distracted by.

The new system worked on tricky measures that were a departure from previous policy; the reopening of indoor dining for customers with a Covid vaccine pass being a prime example. The government had set itself against using the pass system – designed to facilitate the restart of international travel – for a so-called domestic dividend where the vaccinated would enjoy privileges that the unvaccinated did not. Extreme opponents viewed it as modern-day apartheid.

But at the end of June, Holohan and NPHET reversed its advice that indoor dining could proceed from 5 July, recommending that it be delayed until later in the month, but more significantly that even at that stage it should only be allowed for those with a 'non-reproducible and enforceable system of verification of vaccination or immunity status'. Holohan later told opposition TDs that, without this system, indoor hospitality would be closed until the end of September or beyond.

The proposal caused consternation among some ministers. Michael McGrath told the Cabinet that NPHET had 'thrown a grenade on to their desks', while other ministers, including Heather Humphreys, Catherine Martin, Norma Foley and Simon Harris, were all reported to have concerns. The publicly reported narrative was shock and unease within the Cabinet room, which soon spread to government backbenchers. Some former Fine Gael ministers threatened to vote the proposal down and one of them, John Paul Phelan, went missing for the eventual Dáil vote.

But far from hoodwinking the government and reverse-engineering policy, Holohan had quietly worked the back channels before the proposal was formally recommended by NPHET. No one in the know was taken by surprise. Donnelly had been told, as had Watt, who briefed Martin Fraser. The coalition leaders were briefed by Holohan directly the weekend before it went to Cabinet.

In all matters Covid-19, Donnelly retained his formal power and role, and was extensively briefed, but during 2021, some believed he became a more marginal figure when it came to the removal or application of public health restrictions, the centrepiece of pandemic policy. Four senior sources involved in pandemic decision-making, both on the political and the public health side, agreed that the true axis of policy and decision-making ran between the chief medical officer to Watt, to Fraser, and on to the Taoiseach and the two other coalition leaders, Varadkar and Ryan.

It's not unusual for the Taoiseach of the day to take a direct role in the most pressing policy matters – Enda Kenny on economic recovery, Varadkar on Brexit – but this is usually alongside an equally prominent role for the relevant minister (Michael Noonan and Simon Coveney respectively in those instances).

But Donnelly was often left out of Covid-19 press conferences announcing the relaxation of restrictions or big policy shifts. Cabinet memos on Covid-19 were brought almost universally by the Taoiseach and his department. While Donnelly frequently appeared across the media to talk about the decisions government had taken, there was, insiders reported, no sense that he had the same role in decision-making that a health minister might be expected to have. Micheál Martin, for his part, rejected this entirely. 'You can't bypass the Minister for Health; he has to make decisions on this.' Donnelly, likewise, rejected this – his spokesperson argued that he led on a wide range of Covid-related programmes in the department and engages widely on a political level with the Taoiseach and others.

—

Towards the end of the summer of 2021, even though cases were climbing, serious conversations started within government about winding down NPHET. Alongside the disbandment of COG and the vaccine taskforce, the intention was to 'normalise' the pandemic.

This went hand in hand with a detailed battle plan for a full and final shift away from the acute emergency phase that took hold of the nation in March 2020 and held its grip tightly on its citizens for over a year. The hope was that Covid-19 would fade into the background.

Informed by work done by Martin Cormican, the HSE lead on infection prevention and control, Colm Henry, the executive's chief clinical officer, drew up a series of papers for Reid and the HSE board on what a post-pandemic vision for the health service would look like.

After lockdowns, variants, dramatic loss of life and economic and social disruption, there had been a 'realisation that vaccination would be the only plausible "exit" solution from the pandemic', one of the papers said. However, Covid would remain indefinitely. 'It will not be eradicated or eliminated [...] we will transition from the current pandemic to a steady, but much lower, endemic rate of infection.'

The HSE leadership was told, 'We need to transition from pandemic management towards living with Covid-19 as one of many endemic diseases.' In layman's terms, Covid-19 was here to stay, but the crisis phase of infection was approaching an endgame. People would still get sick, as they do with other endemic diseases, but society would not 'resort to exceptional measures such as lockdowns, social distancing and interruptions to normal services'.

The paper stated that lockdowns had ultimately 'saved lives and prevented our healthcare system from becoming overwhelmed', but Ireland had 'endured a profound shock to its social and economic life'. There was a medical cost as well: waiting lists; unscheduled care presentations; undiagnosed disease, including cancers; mental health impacts. 'There is no person or part of society that has not been impacted by Covid-19.'

The need now was to 'transition to harm reduction strategies to allow life to go on as "normal" as possible in a world where Covid-19 is endemic'. Some of the most visible aspects of the pandemic response would be broken up: testing, which had been designed to find the maximum number of cases, whether they were symptomatic, serious, or neither, was now 'increasingly inappropriate'. A transition to 'targeted testing' similar to other endemic diseases was needed. Rather than track every case, the system had to watch for overall incidence, severity and whether the prevalence or dominant strain of disease was changing.

The paper advised that test and trace capacities should be retained to the end of 2021, but then a 'phased approach to scaling down' was advised, again with the capacity to scale back up quickly. Testing would be narrowed to symptomatic people at the request of a doctor – a radical break from what had effectively become an on-demand, population-wide self-referral system designed to aid real-time detection of cases. Contact tracing would also be retained, but it would be led by public health, who would direct it, rather than the industrialised model of the peak pandemic.

Covid boosters would become part of the routine national immunisation programme. Extra vaccinators and other resources would be needed as 'pre-pandemic capacity will not be sufficient', but there would be a shift from the emergency vaccination programme. Underpinning it all would be, the paper said, a totally reformed public health system: a 'fast, dynamic and agile, integrated and intelligence-led public health response, organised at local level'.

—

Tony Holohan's letter to Stephen Donnelly on 25 August, right at the end of a summer that had seen life return to the closest thing to normal since February 2020, outlined a final shift into a new phase of managing the pandemic, enabled by vaccines.

In typical Holohan style, he still managed to irk the government by outlining five criteria, including some really vague ones, that had to be met in order to move to a new reality. 'I didn't like it at all because I thought the five criteria would be extremely hard to achieve,' Leo Varadkar bluntly stated in early November 2021.

The letter was in some ways intentionally vague, leaving room for interpretation, for a shift towards flexibility as opposed to restrictions based on constant and exhaustive measurement of the disease. In this way, it was in line with the wider demobilisation of emergency structures outlined in the HSE's strategy. The government set out a series of final relaxations, which would culminate on 22 October, when all restrictions apart from wearing face masks would be lifted.

The idea that Covid was on the retreat was both alluring and logical. Through summer, the disease had surged again, but had not snapped out of control. It grew mainly among younger people at first. As college exams and the Leaving Cert ended, social activity and travel picked up, just as Delta was getting the upper hand, driving its transmissibility advantage home among these younger unvaccinated groups.

Donnelly warned the Seanad in mid-July of 'roaring' case growth, with projections of up to two thousand cases a day by the end of the month, just as the government was trying to figure out how to reopen indoor dining. Cases did briefly tip over that threshold, but not until later in August, before vaccination caught up with Delta.

Just as Holohan was sending his letter with the five criteria, as the HSE was planning for a post-pandemic future, and as it looked as though the government was finally about to shut NPHET down, Covid-19 cases settled into a steady decline that lasted almost all of September.

The first attempts to decouple daily life from the pandemic were made: large numbers of healthy children who would have been deemed close contacts were no longer told to stay off school. The disease was no longer setting the pace.

It seemed, for a vanishing moment, that Covid-19 was becoming a thing of the past. At the start of October, Philip Nolan declared on RTÉ Radio's *News at One*, 'We seem to have come close to suppressing what is a very transmissible virus.' There was nothing, he said, in the numbers of new cases, hospitalisations or ICU admissions that would make NPHET change the advice it had given at the end of August to open up everything later in the month.

However, before he made those remarks, the disease had quietly started to take off again. 'Everything starts to take off from late September,' Nolan later said. 'There's a change point [following] the major relaxation on the twentieth of September, and that just precipitates too much social mixing across everybody. There's no smoking gun here.'

Infection surged back, finding its foothold among the small number of adults and children who were unvaccinated, and among socially active 19–24-year-olds. This drove breakthrough infections among the unvaccinated population. A booster or third dose programme began at the end of September at a time when over a thousand new cases were being reported every day. Society was largely open or opening, and vaccines had dramatically reduced the levels of serious illness and hospitalisations, but they had been less successful in preventing transmission of the virus.

Nonetheless, in October, with NPHET's blessing, the government allowed nightclubs to reopen, though entry was limited to those with a vaccine pass. It followed a very public advocacy campaign for the sector by arts minister Catherine Martin, which rubbed some of her colleagues up the wrong way. Some of the public health doctors on NPHET warned against the idea. But it was viewed as safe, and, in any case, the passes were to continue well into 2022. Perhaps more important, it was viewed as unavoidable. If not now, with these levels of vaccination, then when?

The plan remained to keep moving forward, incrementally if needs be, but forward nonetheless. The Taoiseach told the *Sunday Independent* on 17 October, 'We are not contemplating going backwards.'

However, winter was coming. and would bring an entirely new threat with it.

CHAPTER 32:

OMICRON

26 November 2021
Cases: 551,528
Deaths: 5,652
Seven-day average of daily cases: 4,672

U rsula von der Leyen was worried. 'The scientists are very concerned,' the European Commission president told Micheál Martin in a phone call on the morning of the last Friday in November.

A new variant of Covid-19 had had been found in South Africa, Botswana and Hong Kong. One case had already been confirmed in Belgium. The response of many countries was to halt travel to and from parts of Africa. Later that day, Minister for Health Stephen Donnelly announced that arrivals from seven southern African states would have to undergo mandatory 'home' quarantine and signalled plans to bring back laws allowing for hotel quarantine.

Not unlike March 2020, the fear of the unknown was driving the State's response. After more than a year and half of struggling against the virus, it seemed like Ireland was again losing the battle. The early and incomplete evidence was that this new variant had a larger number of mutations, could reinfect people who had already had Covid-19, could potentially evade the vaccines, and was far more transmissible. It would inevitably arrive in Ireland, but for the time being that arrival could be slowed, marginally, with new travel restrictions. There was no resistance at political level to these measures.

The Taoiseach had a strong working relationship with von der Leyen, a former German cabinet minister, who had been Eurpean Commission president since December 2019. They were in frequent contact not just on Covid, but often on the disputes between the EU and the UK on the post-Brexit arrangements for Northern Ireland. During particularly acute phases of the seemingly intractable Brexit rows, they would be in touch every day, texting and calling each other.

As was so often the case with Covid-19, there was a shiver of dread and uncertainty among policymakers. 'Deeply, deeply worried,' was how the Taoiseach characterised von der Leyen's mood later that day: 'They're concerned about its [the variant's] potential to escape the vaccine, which could then have you back to square one.'

Martin cut the figure of a genuinely worried man as he sat by the fireplace in the Taoiseach's office. Outside, in the courtyard of Government Buildings, the first winter storm, Storm Arwen, was beginning to make its presence felt.

By that evening the World Health Organization had designated this new highly mutated strain a 'variant of concern' and had assigned it a name from the Greek alphabet – Omicron.

—

Tony Holohan went on holiday at the start of October when the country was moving steadily through what everyone hoped was the final chapter of the pandemic. But as he was enjoying the southern Spanish sunshine, somewhere between Malaga and Marbella, a shockwave came through the data. At a meeting of the Covid Oversight Group on Wednesday 13 October, Ronan Glynn, (deputising for Holohan) and Philip Nolan took the assorted mandarins and the three coalition leaders' chiefs of staff – Deirdre Gillane for the Taoiseach, Brian Murphy for the Tánaiste and Anna Conlan for Green Party leader Eamon Ryan – through the latest figures.

Suddenly, every single indicator was going in the wrong direction. The Delta variant was continuing to cause havoc. The demand for testing and the positivity rate were rising across all age groups, with a bias towards older people. The number of people in hospitals had started to increase and, with some people having received their vaccination ten months earlier, there was growing evidence of waning immunity. People mixing indoors was, once again, fuelling the fire. NPHET officials at the COG committed to undertake a more complete analysis by the following week – they still weren't sure if this was a blip or a trend.

On the government side, there was a resolve to go ahead, in some shape or form, with the planned 22 October reopening of nightclubs. But as the meeting broke up, its chair, Martin Fraser, the secretary general in the Department of the Taoiseach, told the group, 'I think you all need to brief your political masters now.' The politicians had to be told that the trajectory of the virus had taken a turn for the worse. It was not the message they would want to hear. In the days that followed, there was an emerging frustration with NPHET and its tactics, though senior people on the public health side later wryly noted that this often came in the wake of negative advice. Two days after that COG meeting, Glynn posted a video to Twitter, seemingly recorded in the Department, advising people to work from home – contrary to the agreed government policy at the time. Ministers privately fumed, one observing that it 'would appear he is not working from home himself'.

NPHET's concerns were shared within the senior echelons of the HSE. One senior figure privately confided that if case numbers continued growing, the health service would be facing a huge problem. Paul Reid began a media offensive, urging the public to 'hit the reset button' and remember the basic public health measures.

Holohan was back from Spain by the time NPHET met the following Monday, 18 October. Yet despite the fears over increasing case numbers, and the reservations of some members at the meeting who said it should be paused, it recommended that nightclubs should reopen, albeit with the proviso that people had to display vaccine passes to be admitted. That reopening, as it transpired, was somewhat chaotic. Long queues formed outside Copper Face Jacks on Dublin's Harcourt Street and elsewhere on the first weekend of reopening. New rules were sprung on the industry with little notice, including one that you had to book a ticket at least an hour before entering a club in order to facilitate contact tracing.

Four days after nightclubs reopened, on 26 October, Stephen Donnelly gave the Cabinet subcommittee on Covid-19 a stark warning that a peak in cases, which was projected in the coming weeks, would not necessarily be followed by a rapid fall. It was not even Halloween, but already the prospect of high case numbers in the run-up to Christmas was playing on the minds of the pandemic policymakers. The health minister warned that the number of new cases in the previous week had been the fourth highest of the entire pandemic. There had been a 40 per cent increase in hospitalisations, and the same increase in ICU admissions, in less than two weeks.

There was no talk of reintroducing restrictions at that stage. But Holohan began to sound the alarm as loudly as he could. The following day he told a NPHET media briefing that there had been 'slippage' in adherence to public health measures and urged people to double-down on mask-wearing, distancing and hand washing.

A week later he appealed to the public to 'ration' their discretionary activity and reduce the number of people they planned to meet. But by 10 November, the chief medical officer admitted that none of his advice appeared to be landing. 'We're still seeing high levels of socialisation across the population,' he said. Privately, senior NPHET figures feared they had lost the room.

—

Just as he had in the spring and summer of 2021, Stephen Donnelly continued to vigorously pursue the wider use of antigen testing throughout the autumn and winter. On 1 September, his secretary general, Robert Watt, had emailed Holohan and two other department officials asking that they consider Donnelly's request to implement serial antigen testing in nursing homes, their deployment at airports and their mass availability in pharmacies.

On the face of it, Donnelly's approach appeared to be wearing down Holohan and his team. While retaining strong reservations about their wider use in society – which Holohan articulated in a series of strongly worded emails and letters across October and November 2021 – NPHET ultimately recommended on 18 October, the same day it greenlit night-clubs reopening, that the HSE send vaccinated close contacts a rapid antigen test. Later in November, it advised those going to nightclubs to serially antigen test themselves. This was in line, NPHET officials believed, with their long-held view that antigens could be used, but just not to 'green-light' activities – to enable someone with a negative antigen test result to do an activity that would otherwise be seen as too risky.

That same day, Donnelly emailed Paul Reid asking that the HSE, 'as a matter of urgency', make available public information such as instruc-tional videos, FAQs and infographics about how to use the tests. He also asked for an estimate of future orders on rapid tests, 'given current stock levels and estimated demand given the new NPHET advice'. Reid responded that he was still waiting for the Department of Health's comm-unications and legal teams' disclaimer reviews on the material.

In the weeks that followed, Donnelly pushed for even more, includ-ing a proposal to subsidise antigen tests, some of which were retailing for as much as €8, being sold in supermarkets and pharmacies.

Holohan was dead set against the idea. In an email to Donnelly on 17 November he cited data from an Amárach survey that day showing that the majority of people using antigen tests were symptomatic. Of those who received a negative result, the majority were interpreting that as a green light to participate in activities as normal. He cited reports from public health doctors that symptomatic people were going to crèches and schools after a negative antigen test and thus placing both children and adults at risk. 'With this level of inappropriate use, incentivising the use of these tests at present risks promoting rather than reducing transmission of the disease,' Holohan concluded.

Two days later, he wrote to Donnelly again with the latest Amárach data, and once more insisted that any scheme that incentivised the use of antigen tests 'should not be progressed' until there was much greater public understanding of how to use them appropriately.

Despite the CMO's warnings, a Cabinet memo outlining a plan to subsidise tests was drafted and redrafted. Twice it was heavily trailed in the media, but failed to appear at the ministers' meeting. At one point it was proposed to subsidise tests in pharmacies only, 'with the possibility of other retailers being involved at a later stage', according to an email from Department of Health senior official Fergal Goodman, the man tasked with drafting the memo. The more Goodman worked on options for a subsidy scheme, the more issues came up. It just wasn't coming together. In addition to the expected resistance from Holohan, senior officials, including Robert Watt, weren't on board, viewing subsidised antigen testing as too messy and convoluted. They wanted antigen tests to be used in accordance with the new role that was emerging for them: being sent to close contacts, and then leaving it down to people's own choice as to whether or not to use them privately.

It was also expensive. The proposal that got closest to Cabinet envisaged a cost of about €31m a month, for three months. Ultimately the idea was killed off by the Department of Public Expenditure (DPER), which had been asked to sanction the money. In a letter dated 24 November, assistant secretary Ronnie Downes told Goodman, it 'does not appear obvious from the information provided to date that this proposed major subsidy and associated public expenditure will, in fact, help control the spread of the disease', a view that in effect echoed what Holohan had been saying. Concluding his letter, Downes wrote that DPER had 'identified a number of significant concerns related to value for money, costs, controls and operational and legal issues' with the proposal.

While NPHET advice on antigen tests evolved over the course of November to recommending that people who engaged in high-risk activities such as clubbing should take regular rapid tests, Donnelly's idea that the State should bankroll this was a bridge too far. On 29 December, he slipped into an interview with Claire Byrne on RTÉ Radio a comment that the plan was being abandoned because it was now unnecessary – the market had determined that antigen tests were now cheaply and widely available. 'We got to broadly the price we were targeting without having to spend taxpayers' money,' he declared, while saying little about the internal resistance he had been encountering in the weeks prior.

—

Despite the worrying trajectory of the ongoing Delta wave, NPHET's approach to restrictions throughout November proved less cautious than the government's. It was a remarkable turn of events given what had happened a year earlier. After NPHET recommended some clarifications around public health guidance – including reinstating advice to work from home and asking that consideration be given to extending vaccine passes to other unspecified settings – on 11 November, the government decided to go significantly further five days later.

The Cabinet agreed that all pubs, bars, nightclubs and restaurants would have to close at midnight. Holohan was amenable to the idea when Micheál Martin called to ask him about it. It was viewed as a practical measure that could drive down socialising and effectively shutter the nightclub industry less than a month after it opened.

The day it was announced – Tuesday, 16 November – marked the first step backwards in Ireland's nearly year-long march out of public health restrictions. There was a grim sense of déjà vu. Two days later, Paul Reid sent an extraordinary letter to the chief executives of hospital groups, hospitals and other senior managers asking that they outline what additional 'surge' ICU beds could be created within ten days and that, if necessary, they curtail 'all other activity to facilitate redeployment of staff to critical care areas'. Earlier that week, Reid had told the Cabinet subcommittee on Covid-19 that the situation with Covid-19 in hospitals was 'grave and deteriorating'. The HSE and the government were moving ahead of NPHET advice as the situation deteriorated and senior figures in the health service were getting very edgy. 'Our hospitals are at their limit,' one senior HSE figure observed in mid-November, before Reid sent his letter. The ICUs were 'in big trouble' and GPs were 'exhausted'. Test and trace was already in surge mode.

Christmas was coming – a challenging time even in a non-Covid year. The same person sketched out a typical Christmas in the hospital system pre-Covid. On Christmas Eve, wards are emptying as people are sent home for the holidays, medics are relaxing and having informal parties. Hundreds of beds are vacant. Then, over Christmas Day, the first suicide attempts start to filter in. The trickle grows: sick older people; people who have put getting treatment for an illness on hold over Christmas. Then it becomes a flood – 'the shit hits the fan'. Delayed presentations, assaults, everything imaginable shakes the system to its core. If this happened, with a wave of new Covid-19 cases as well, it could be unimaginable.

The nerves in the HSE prompted the politicians to ask just what exactly was going on with the booster programme. A month earlier, on the advice of NIAC and Holohan, Donnelly had given the go-ahead for all over-60s to be vaccinated. Boosters had begun among immuno-suppressed people in late September, but the vaccine programme was a shadow of its former self.

The mass vaccination centres were gone or being dismantled, deliveries had been slashed, and there were deep concerns that there were over 370,000 people who were unvaccinated or partially vaccinated. Illness among this cohort could, by itself, place pressure on the health-care system, and drive breakthrough infections among the vaccinated.

Ireland was caught in the bizarre situation of having among the highest vaccination rates in the developed world, but again being imperilled by rising case loads and a health service that was struggling to cope.

Holohan felt the booster programme wasn't moving fast enough and frequently expressed this view in meetings in the Department in October and November. Ronan Glynn, who acted as the main interface between the vaccine programme and NPHET, consistently made the same point. It was a frustration shared by Watt and Donnelly. The tensions over the pace of vaccination continued into November. At another COG meeting on 24 November, Watt declared that the vaccination programme needed to move to 'an emergency footing'. On the same day, the number of daily Covid-19 admissions to ICU hit what would transpire to be their peak of Ireland's fourth wave – 132.

At that stage, however, there was little indication that the situation was stable when NPHET met the following day to consider a range of measures, including a recommendation that masks should be worn by children aged 9 and over. That recommendation, coupled with a proposal that children under 12 should avoid indoor community gatherings for the next two weeks, proved controversial. The Ombudsman for Children would later criticise an 'in-built unfairness' in the proposals that effectively curtailed the Christmas pantomime season. The moves irked the coalition again. Days earlier, Holohan had told opposition health spokespersons that he didn't anticipate recommending more restrictions – and then did just that. Holohan did not see it as a lockdown for kids or anything close to it; rather it was a measure aimed at ensuring the schools could stay open. But it was not a welcome message for the politicians or parents.

That NPHET meeting on Thursday, 25 November was notable for another reason. It was the first time that public health officials discussed a new lineage: B1.1.529, which would soon become known as Omicron. The head of the National Virus Reference Laboratory, Cillian De Gascun, said that of the 1,200–1,500 cases a day being sequenced by his lab, no case of it had been found. While there was scant information at that stage, De Gascun reported to the meeting that the characteristics of the variant appeared to be a cause for concern. It could be the worst possible variant. It had 37 mutations in the spike protein, which it used to latch on to and invade a body's cells. While there was no solid data, all the early scientific commentary presented a worrying picture. That evening, as he left the Department of Health, Stephen Donnelly's phone pinged with texts and WhatsApps of Twitter threads about the new variant.

That weekend NPHET advised that PCR testing be reintroduced for everyone arriving into the country, regardless of their vaccination status. Within days, the State was reimposing travel restrictions it had hoped were gone for good. Meanwhile, NIAC recommended that the booster programme, which up to that point had been confined to over-50s and the medically vulnerable, be extended to everyone over the age of 16. The emergency footing Watt had spoken of was now under way. Heading into

December, less than a fifth of the eligible population had been boosted. Within a month, the HSE had vaccinated half of them.

But before that, as November turned to December, the uncertainty around Omicron would soon lead public health officials to conclude that the accelerated booster programme alone would not suffice. More had to be done – and this would lead to one of the most ill-tempered showdowns yet.

CHAPTER 33:

SUBVERSIVES

2 December 2021
Cases: 578,064
Deaths: 5,707
Seven-day average of new cases: 4,451

I t was a cold, wet December night. Laura Casey, a principal officer in the Department of Health working for NPHET, hopped on her bike and cycled the eight-minute journey from Miesian Plaza on Baggot Street to the Department of the Taoiseach on Merrion Street. In her possession was a printed letter signed by the chief medical officer with the latest recommendations from NPHET, which had met earlier that day.

The uncertainty over Omicron had prompted Tony Holohan and his team to recommend a series of new restrictions. Nightclubs were to be closed, strict social distancing reintroduced in hospitality, capacity at indoor events cut to half, the Covid pass extended to gyms and hotels, and household visits kept to a maximum of three other households. Inevitably, such measures would not be popular with the government or the public, but things were still so finely balanced between government and its advisers that Holohan, Robert Watt and others in the department were determined that the recommendations not leak.

They knew that if the government felt bounced into action – again – the backlash could be destabilising. Throughout the pandemic, politicians

steadfastly believed that NPHET would brief the media about its recommendations in order to box the government into a decision. Dozens
of times, the media would document the path from a NPHET meeting
to Holohan writing a letter to Stephen Donnelly that would then go
before the Cabinet subcommittee before the full Cabinet agreed whatever measures were deemed necessary. Every step was riddled with leaks
and briefings and they came from both NPHET and government, who
blamed each other. Leaks became a cipher for the tensions within the
wider relationship. When restrictions were being recommended, this
tension had the potential to go nuclear.

So on that December night, to avoid leaks, a letter was printed off
and Casey cycled through the rainswept streets. She took a copy to the
Taoiseach's department, where it would go to Martin Fraser and Micheál
Martin. She also gave one to Stephen Donnelly's driver, who made sure
that it was handed to the health minister in the Dáil chamber. Donnelly
had already been briefed orally by Holohan earlier that day and was
before TDs that evening dealing with legislation to give effect to new
travel restrictions, including the reintroduction of hotel quarantine.

Holohan had himself become increasingly exasperated by the leaks
and more specifically that NPHET was being blamed for them. However,
even though they felt unfairly targeted, the chief medical officer and
other senior NPHET members had come to the conclusion that at least
one person on the team was consistently leaking from key meetings. They
viewed it as entirely counter-productive to NPHET's aims, which were
ultimately to secure government agreement to their recommendations.
Though the identity of this person has been discussed privately by senior
NPHET figures, they were never confronted. The person in question
categorically denies briefing the decisions from NPHET meetings.

Ahead of the NPHET meeting earlier that day, Holohan and others
on NPHET, including Ronan Glynn, discussed how to smoke out the
mole. It was decided that Holohan would put up a slide displaying on
screen the measures that would form part of his letter, including a proposal to cut capacity on public transport to 50 per cent. But that proposal
never made it into the letter. In fact, it was never under consideration.

The question was, having been shown to the meeting, would the bogus recommendation be leaked?

—

Paschal Donohoe was sitting alone on the front bench of the government side of the Dáil chamber, surrounded by binders and sheets of paper, as he undertook his most complex and hardest legislative job of the year, the Finance Bill, which gave effect to measures announced in the budget. As TDs streamed into the chamber to vote on amendments, Donohoe was approached by several backbenchers who had seen a tweet from RTÉ's Paul Cunningham just after 9 p.m. about NPHET plans to limit household visits, as well as much earlier posts indicating that it was considering reimposing hospitality restrictions.

Donohoe was furious, believing that the NPHET letter had been made available to RTÉ before it had been given to ministers. If there were new restrictions on hospitality he should have known about them, given that he was responsible for the financial supports underpinning the sector. This view became widespread among cabinet ministers, as did the assumption that the leak had come from NPHET. The truth was more complicated.

In fact, a government source had been briefing the likely outcome of the NPHET deliberations to some political correspondents that evening, including lines strikingly similar to those that were reported by Cunningham and that caused such consternation on the government benches.

But more was to come. John Lee, the veteran political correspondent, appeared on Virgin Media Television's *The Tonight Show* just after 10 p.m. with a scoop: the full rundown of the NPHET recommendations. But his story, which appeared in the *Irish Daily Mail* the following day, contained one measure that wasn't actually in the letter: the 50 per cent reduction in public transport capacity.

Lee's story could ultimately only have emanated from someone who had been shown the slide with the bogus recommendation to cut public transport capacity by 50 per cent – which strongly suggested the NPHET ship was leaky. But it was also the case that government, or at least one person within it, was briefing on the expected public health restrictions from NPHET.

The careful steps taken to avoid a leak had failed spectacularly, and the stage was set for a confrontation that would only be paralleled by the ugly meeting on 5 October 2020.

—

Anger on the political side had not subsided by the following morning when, in a rare move, only Holohan and Philip Nolan, NPHET's head of modelling, were invited to the Cabinet subcommittee meeting, via a text from Liz Canavan in the Taoiseach's department. Ronan Glynn was excluded, while Paul Reid from the HSE and Brian MacCraith from the vaccine task force were not invited either.

It was a virtual meeting, the politicians and their advisers sitting in the Sycamore Room in Government Buildings, with the secretaries general of their departments also on the call. Holohan and Nolan were beamed on to the screen from their respective homes. It became clear almost immediately why the list of participants was kept shorter than usual. After the Taoiseach opened, he departed from the custom of allowing Holohan to present the NPHET assessment and recommendations and instead invited the Tánaiste to speak.

Leo Varadkar was furious. He let rip, accusing NPHET of acting in a 'political' manner. He said it was unacceptable that the government had been put in a position where it had no alternative but to do what the public health officials recommended. It was clear to those in the room and on the screen that Varadkar was angry and annoyed that decisions were out in the public domain before they had been discussed. He said that NPHET had undermined and disrespected the Taoiseach. To Holohan and Nolan, the clear implication of those words was that someone on NPHET had leaked the recommendations.

Furthermore, Varadkar questioned the need to tighten restrictions when the public health situation appeared to be improving. Government and NPHET should listen to the doctors on the ground in South Africa, who were at that stage saying that Omicron was not having a severe impact on hospitals, he argued. He also pointedly told the meeting that the public health team and ministers should have listened to the Indian doctors who said that Delta was serious while, in his view, NPHET was still waiting for evidence before acting. He also criticised Philip Nolan's models, saying that they would be overly pessimistic again as they assumed Omicron would convert to hospital/ICU admissions and deaths at the same rate as Delta, which, the Tánaiste believed, was unlikely to be true. It was a scathing assessment of Holohan and the NPHET team.

Eamon Ryan, the Green Party leader, was next up. He said he largely agreed with what the Tánaiste had said. Ryan, who throughout the pandemic was viewed by colleagues in government as a libertarian when it came to restrictions, talked about the deep anger among younger people about the effect of the pandemic on their lives.

Catherine Martin, Ryan's deputy and the minister with responsibility for the hospitality sector, asked whether NPHET's proposals had been 'mental-health proofed'. She queried the science behind the six-to-a-table rule in hospitality and 50 per cent capacity limit for indoor events. She asked where the evidence was to back up the rules NPHET were recommending for the sector she represented. Helen McEntee, the justice minister, was not pleased either. 'It's not helpful that I am talking to you and I haven't seen the letter,' she had told *Morning Ireland* earlier that day when faced with questions about the new recommendations. As he had been the night before, Paschal Donohoe was livid. 'Why was I, a member of government, finding out about this in the Dáil chamber after RTÉ?' he asked.

Nolan and Holohan furtively communicated about how to handle the onslaught. Holohan even sought advice from Robert Watt as the meeting was in progress. It was agreed that the chief medical officer would go ahead with his presentation outlining the rationale for the measures.

But when it came to the politicians again, Donohoe wasn't finished, interrupting Holohan to ask him to address a question he had raised about the leak. The CMO denied that it came from NPHET or at the very least from its senior membership. 'It's not in our interest and I've no idea where it came from and I have no explanation for it,' he said. 'Any investigation of any kind, I have absolutely nothing to hide, I am quite willing to be part of that.'

At that point, Varadkar interjected and said it would be a pointless exercise unless phones were going to be examined and, in his view, that wasn't going to happen. It was not considered a serious remark by those in the room – rather it was indicative of the Tánaiste's level of anger. Some later noted Varadkar's own predicament over leaks. His own phone had been seized earlier that year by Gardaí investigating his leak of a confidential document.

The meeting was, in the words of one participant, 'carnage'. There was a sting in the tail when it came to addressing the row over leaks. Watt told the politicians after Holohan and Nolan had left the meeting that he would deal with the leaking matter. Before that could even happen, at the full Cabinet later that day ministers agreed that all communications would now be managed and run centrally through the Government Information Service, which would be 'coordinating all media by civil and public servants and members of advisory bodies in respect of Covid-related matters'. It was unusual, to say the least, that communications strategy was the subject of a full cabinet decision, which was seen, in effect, as a gagging order on the public health team.

The leak, and the meeting itself, had had a profound effect. The NPHET team was taken aback at the level of anger in the room and in particular from Varadkar afterwards. People who dealt with him felt Holohan was personally shaken by it. Senior figures said that in its aftermath, relations were worse ('way worse') than at any time in the pandemic. Some among the senior echelons of NPHET felt that Holohan and Nolan stood accused of being subversives who had actively sought to undermine the government and bounce ministers into making decisions. An accusation that civil servants have attempted to subvert the democratic power vested in the government is a serious matter. It would have been anathema to Nolan, the son of two civil servants, and Holohan, the son of a guard who served along the border during the Troubles.

The politicians, meanwhile, were genuinely angry and upset. However the news emerged, they were again being hit with advice to impose new restrictions at high speed, again on the back foot, reacting rather than leading. The mechanism for making pandemic decisions was wearing out. How long could this be sustained? Yet, despite the acrimony, it was not October 2020 all over again. The government accepted the public health advice in full and the Taoiseach later announced the measures would come into effect from the following Monday.

The gagging order in particular caught the public's attention, with broadcasters struggling to secure interviews with NPHET members. However, in the background, Micheál Martin was quietly working to defuse the situation. The following day, Saturday, 4 December, he called Holohan to discuss the decisions made the previous day. During the call – which the CMO later briefed colleagues on – the Taoiseach told him that he appreciated and supported NPHET's work, notwithstanding the acrimony that had spilled out the previous night. It was a deft intervention. Martin had poured oil on troubled waters.

—

The surge in cases caused by the more transmissible Omicron variant created massive pressure to get more booster vaccines into arms. While none of the mass vaccination vaccine centres was closed, some were effectively mothballed, running part time, a few days a week. The number of vaccinators available for work dropped significantly, from around 1,350 to circa 750, as people drifted back to other parts of the health service.

The character of the vaccine programme had shifted from carpet-bombing to laboriously targeting small groups where uptake was low, among migrant communities and marginalised populations. Towards the end of September, the HSE began rolling out boosters to nursing homes and to some immunocompromised people, but when NIAC cleared the way for the over-60s to be boosted from the middle of October, there were hundreds of thousands of people eligible again, on an age-based approach.

The public's appetite and enthusiasm for the booster shot was less than it had been with the original vaccination. Across October and early November, with society largely reopened, it was not seen as urgent for many people. There was a spike in no-shows, but there were logistical and technological quirks that frustrated people. Someone could be boosted by their GP, but still receive several appointments via text for a vaccine centre.

The HSE had been planning to run the entire booster programme in about 20 weeks, around the same timeframe for the winter flu vaccine programme. But Omicron changed the game and the health service was now being told it had to be done in about 6 weeks.

In mid-November, Martin Fraser called Brian MacCraith and asked him to reconvene the high-level vaccine taskforce, which was rechristened the booster oversight group. The message landed with the HSE. 'That was the week where they were getting fucking pissed off,' one senior official later recalled.

The urgency to boost meant that once NIAC had cleared the way for everyone over 16 to receive a booster, towards the end of November many of the barriers that had existed during the first rollout were dispensed with. The entire programme was condensed into a single fast phase, with GP surgeries and pharmacists brought into play. Vaccines effectively shifted from constrained and planned rollout to open access in the run-up to Christmas. Instead of tightly planning how many vaccines would go to each setting, the attitude, characterised by one source, was 'How many do you want? No problem. Here you go, we've got loads of it. Use as much as you can.' Stocks were pushed so enthusiastically that, by early 2022, many hundreds of thousands that had been sent out to fuel the pre-Christmas rush went out of date and had to be destroyed by the HSE's national cold chain service.

—

In mid-December, with much about Omicron still unknown, NPHET met to consider more restrictions as the new variant slowly became dominant. While there was some evidence that it was milder, there was not enough that NPHET felt it could rely on. At a meeting on 16 December, modelling scenarios were shown with cases in excess of 20,000 per day. If Omicron spread faster but made people just as sick, it could be as bad as January 2021 or worse, with more than 400 people needing critical care.

NPHET's most draconian recommendation was to close all hospitality, sporting, theatre and cultural venues at 5 p.m. During the meeting, some questioned the necessity of the measure several times. Nonetheless, the meeting ended with a consensus.

As had happened two weeks previously, news of the recommendation leaked that night. There was a predictable backlash from the hospitality sector and government backbenchers began to line out against the early closing measure. But within the senior ranks of the coalition there was little resistance, given the potential danger of Omicron and fears of another nightmare Christmas. With Holohan's backing, the closing time was extended to 8 p.m., but all the other advice was accepted. It was all geared towards driving down socialising in the run-up to and the period over Christmas. 'None of this is easy,' an exhausted-looking Micheál Martin told the country. 'The level of concern is the highest that I have ever seen.'

—

On Christmas Eve, the previous record for daily case numbers was smashed, hitting 11,182. On Christmas Day, there were 13,765 cases of Covid-19. Omicron meant Covid-19 was spreading like wildfire among the population. The positivity rate – the percentage of cases detected from testing – shot up as demand also spiked. This meant that there would be lots of cases, but those positivity levels also meant there were simply unprecedented levels of Covid-19 in the community, and much of it wasn't being detected. NPHET estimated there might have been 500,000 cases in the run into Christmas, many more than had been diagnosed. By the early weeks of January 2022, the public health team estimated there may have been 500,000 infections in a week – around twenty times the number diagnosed in the entirety of the first wave in 2020. Barely a family around the country was untouched by Covid-19 over that period, with Christmas plans upended by a positive test or a close contact notification. With so much virus circulating, NPHET advised even greater use of antigen testing. So much so that by mid-January 2022, anyone aged 39 and under was advised not to seek a PCR test and to rely on antigen tests instead.

NPHET's fresh advice on antigen testing was widely viewed as a U-turn after a year and a half of resistance. But Holohan and other senior figures felt that high case numbers – that a PCR testing system alone could not cope with – was always the point at which the rapid tests could be used.

But while cases were spiralling to record levels, Covid-19 hospitalisations remained relatively stable over the Christmas period and a growing percentage of admissions were people with other health issues who had subsequently tested positive for the virus. Just as important, ICU admissions were also steady. Many of the people in ICU were infected with Delta, not Omicron. Vaccines meant that those who became infected did not become seriously ill and ICU admissions fell below 100 on 22 December and remained below 100 into the new year.

Early in January, Holohan began to quietly form the impression that the Omicron wave would not threaten the health service. There was vaccine protection from an accelerated booster campaign and the enormous case numbers meant that hundreds of thousands of people had acquired immunity.

On 4 January, the CMO met the Taoiseach and told him no further restrictions would be likely.

Two days later at a NPHET meeting, some of the more liberal-leaning members could already see no reason for keeping the restrictions. Towards the end of the second week in January, the data on Omicron became irrefutable. Donnelly was briefed by Holohan and his team that the peak had passed.

By the time NPHET met again on Thursday, 20 January, there was talk of reopening pubs that weekend. However, there were still some unknowns. Caution and precedent suggested there could be a phased reversing out of restrictions – a view some members of the team argued for at the meeting. But in the end, consensus was once again reached around the viewpoint Holohan had when he entered the meeting.

NPHET advised that all restrictions be dropped at 6 a.m. that Saturday. It was a remarkable turnaround. The pandemic was not over, ministers were warned: 'The emergence of new variants with increased levels of transmissibility, immune escape and/or virulence remains a risk both nationally and globally,' the Cabinet was told in a memo the following day. But the public's response over Christmas had been extraordinary. Even without a lockdown, survey data showed that the change in public behaviour from mid-December to early January 'was the largest recorded since the study began a year ago. People socialised less and were more careful when they did,' the memo stated.

Ordinary people, not politicians, were responsible for much of the positive difference compared to a year earlier, by virtue of both their caution and their willingness to buy into the vaccination programme. In the four and a half days leading up to Christmas Day, 470,000 booster doses were given. By the time the Cabinet met to consider unwinding nearly all remaining public health restrictions, on Friday, 21 January, a total of 2.6 million booster doses had been given.

That same day, the Cabinet was told there had been 66 Covid-related deaths up to that point in January 2022. It was way down on 196 the previous month, 246 in November and 224 in October. Given the scenario in front of them, and the advice from their medics, the government pushed ahead with reopening.

For what all concerned hoped would be the last time, Micheál Martin addressed the nation from the front steps at the front of Government Buildings. 'I have stood here and spoken to you on some very dark days,' he said. 'But today is a good day.'

He spoke of how trust in the State had enabled the most extraordinary response – and how repayment of that trust now demanded the rapid removal of restrictions on personal freedoms. Spring was coming, he said; it was time to see each other again, to smile and sing again.

'It is time to be ourselves again.'

—

17 February 2022
Cases: 1,260,329
Deaths: 6,402
Seven-day average of new cases (PCR confirmed): 3,538

In almost every other way, it was a normal NPHET meeting. There was a detailed review of the epidemiological situation and a discussion on the public health measures. Then, at the end, Holohan spoke. He had told Stephen Donnelly, the health minister, that NPHET, in its current form, was no longer necessary.

In many ways, this chimed with the entire spirit of the meeting, which came to the conclusion that many of the interventions that had become part of daily life were no longer necessary. Mass testing should be scaled back and targeted at the over-55s and the vulnerable. Symptomatic people would no longer take a test, but would be asked to isolate themselves. The entire regulatory apparatus, with legal enforceability, of mask-wearing should be dismantled. Masks, the most visible and omnipresent reminder of the disease, were no longer mandated.

The reality – even if it might prove to be only fleeting, before vaccines waned, or before the next variant, or the next pandemic – was that there could be 20,000 cases of Covid-19 per day, and the hospitals and ICUs could handle it. There would be disease, and death, but the costs of interrupting it with restrictions and even lockdowns would be too great.

Omicron had crystallised a reality that had been slowly forcing its way into pandemic policymaking over the previous six months. Variants were becoming too transmissible to be contained without the strictest lockdowns. But the strictest lockdowns were also becoming politically, economically and socially unacceptable, particularly since the vaccines were reducing harm enormously.

The disease could be tolerated, even at massive levels, without overwhelming the HSE. The point of lockdowns had never been to save every life. It had been to avoid catastrophe, and now catastrophe was not coming. That being the case, the realisation among NPHET members that day when they discussed masks and testing was, as one participant later recalled, 'There's no reason any more for all of this stuff, including us.'

There had been no forewarning for members that this could be their last meeting. It was the 103rd full meeting of NPHET, just over 750 days after its first. Holohan imparted the news imperfectly. Some felt it was hard to discern exactly what he was saying – his speech was so full of subordinate clauses, conditionals, complexity and nuance that even immediately afterwards some people couldn't quite grasp what had been said. He was eager to ensure that people knew that whatever happened next was not up to him; it was up to the minister, who would review his proposal.

Allies of the chief medical officer were of the view that the approach outlined should be tightly adhered to, but Donnelly, as ever, was anxious to put his own stamp on things. He had already been working on his own list of people to advise him directly, rather than providing advice to Holohan to impart to him. But that was a battle for another day.

The last NPHET meeting was light on sentimentality. Holohan said there would be a time to properly express gratitude, but given that it could be the last meeting of the group in its current form, he thanked the members for their service. Máirín Ryan, the acting head of HIQA, thanked Holohan for his leadership, mentioning Glynn and the other members as well.

It was imperfect, and undramatic, and in some ways unclear. But the important message got through. The emergency phase had largely passed, there was a need to normalise and hand over to a group of people whose day-to-day job would be pandemic management.

Covid was not gone. The pandemic was not over. Disease doesn't end neatly. But it was an ending of sorts. Whatever had happened in the last two years, it was as over as it was ever going to be. Immediately afterwards, one member of NPHET said simply, 'We're done.'

EPILOGUE

I n late January 2022, Tony Holohan changed his phone number. Someone had obtained his work number, and he got a flurry of phone calls from numbers he didn't recognise. A few left threatening messages. 'You fucking cunt,' one person said. 'We're coming for you, your day is up.'

One Sunday in early October 2021, a small group of anti-vaccine protesters turned up outside his home near Bushy Park in Terenure. Gardaí were called and the protest dissipated. Though these were small demonstrations and very much against the mainstream, Holohan's prediction to Deirdre Watters in April 2020 that his superhero status among the public would change had transpired.

It wasn't just Holohan. As Covid wore on, anti-lockdown and anti-vaccination protestors congregated outside the homes of Leo Varadkar and Stephen Donnelly. The minister for health had to install a security fence around his house, where his young children live. Paschal Donohoe was pursued down the street in October 2021 by a crowd of protestors who called him a 'fucking murdering cunt'.

These were the actions of a minority who turned their face away from the public health response and demonstrated an unacceptable level of verbal and physical hostility. They illustrate, nonetheless, how contentious and polarising the debate became, as the pandemic evolved and the State's system for policymaking came under strain.

With NPHET effectively stood down in February 2022, it is important to describe what happened over the course of the two years it existed.

This task is challenging, as the pandemic and the response was too all-encompassing and too vast to be neatly packaged. It is also arguably a little unfair on NPHET members, who never asked for this to happen and worked tirelessly with little relief.

In particular, Holohan was forced to deal with this unprecedented professional challenge at the same time as an enormous personal tragedy, the death of his wife, Emer Feely, following a long battle with cancer, in February 2021. 'The personal side was the worst part of all this,' he reflected a year later. He disputes suggestions that it might have clouded his judgement. 'I didn't have any other intention other than just doing the job to the best of my ability. I did the job and then tried to manage what I had to manage alongside that at home.'

However, it is undeniable that, over the course of the pandemic, NPHET, and Holohan in particular, grew to something beyond themselves, what they asked for, and what was intended. They became freighted with the fears, invested with the hopes, and targeted by the frustrations of the country. Above all, they were a reification of how a disease became the centre of the entire political and public discourse of the State for two years, and of how everyday life was medicalised in unimaginable ways, during a period of unprecedented stress, pain and trauma for the nation. This occurred against a backdrop where there was no actual decision taken that this would be the best model to make pandemic policy.

There was no Cabinet approval or even a ministerial order underpinning NPHET's establishment in late January 2020. Both health ministers, Simon Harris and then Stephen Donnelly, tried to attend meetings but were sharply rebuffed by Holohan, who for the most part decided who was on NPHET. Its meetings were held in private and minutes were released weeks, if not months, after they happened.

Existing State emergency response structures such as the National Emergency Coordination Group (NECG), on which ministers usually sat, were not utilised. NPHET, almost by a quirk of the emergency nature of the situation itself and without much prior discussion, became the pre-eminent body responsible for managing the pandemic. Its decisions dictated an unprecedented societal and policy response.

This was at its height during the first wave in 2020, when there was no political opposition, when the government had no mandate, and when the apparatus of the civil service, the health service and the wider State was universally organised to confront a single threat. They, and other officials, were immensely powerful. While political and constitutional authority remained vested in the government, the agenda-setting power of NPHET, the capacity of its meetings and recommendations to frame the entire process of pandemic policymaking, was unprecedented.

The power this non-elected body exerted over political choices has some comparisons with how the Troika dictated budgets after the financial crash. But while that arrangement was repugnant in a way that could never be applied to the mission of providing public health advice, it was at least done under a framework that had parameters and which successive governments signed up to.

There was no such framework for the pandemic other than the oft-cited credo 'NPHET advises, government decides'. But this was woefully inadequate when it comes to understanding or describing the real contours of how Covid-19 policy was developed. At a bare minimum, political choices were made that the government did not want to make, such as when it implemented Level 5 lockdown two weeks after having rejected that recommendation from NPHET in October 2020. That is not a comment on the advice given or the decision itself, but it is the reality of it.

Some of the most drastic, expensive and cruel policies ever imposed by the State were arrived at within a system that was ad hoc and could be haphazard. When it misfired, it could be costly. While the political side had identified some of the flaws by the summer of 2020, when daily case numbers were the lowest they have been at any point since the pandemic began, and when Varadkar formed the view that NPHET was 'suboptimal', they did nothing to change it.

This meant that the whole process from then on was characterised by a near-ridiculous situation where public health advice was formulated in secret, but under great public scrutiny, often leaked, and then handed to a government which then had to make decisions rapidly and, again, under massive scrutiny. This is a bad way to make any policy; it's a worse way to decide on something as massive as lockdowns.

Given the war-like conditions that existed, there is a benefit to acting fast, and formal considerations of how policies are made sometimes have to be relegated to a second tier. However, this era lasted for two years, and during the pandemic, substantial strategic choices were made without being explicitly articulated. The disposal of the five-level *Living with Covid* plan in 2021, in favour of an approach which relied entirely on substantially vaccinating the population before relaxing restrictions, was never fully explained.

Similarly, there was a pivot during the autumn and winter of 2021/2022 when it was quietly accepted that increased infectiousness of the Delta and Omicron variants meant interrupting transmission would no longer be the organising principle of the response. People would get infected, and that would be tolerated, because harm rather than infection would be the key metric. Whether this is right or wrong or indifferent, it was never clearly explained.

When civil and personal liberties are suspended, there are obligations on policymakers to explain clearly and honestly what is going on. It is worth dwelling for a moment on the criticism of how pandemic-era restrictions were designed and imposed by Trinity College Dublin's Covid-19 Law and Human Rights Observatory, which highlighted 'severe lack of clarity in government communication regarding what was law and what was merely public advice', including the enforcement of a criminal prohibition on holding religious services when 'in our view, no such prohibition actually existed in law. Far from mere technicalities, these basic issues of accountability and rule of law compliance go to the heart of a just legal system. Even if many agreed that the measures adopted were necessary, the manner in which they were adopted and enforced left much to be desired.'

—

The nadir of the Irish model for handling the pandemic was when Holohan returned with his Level 5 recommendation in October 2020, damaging relations between NPHET and government. Then the disaster of the 'meaningful Christmas' was set in train by policy choices made by a coalition newly determined to assert itself within this framework. Despite the Taoiseach and ministers maintaining a strident defence of their actions in October, November and December 2020 during interviews for this book, any objective assessment of what happened in that period would undoubtedly call into question the government's decisions.

Ministers defied the public health advice and delayed locking down in October 2020; they opened up more than the public health advice said would be sensible in December; and then delayed several days before locking down fully again before the end of 2020, even as Holohan and NPHET warned of the perilous situation facing the country. What followed across January 2021 was the darkest moment in Ireland's pandemic experience.

But the blame for what happened does not lie totally with the politicians. Holohan failed to effectively communicate to the politicians his advice to lock down in early October, resulting in a row that damaged relations for the rest of that year. NPHET's recommendation to permit household visits even earlier in December 2020 than the government decided, while keeping hospitality closed, could well have driven just as many infections.

Holohan's personality and style are also an important part of this story. The majority of the big calls were correct – and this may be a function of that style. But it is worth reflecting on, as is how it played out in some specific examples. It was such that meetings could run for hours in a bid to achieve what he, and allies, described as consensus but what others viewed as a war of attrition; wearing them down to come round to his way of thinking. Within NPHET existed a closer-knit group, clustered around Holohan.

NPHET's advice was far from infallible and a pattern of medical paternalism emerged in its attitude towards face coverings and antigen testing in particular. The broad view was that the public could not be trusted with either, which resulted in the use of face coverings not being widely advised until long after the first wave. The debate over antigen testing went on for over a year and resulted in bitter acrimony and the extraordinary situation whereby a health minister felt it necessary to reverse-engineer clinical governance in the face of strident opposition from Holohan and others on NPHET. While they had a reasonably solid scientific basis for their opinions they exhibited an, at times bizarrely trenchant, opposition to the wider use of such tests.

Far more important than masks and rapid testing was what happened in Ireland's nursing homes across February, March, April and May 2020 and again in January 2021, which might well have been avoided with better decision-making.

The decision, for example, to clear out hospitals to prepare for a surge in admissions by decanting large numbers of elderly and vulnerable patients into nursing homes shows how the response was overly focused on the acute hospital system, rather than where the virus did the most damage.

Ultimately, far removed from the decisions in that period, it is undoubtedly the case that the virus was able to exploit the weaknesses that long existed because of the way in which the State cares for its older population. That system of care is a patchwork of private and public nursing homes in which elderly and vulnerable residents are brought together in large congregated settings rather than being incentivised and enabled to be cared for in their own homes. This model of care is a perfect breeding ground for an infectious and deadly virus. As a result, Covid-19 killed hundreds of nursing home residents in the spring of 2020 and it killed hundreds again in the winter of 2021. There has for years been much discussion and debate around overhauling this model, but there is still little to indicate that fundamental change is imminent.

Notwithstanding any inadequacies in how the response was put together, any assessment of how Ireland handled Covid has to be comparative. 'We had a bigger problem in Europe than most other continents, [and] we fared relatively well compared to most countries in Europe,' Holohan said.

Measured by the Our World in Data website, Ireland had a cumulative total of 1,284 Covid deaths per million people. The European Union had 2,214; the United Kingdom 2,348; the United States 2,806. There is a real element of the ends justifying the means here. Lockdowns are impossibly brutal, their costs nearly incalculable; and yet, on their own terms, they were justified in that they certainly preserved human lives.

Public health restrictions were underpinned by social cohesion. They are ultimately a function of how people behave, not what policies are decided on. And Irish people by and large bought into the response, even if tensions existed within the policymaking bubble. Regular surveys across 2020 and 2021 showed that the majority of the public supported measures to curb the spread of the disease, including restrictions. Polling also showed greater support for Holohan than for political leaders. 'Every time we asked anything of the wider public,' Ronan Glynn said in autumn 2021, 'they seemed to understand what was happening, the direction of travel and the pace at which things were happening and why.' The response in Ireland was characterised by public buy-in and by social cohesion. Holohan argued in February 2022 that in simple terms it goes back to the relationship of trust between a doctor and their patient. In the context of the pandemic, the entire population was the patient and NPHET – perhaps more precisely Holohan – was the doctor. 'I think there was trust and confidence in what they were being advised and what they were being asked to do and people bought into it within all the limits of reasonableness,' he said.

Maybe this is unsurprising. Faced by novel threats, in times of crisis, particularly in an era when confidence has ebbed away from institutions, empowering experts or technocratic bodies is an attractive option. It is also useful for politicians to have someone else to blame when they have to impose extreme or unpopular policies. This was in turn enabled by a massive political and State response. An unprecedented amount of financial firepower was summoned to pay millions of people to stay at home and keep thousands of businesses on life support. It was maintained through all of 2020, 2021 and right through to spring of 2022. Without it, the public's compliance with what was imposed on them would not have lasted as long as it did.

—

There is no 'right' way of handling a pandemic. Some countries chose a zero-Covid approach, and while that option was fleetingly available in the summer of 2020, it is clear that it was not possible for Ireland, and faced too much entrenched resistance on the grounds of geography and politics. The question is whether the State has been changed by the pandemic and the consequences of what was done, and whether the lessons learned will now be acted upon. There must also be a particular focus on the utility, costs and sustainability of lockdowns as a central policy response to pathogenic threats.

Delays in diagnosing and treating cancers and other serious illnesses as a result of the Covid-19 restrictions are likely to have adverse outcomes for thousands of people for years to come, as will the mental health issues brought about by long lockdowns.

The complete closure of the construction sector twice in two years compounded an already dire housing crisis that is freezing a whole generation of people out of the market, perhaps for good. The closure of schools, in particular the long closure at the beginning of 2021, had a profound effect on all children and, in particular, those with special needs. Their paths in life were changed irrevocably by what happened in 2020 and 2021.

Lockdowns also created a new type of childcare crisis and women ended up bearing the brunt of this. A global study found that women did three times as much caring for children as men. It was no different in Ireland, where women were disproportionately affected in a variety of other ways. There was a huge increase in calls to Women's Aid and a surge in domestic violence orders. It was also striking how comparatively few women occupied leadership positions in pandemic decision-making. Both Taoisigh, both Tánaistí, both health ministers, the chief medical officer, his deputy and acting replacement, the head of the HSE, the head of the civil service and even the chair of the vaccine taskforce were all men. Many women served with them, but not at the very top of the decision-making apparatus.

Covid-19 also brought about a series of drastic policy shifts by the government, but there is little evidence to indicate that many of them will be sustained beyond the acute phase of the pandemic. The freeze on evictions and rent increases were scrapped once restrictions were eased, while the ground-breaking decision to cancel the Leaving Cert in favour of a calculated grade model failed to spark a more fundamental rethinking of the much-criticised exam.

Remote working was a policy necessitated by lockdowns and actively encouraged by the government, and while there has been policy and regulatory reform in this area, it is unclear if such changes will prompt radical rethinking by employers, or if all workers will be able to really insist on hybrid working models.

The health service and the people within it did remarkable things during the pandemic. But it does not solve Ireland's problem with health policy, vividly illustrated by an audit of child mental health services that showed hundreds of children were in receipt of risky treatment and had been prescribed inappropriate medication. The delivery of a more fundamental overhaul of the provision of healthcare in Ireland through the cross-party Sláintecare plan stalled during the pandemic and there are doubts about whether those tasked with delivering it are able to.

Ireland's pandemic response was in many ways shaped by how the key power relationships functioned at important times. There is arguably as much to learn from the decisions taken when those relationships functioned as there is when they broke down, particularly when they involved monumental moves that impacted the lives of everyone in Ireland.

If, as the Taoiseach asserted to the authors in late November 2021, Covid-19 is not the last pandemic, then the State and its institutions must now be as agile as they proved to be over the last two years in implementing the lessons of this one.

A NOTE ON SOURCES

The majority of interviews that took place for this book in 2021 and 2022 were conducted under the journalistic ground rule of 'deep background'. This means that all the information people told us in interviews could be used, but it could not be said who provided it. Interviews were digitally recorded to assist us in writing what we intend to be the most accurate and best obtainable account of Ireland's response to the Covid-19 pandemic. A smaller number of interviews with key participants were carried out on the record, and some participants also agreed, after their background interviews, to put their views on the record.

The book draws on hundreds of hours of interviews with first-hand participants in and witnesses to the events described, as well as confidential government records and thousands of pages of previously unpublished documents.

Where exact quotes, thoughts or conclusions are attributed to participants, the information is drawn from that person, from a colleague or colleagues of theirs who has direct knowledge, or from contemporaneous meeting notes, personal diaries, files, emails or documents.

ACKNOWLEDGEMENTS

The authors would like to thank everyone at Gill Books for the opportunity to write this book. In particular commissioning editor Seán Hayes for the faith he showed, the invaluable advice he gave, the wisdom and counsel he offered at all times and the pints he bought. They would also like to thank Aoibheann Molumby for her patience and understanding, along with Teresa Daly, Fiona Murphy, Jane Rogers, Michelle Griffin and Kieran Kelly.

Thanks also to Kevin Cunningham for the work he did in putting together the graph at the front of this book and Barry J. Whyte for his insight and feedback on early drafts.

The authors would particularly like to thank the many dozens of people who generously gave their time for the book. All of them were part of an incredible period in Irish history when the pandemic pushed men and women who were working in the public interest well beyond what could reasonably be seen as their breaking point. Their tolerance and regard for this project during an unimaginably trying time is greatly appreciated.

The authors believe that journalism is vital to democracies, and hope that this book helps people understand something of what happened over the nearly two-year period it covers. But journalism is nothing without sources, and the authors are in their debt for their time and, more importantly, their absolute honesty.

—

Jack Horgan-Jones would like to thank his parents, Mary Jones and John Horgan, for their encouragement and support, not only for this book, but at all times. To his siblings, Conor, Kate and Adam, and especially his sister Jane for her support, friendship, and for reading countless passages WhatsApped to her at any and all hours.

Acknowledgement is due to all colleagues at the *Irish Times*, to his senior editors Mark Hennessy, Deirdre Veldon and Paul O'Neill. Thanks to all those in the newsroom, but especially to the political team – Pat Leahy, Jennifer Bray, Cormac McQuinn, Harry McGee, Marie O'Halloran and Miriam Lord. Special thanks is due as well to his colleagues Martin Wall and Simon Carswell, whose skill, expertise, and enthusiasm for journalism is evident in their own reporting, and is matched only by their patience and kindness in discussing and fine-tuning the themes, concepts and stories that run through this book.

More than anything, Jack is grateful to his family. To his amazing daughters Olivia and Eve – the latter who was born just six days after the first draft of this book was submitted. Above all to their mother, his wife, Kate, who carried not only Eve but also their family through the period this book was written, while maintaining her own busy professional life. Her patience, belief, intelligence, good humour and counsel have sustained this effort. She is brave in difficult times and brilliant at all times.

—

Hugh O'Connell would like to thank his mother, Bernadette McHugh, for her endless patience and support, and his father, Fergus O'Connell, whose constant guidance on the project and painstaking proof-reading of the earliest drafts was essential. Thanks also to his sister Ferga for being an important sounding-board and, in general, a rock of sense.

There are numerous colleagues across the *Irish Independent* and *Sunday Independent* to acknowledge, but in particular his political editor, Philip Ryan, for his constant support and wise counsel, along with colleagues on the political team, Gabija Gataveckaitė, John Downing and

Senan Molony. They were all on hand for advice and offered a wealth of information and tips. He'd also like to thank Paul Sheridan, Alan English, Fionnán Sheahan and Maeve Sheehan, who all helped along the way to make this book possible.

Enormous thanks are also due to Jennifer Schweppe, John Mathews, Clarissa Diniz and Sinead O'Carroll.

Most of all Hugh is and will always be eternally grateful to his gorgeous wife, Theresa, who made this book possible by sacrificing an enormous amount over an intense eight-month period. She is a bastion of strength, common sense, fun and support. She is also most importantly an incredible mother to their wonderful daughter, Mary-Jane, who, thankfully, won't remember that period in the first year of her life when Dada was disappearing off to do book work.